Five Hours with Mario

Also available in the

FIVE HOURS
WITH MARIO

by Miguel Delibes

Translated by ❋ ❋ ❋

Frances M. López-Morillas

COLUMBIA UNIVERSITY PRESS · NEW YORK

COLUMBIA UNIVERSITY PRESS
NEW YORK   GUILDFORD, SURREY
COPYRIGHT © 1988 COLUMBIA UNIVERSITY PRESS
ALL RIGHTS RESERVED

Library of Congress Cataloging-in-Publication Data

Delibes, Miguel.
[Cinco horas con Mario. English]
Five hours with Mario / by Miguel Delibes;
translated by Frances M. López-Morillas.
p.   cm.—(Twentieth-century Continental fiction series)
Translation of: Cinco horas con Mario.
ISBN 0-231-06828-X
I. Title.   II. Title: 5 hours with Mario.   III. Series.
PQ6607.E45C513 1988
863'.64—dc19   88-16949
                                                          CIP

Columbia University Press wishes to express its appreciation
of assistance given by The Program for Cultural Cooperation
Between Spain's Ministry of Culture and
United States' Universities in the
preparation of this translation.

Book design by Jaya Dayal

Casebound editions of Columbia University Press books
are Smyth-sewn and printed on permanent
and durable acid-free paper

PRINTED IN THE UNITED STATES OF AMERICA

for José Jiménez Lozano

Note

In the Spanish original, the protagonist's style of speaking is a faithful reflection of her social and educational background. The translator has been at pains to convey this background in colloquial and occasionally careless English.

All the biblical quotations are taken from the Douay Version.

Five Hours with Mario

PRAY TO GOD IN CHARITY

for the soul of

DON MARIO DIEZ COLLADO

Who rested in the Lord
Sustained by the Rites of the Church
on March 24, 1966
at the age of 49 years

— R. I. P. —

His grieving wife,
Doña María del Carmen Sotillo;
children, Mario, María del Carmen, Alvaro,
Borja, and María Aránzazu;
father-in-law, Ilustrísimo Señor Don Ramón Sotillo;
sister, María del Rosario;
sisters-in-law, Doña Julia Sotillo
and Doña Encarnación Gómez Gómez;
uncles, aunts, cousins and the rest of
the sorrowing family, announce
their grievous loss and request a
prayer for his eternal repose.

Funeral Mass: Tomorrow, at 8:00 A.M.,
Parish Church of San Diego
Departure for the cemetery: at 10:00 A.M.
Gregorian masses to be announced at a later date.
Mortuary services: Alfareros, 16, ground floor.

Printing: PIO TELLO

After she has closed the door on the last visitor, Carmen lightly rests the nape of her neck against the wall until she can feel the cold contact with its surface, and blinks several times as if bewildered. She can feel the ache in her right hand and her lips are swollen from so much kissing. And because she can think of nothing better to say, she repeats the same thing she has been saying ever since morning: "I still can't believe it, Valen, mind you; I just can't get used to the idea." Valen takes her gently by the hand and, preceding her, draws her unresisting down the hall to her bedroom.

"You have to sleep a little while, Menchu. I'm delighted to see you being so brave and all, but make no mistake, you foolish girl, this is absolutely artificial. It always happens. Your nerves don't let you rest. You'll see tomorrow."

Carmen sits on the edge of the big bed and obediently takes off her shoes, pushing the right shoe off with the tip of her left foot and vice versa. Valentina helps her to lie down and then folds back a triangle of bedspread to make it cover half her body, from the waist down. Before she closes her eyes Carmen says, suddenly rebellious, "I can't sleep, Valen. I don't want to. I have to be with him. It's the last night. You know it is."

Valentina's attitude shows that she is willing to humor her. Her voice—both the content and volume of her voice—as well as her movements, infer inexhaustible efficiency.

"Don't sleep if you don't want to, but relax anyway. You've got to relax. You've got to try to at least." She glances at her watch. "Vicente won't be long now."

Carmen stretches out under the white bedspread, closes her eyes and, as if that might not be enough, covers them with her bare right forearm, very white against the black sleeve of the sweater that covers it to the elbow. She says, "It seems like a hundred years since I called you this morning. My God, the things that have happened since then! And I still can't believe it, mind you; I just can't get used to the idea."

Even with her eyes closed and protected by her forearm, Carmen keeps seeing faces filing by, some of them woodenly inexpressive and others deliberately mournful. "So sorry"; "Try to resign yourself"; "Take care of yourself, Carmen, the little ones need you"; "What time are they coming for the body tomorrow?" And she: "Thanks, So-and-So," or "Thanks, dear," and, if the visitor were socially prominent, "How happy poor Mario would have been to see you here!" The people were never the same but the density didn't diminish. It was like the flow of a river. At first, everything was heavily conventional. Long faces and pregnant silences. It was Armando who broke the tension with his joke: the one about the nuns. He thought that she hadn't heard him, but she had, and independently of her so had Moyano; he reproached Armando with an acrid, silent glare out of his milky pallor, his face framed in a black, silken rabbinical beard. But after that nothing was as tense as before. Moyano's beard and his deathly pallor were appropriate to a wake. By contrast, the white streak in Valen's hair seemed out of place. "When they told me I couldn't believe it. Why, I saw him yesterday." Carmen leaned forward and kissed her on both cheeks. Really, they didn't kiss; they crossed heads in a studied gesture, first on the left side and then on the right, and kissed the air, or perhaps a stray hair, so that each of them felt the little popping sounds of the kisses but not their warmth. "Why, I can't believe it myself. Last night he had supper just as usual and read till all hours. And this morning, well! How was I going to imagine anything like this?" Moyano's beard was perfectly in tune with the atmosphere. And his waxen, taut scholar's complexion. It was the only thing that Carmen could be grateful to him for. "Do you

mind if I go in and look at him?" "Of course not, dear." "So
sorry, Carmen." And the two women crossed heads, first on
the left side, then on the right, and kissed the air, kissed
nothing, perhaps some loose strand of hair, so that both felt
the breath of the kisses but not their warmth. "I've never seen
a corpse look like him, I promise you. He hasn't even lost
color." And Carmen felt a swelling sense of pride about her
corpse, as if she had made him with her own hands. No other
one was like Mario; he was her corpse; she had manufactured
him herself. But Valen was reluctant. "I'd rather remember
him alive, see." "I can tell you that it's not the least bit
upsetting." "Even so . . ." And Menchu too, but she was Carmen's daughter and couldn't refuse. When she came home
from school Carmen, with Doro's help, had made her go into
the room and forced her to open her eyes, which she obstinately kept shut. "Leave her alone, for heaven's sake, she's still
a child." "She's his daughter, and she's going in this minute
because I tell her to." Hysterical, that's what she was. Menchu
had acted like a hysteric.

"Ungrateful children."

"Leave it alone, Carmen; relax, come on, try to relax. Don't
think about anything right now."

Most of them were dark shapes with staring identical eyes.
What they had in common was a vague feeling of responsibility, a comfortable sentimentality, and a greedy desire to hold
on to her, Carmen, with their fingers or their lips. They came
in wondering what to say, anxious to get it over with: "When
they told me I couldn't believe it; why, I saw him yesterday."
"Poor Mario, so young!" Valen's white streak jarred like the
crack of a whip. The books too, behind the coffin, struck a
jarring note with their bright red, green, and yellow spines.
After the undertaker's men had left she patiently reversed, one

by one, all the books with brightly colored bindings that stood out against the black cloth. When she finished she felt strangely pleased, and her fingers were covered with dust.

"So sorry." "God grant you health to pray for his soul." After all, she'd done the right thing in sending Bertrán to the kitchen. A mere usher oughtn't ever to be in the same place as the professors. And then, the scene. It was his fault that Antonio had been so embarrassed. Why did deaf people have to show up at these things? Antonio had merely said, "The good ones die and we bad ones are left," and actually, he didn't say it; he sort of muttered it, but Bertrán said, "How was that?" and Antonio said it again quietly, first glancing suspiciously to one side and the other, and Bertrán shrugged his shoulders and raised his voice and said, "I don't under-stand you," and looked toward the others for support, and Antonio looked at the corpse and then at the group, but he said it again and again, his voice getting louder each time, while silence gradually took over in the groups of people, so that when he shouted, "We bad ones are left and the good ones die!" and Bertrán answered, "Oh, I didn't understand you, excuse me!" everyone realized what had happened.

Some groups came in and others left. What they had in common was a vague sense of responsibility and hypocritical eyes, suddenly grieved. It was Bene, Antonio's wife, who said, taking advantage of an unnatural silence and after a sigh so prolonged that she seemed to be collapsing like a spent bal-loon, "The heart's very treacherous, everyone knows that." And it was like a liberation. People's eyes gradually lost their grieved expression and, little by little, their faces grew less long. A culprit had been found. But she merely said to Bertrán, "Bertrán, go along to the kitchen; we can hardly budge in here."

"You can't imagine what it was like in the kitchen, Valen. A madhouse. Mario always did make a big hit with people like that, of course."

"Yes, sweetie; now be quiet. Don't think about anything. Try to relax, I'm asking you please."

"It seems like a hundred years since I called you this morning, Valen."

She had phoned her almost as soon as she discovered him. And Valen came right away. She was the first to arrive. Carmen had poured out her heart to her for an hour and a half. *It was later than usual for him, but when I opened the outside shutters I still thought he might be asleep. I was surprised by the way he was lying, honestly, because Mario usually slept on one side with his legs drawn up, he didn't take up even half the bed, lengthwise, of course, crosswise it was uncomfortable for me, just imagine, but he would curl into a ball, he says he's always slept that way, since he was little, ever since he can remember, see, but this morning he was lying face up, looking normal, of course, no change of expression, Luis says that when they have the attack they notice instinctively that they're choking and turn over, searching for air apparently, I figure it's like fish when you take them out of the water, something like that, you know how their mouths move? But as for color and all, as if nothing had happened, absolutely normal, not even stiff, just exactly as if he were asleep . . .* But when she touched his shoulder and said, "Come on, Mario, you're going to be late," Carmen pulled back her hand as if she had burned it. "The heart's very treacherous, everyone knows that." "What time are they coming for the body tomorrow?" "Why, I can't believe it myself. Last night he had supper just as usual and read till all hours . . . and this morning, well! who could have told me something like this would happen?" And she asked Valen (for she was on close terms with Valen),

"Valen, do you know if Mario has the courtesy title of 'Ilustrísimo Señor'? It's not out of misplaced vanity, you understand,
just imagine at a time like this, but it's for the funeral notice,
you know? because a funeral notice without a title, just plain
that way, seems like a snub." Valentina did not answer. "Did
you hear me?" She had the fleeting impression that Valen was
crying. "Why, I don't know, think of that," Valen suddenly
answered, "you've got me stumped. Wait a second, I'll ask
Vicente." Carmen heard the earpiece bang down, and Valen's
rhythmic steps, growing fainter and farther away, in the hall.
And at last, "Vicente says no, the 'Ilustrísimo' is only for
administrators. Sorry, sweetie."

They were persistent, tenacious shapes, which clamped onto
her hand like suction cups or obliged her to lean forward, first
on the left side, then on the right. "You don't know what a
shock it was for me; I couldn't eat my dinner. Angel told me,
'Go on, eat, girl, you won't mend matters that way.'" *But
children don't give you anything but trouble from the time they
force their way out, tearing a woman apart down there; thankless
children. You take Mario, not a tear. Won't even wear mourning
for his father, can you beat that?* "Leave me alone, Mother,
please, that doesn't help me. Those things are stupid conventionalisms, leave me out of it." Half an hour crying in the
toilet. *It's like this sweater, Valen, don't tell me, it's from when I
was wearing mourning for poor Mama, may she rest in peace. But
I look awful, it's too small for me now, and the worst of it is that
for the moment I don't have another one.* Carmen's black sweater
looked white over the tips of her breasts because of their
swelling bulk. Strictly speaking, Carmen's breasts, even black-
covered, were much too aggressive to go with mourning. The
suspicion fluttered in Carmen's subconscious mind that everything strident, bright-colored or aggressive was inappropriate

to the occasion. *I would have been glad to give him mouth-to-mouth resuscitation, I wouldn't have minded at all, other women say how disgusting but not me, anything but letting him slip away like that, but to tell you the honest truth I've only seen it once on the newsreel and I didn't dare, because it's one of those things, you know, that you don't pay attention to, it's like watching firemen, didn't register with me, that just doesn't seem to be my thing, I don't know how to tell you, it's the last thing you think of."* "The heart's very treacherous, everyone knows that." "It's not just because I say so, but he'd never been sick in his life." "I'm not a bit surprised by Mario's reaction, Menchu; they were so close." Valentina started to laugh: "Have you tried putting on a black slip and bra?" That made a big difference. The sweater was still small and her breasts large, but you couldn't see through the sweater stitches any more. *My bust has always been my big defect. I always had a little bit more than I wanted.* Valentina and Esther didn't leave her for a moment. Esther never opened her mouth, but kept watching her for signs of weakness. Valentina, from time to time, kissed her on the left cheek: "Menchu, sweetie, you don't know how pleased I am to see you being so brave." And to cap the climax, Borja came home from school yelling, "I wish Daddy would die every day so I wouldn't have to go to school!" She had slapped him without mercy, until her hand began to hurt. "Leave him alone, señorita, the poor little thing doesn't realize; you're going to hurt him." But she kept on slapping relentlessly, blindly. And then the shapes that arrived, with two round, surprised-looking eyes, pressed that same swollen, tender hand, or crossed heads with her, first on the left side, then on the right, and said, "I heard about it by pure chance"; "When they told me, I couldn't believe it. Angel said to me, 'Eat; you won't mend matters by not eating.'" But nobody kissed Mario or shook his hand. His friends hid their faces distractedly against his shoulder and frantically pounded his back with their right hands, as if they were trying to beat the dust out of his blue sweater. "I'm not a bit surprised; they were so close. Poor Mario!" "The father or the son?" By this time she didn't know what she was saying. "Both of them. Now I come to think of it, both of them." He was her corpse; she had manufactured him. She shaved him with the electric razor and combed his hair before the undertaker's people put him in the coffin. "He hasn't lost color or anything. He doesn't look like a dead man. I never saw anything like it, don't you agree? And after all, we're used to seeing them." "So sorry." She bent her head forward, first on the left side and then on the right, and kiss-kissed into the air, kissed nothing, so that the other woman could feel the little explosion of the kiss but not its warmth. "Don't tell me you're going to leave our master in a business suit, just like it was every day." "Why not, Doro?'" Doro crossed herself. "Well, honestly, and with brown shoes too. Not even for the poorest of the poor." Carmen sent her off to the kitchen. She didn't have to give explanations to a servant. She told Bertrán, "Go along to the kitchen, Bertrán; we can hardly budge in here." When Bertrán came in, his nearsighted, bleary eyes set flat in his face, he had told her, "He wasn't just good; he was a man through and through, which is different. Don Mario was a real man, and there aren't many real men to the pound. Understand, señora?" She pushed him away vigorously because he seemed to be about to try to kiss her. Carmen shaved Mario with the electric razor, washed him, combed his hair, and dressed him in the dark gray suit, the one he'd worn to give the lecture on Charity Day, opening it a bit along the side seams because, although the body bent easily, it weighed too much for her to manage alone. Then she put on the black and brown striped tie with the thin red line, but it didn't turn out to her satisfaction because the knot was too soft. Finally the undertaker's people put him into the coffin and carried it to the study, which was no longer Mario's study but his funeral chamber. And Mario said, "Why now?" But when he rushed home from the University he had already guessed. Maybe Bertrán. His eyebrows were drawn right down to his eyes and gave him a sullen, gloomy look, as if the weight of his brain was an unbearable burden and had pressed the curves of his eyebrows down onto his features, flattening them. *But he had already pretty well taken it in, just imagine, we'd never sent for him to come home before, I simply told him, "Daddy," and he was quiet, never said a word, Mario scares me sometimes, Valen, he's a boy who's too much in control of himself for his age, and that's not to say that I don't admire courage, of course, but you have to make allowance for your feelings too, because later it all comes out and then it's worse, but he acted as if it wasn't anything, like a statue, just exactly, and I said to him, "Suddenly. He didn't even wake up. Luis says a heart attack," and I couldn't hold it in and I started to cry and I hugged him, but you can't imagine how it hurt, Valen, because for quite a few minutes it was like hugging a tree or a rock, just exactly, and all he said was, what a remark to come out with, "Why now?" but no tears, absolutely zero, look, a father, what could be more natural, but nothing, like I'm telling you.*

"Thankless children."

"Stop talking; rest now."

Pío Tello was really overcome. *Of course, Mario always did make a big hit with lower-class people. It was too bad about the 'Ilustrísimo Señor,' though. You might not think so, but just to have those two words at the top really dresses up a funeral notice, Valen, don't tell me it doesn't.* "So sorry." "Take care of yourself,

Carmen, the little ones need you." "When they told me I couldn't believe it, I assure you." "Why, I can't believe it myself . . ." Encarna stole the show from her, though. Encarna's bursting in was a crude and senseless action. "So sorry." "Thanks, sweetie." Carmen bent forward and both women crossed heads, first to the left side and then to the right; and both of them felt the little explosions of conventional kisses but not their warmth. She had an instinctive loathing for funeral posters, *I didn't intend to put one up on the street door, understand, I just hate them, I think they're in terrible taste, but you see, at the time it happened, I had no choice, the big thing was for people to find out, because as far as he was concerned, I know, what're you going to tell me, he could have died like a dog, he was like that, but you have to keep up appearances, Valen, because if it comes out in "El Correo" tomorrow that the burial's at ten, it'll be no help, because lots of people rush off to the office and don't even find out, you can be sure of that, so I ordered half a dozen, one for here at the house, one at the High School, one at the newspaper and another place or two, not counting the fact that it'll be announced on the radio after the news program.*

Carmen was convinced that the recovery of Mario's last hours depended on her. The book was lying there on the night table and, inside its covers, Mario's last thoughts, as if canned. As soon as she could get away from the cloying black shapes, Carmen would rejoin him. Encarna was the chief obstacle, but Charo had taken her away. Charo didn't turn up until the younger children came back from school. She had gone to pick them up. Borja had come in yelling, "I wish Daddy would die every day so I wouldn't have to go to school!" Her hand hurt. Carmen didn't know whether it was because she had hit him so hard or because of the relentless shapes' insistent pressure. Her lips were swollen from so much kissing. "So sorry." "Who could have imagined a thing like this?" "What time are they coming for the body tomorrow?" But not Encarna. Encarna hadn't changed. She invaded the house like a whirlwind, elbowing her way through the crowd. And she shrieked, "My God! This one's left me too! This one too!" And the dark groups shrank together and stared and whispered and Encarna made them all into witnesses of her abandonment. Like a crazy woman. "A demented look," Antonio had said. And then, when she knelt, she came out with, "What have I done, Lord, to deserve this punishment?" And the groups opened and closed, folded and unfolded. They whispered, "Who is she?" And their eyes' comfortable sentimentality changed to avidity, they stood on tiptoe to see better, the spectacle fascinated them. But there was no use arguing. "For Don Mario, I wouldn't dream of it." Carmen insisted. "What do you mean I'm not to pay you for the notices?" "Don't insist, señora, Don Mario stood up for the poor without getting rich himself, and make no mistake, that's worth something." She gave in, though she knew that Pío Tello was having hard times, in the damp basement, on the old rotary press that had belonged to *El Correo*, printing funeral notices and posters by hand. "There just wasn't a better man than our master, and look at him lying there . . . !" Carmen had cut her short: "I don't want any scenes, Doro, keep your tears for a better occasion!" It was immoral to have maids and typesetters cry for him and for the children not to. "I don't want any scenes, Doro! Don't you hear me?" And Doro went off to the kitchen blowing her nose loudly and drying her eyes. The noise level rose like the noise of the sea when waves are building up. One conversation got mixed up with another and the cigarette smoke seemed to submerge them in stale air. "It's warm." "What do you say we open up a trifle?" "The atmosphere's very close." "There wasn't a better man than he was." "Open up." "That's the way, so there'll be no draft." "Drafts are very dangerous." "The heart's very treacherous, everyone knows that." "I'm afraid of drafts." "Well, my father, see, a draft, that's all it was, and it's not just because I say so, but he'd never been sick a day in his life." "So sorry." "Health to pray for his soul, Doña Carmen." Carmen leaned forward, first on the left side and then on the right, puckered her lips and let the kiss go, so that the other woman felt its little explosions but not its warmth. *I think I actually hurt her, but I'm not sorry, do you think, Valen, perfectly honestly, that a daughter can let her father slip away just like that, without even saying good-bye? Because all she did was scream, like a hysteric, the same words, "Please, it terrifies me, leave me alone!" but Doro and I, with all our strength, made her open her eyes and everything, that would have been a fine thing, some day she'll thank me for it.*

Carmen didn't know if he was praying or what. He stood motionless, slightly hunched, at the foot of the coffin and stared at his father with an imploring, commiserating attitude. It was Aróstegui who said, "He was a good man," and then Don Nicolás turned toward him suddenly: "Good, for whom?" And Moyano, from behind those filthy whiskers of his, murmured, "He didn't just die; he suffocated." Don Nicolás noticed her: "Excuse me, Carmen, were you there?" But she didn't say anything because those men were speaking in code and she couldn't understand them, nor had Mario, when he was alive, ever taken the trouble to explain their language to her. "Do you mind closing the window a trifle?" "Like that, thanks." "You feel the night chill at this hour." "It was cold yesterday." "Take care of yourself, Carmen, the little ones need you." "The atmosphere's very close." "When they told me I couldn't believe it; why, I saw him yesterday." "I can't believe it myself." She said to Pío Tello, "Write it down. Ready? Pray to God in charity . . ." For a moment Carmen allowed herself the weakness of feeling like the chief actor, and thought, "For Doña Carmen Sotillo," but caught herself in time. "Shall I go on?" Pío said, "Didn't Don Mario have the courtesy title?" "No, as you see. Only administrators." The voice over the phone sounded annoyed. "Others have titles and deserve them less." "Look, that's how things are, what do you want me to do about it?" Pío Tello slowly wrote everything down. At the end, Carmen emphasized, "A good heavy black border, Pío, please." "Don't worry, I'll take care of it." Only the fanatical observance of mourning and the book on the night table linked her to Mario now. Ah! and his corpse. "He hasn't lost color. If you didn't tell me, I wouldn't believe he was dead, I swear by all that's holy." "Do you mind closing the window a trifle more?" "It's really cold." "Like that, thanks."

"Is the book there, Valen?"

"Ssh! Here it is. Don't worry, silly girl. Just relax now, come on, I'm asking you pretty-please. Nobody's going to take it away from you."

Valentina stands up, puts a hand under Carmen's neck and helps her to lie down again; then she gently covers her with the white bedspread. She stays on her feet, does Valentina, and looks around her, the faded flower prints, the crucifix over the bed and, at her feet, the tattered rug with its signs of many years of wear, covering a rectangle of flooring. She slowly, quietly steps along it and scrutinizes herself, in the half-light of the room, in the wardrobe mirror, first full face and then in profile, patting the little curve of her stomach three times. Her lips sketch an expression of distaste. As she turns, her eyes fall on the book again, the tube of nose drops, the bottle of tranquilizers, the little bunch of keys, the wallet, and the old alarm clock. She sighs imperceptibly. Carmen has covered her eyes again with her white, white forearm. She sits down again.

"Are you still there, Valen?"

"Yes, sweetie, don't worry, I won't budge an inch, I promise you, but now relax. Make an effort, come on."

Doro, her eyelids and nose all reddened, had protested obstinately, "Aren't you going to wrap our master in plastic or anything? Gracious, he looks just awful! In my home town the poorest of the poor would have that, just like you're hearing it. And see, they dressed up Don Porfirio, the Boss, like a Franciscan." Carmen got furious with her. It was one of her principles not to let maids lecture her. *I still can't believe it, mind you; I just can't get used to the idea.* "Menchu, I'm so pleased to see you being so brave." The way Mario was acting was really too much. How to reconcile Pío Tello's six-pica black border with his blue sweater? His friends buried their faces in his shoulder and slapped his back heedlessly, as if they were trying to beat the dust out of his blue sweater. "Close it all the way. It's better to close it all the way." "It's cold." "Drafts are very bad." "Like that, thanks." "The heart's very treacherous, everyone knows that." "So sorry." "A good heavy black border, Pío, please." It wasn't as if she really liked funeral notices, but if a thing's to be done, it might as well be done right. *And he just stood there in front of me like he was defying me. I swear, he scared me. "Who turned the books around?" "Why, I did," I said, and he said, "The books were him," what a remark to come out with, see, the books so showy like that, with those bindings, aren't mourning or anything like it, because you know, Valen, the way they make books nowadays, they could be anything, chocolate boxes or something like that, you feel more like eating them than reading them and that's the truth, we're living in*

a period of packaging, honey, don't tell me, the outside of every-
thing is worth more than the inside, it's a swindle and a shame,
just imagine a situation like that, you tell me, with a body in the
house and bright colors all over the place, the devil himself wouldn't
have thought that one up, so I, you know how I am, had the long-
suffering patience to turn the books around one by one, thank
goodness the black swags covered most of them, if not it would've
taken all morning, I'm telling you, some little job that was, you
had to see it to believe it. And you should've seen the shape my
hands were in, the dirt those books collect, that's what books are
good for, like I say, the only thing I'm sorry about is not realizing
in time, because if the undertaker's people had helped me, just
imagine, in a jiffy, of course what are you going to ask of those
people, they didn't even notice, it's natural, see, no attention to
details, they do their job and so long kid, they don't care if they
never see you again. "I've never seen a dead man look like him,
I promise you. He hasn't even lost color!" "Don't you want to
go in and see him, Valen? I can tell you it's not the least bit
upsetting." "No, really not, silly girl. I'd rather have a memory
of Mario alive."

The shapes came in and went out again. The ebb and flow
was constant, like changing the water in a swimming pool.
"You can hardly stand it for the smoke." "You'd think they
could show a little more respect." "So sorry." Carmen leaned
forward, first on the left side and then on the right, and kiss-
kissed without the slightest emotion, purely as routine. "Thanks,
sweetie, I'm ever so grateful." The shapes had bulging, crazy-
looking eyes, but when another seated shape sighed noisily
and murmured, "The heart's very treacherous, everyone knows
that," the latest shapes to arrive, and their eyes, quieted down
and started to look like the shapes and eyes around the corpse.
But despite his good color—Mario is the healthiest-looking

corpse ever made by human hands—Mario wasn't Mario. Carmen had noticed it after she'd washed him. He didn't look like himself. She was doubtful. The dead man was an acceptable dead man, suitable, even looking heavier, but he wasn't Mario. Suddenly, as if some compassionate onlooker had put it into her head, she was struck by the idea: his glasses! Carmen went and got them and put them on him. Then she noticed the stiff pallor of the ears. Still pleased with the cleverness of her idea, she stepped back four paces trying to find a favorable perspective. But no. Doro was following her like a whipped dog: "Either open his eyes or take the glasses off our master. Can you tell me what good they're going to do him with his eyes closed?" The shapes crowded together and stretched their necks: "Look at me, Mario! I'm alone! Alone again! Alone all my life! Do you realize that? What have I done, Lord, to deserve this punishment?" And the groups stirred and whispered: "Who is she?" "Quite a scene she's putting on"; "Bet she's his lady-love"; "Apparently she's his sister-in-law"; "I don't know, I don't know." Encarna was kneeling, and emptied her lungs with every sentence. "Close it all the way, it's almost better." "Heavens, what shrieks!" Carmen didn't know what to do. "Like that, thanks." She hesitated: "What a lot of smoke!" She took off the glasses. "Maybe you're right, dear. It doesn't look like him." Mario wasn't there any more. He was in the book and in the black sweater stretched out of shape by her aggressive breasts, *don't tell me, Valen, these breasts of mine are downright brazen, they're not a widow's breasts, are they?* and in the black border of Pío Tello's funeral notice and maybe in the church, *he didn't even have time to confess, just imagine how awful!* Antonio, the principal, stepped out of the group and took hold of Encarna by the armpits. She twisted in his grasp. They struggled. "Help me. We've got to get her out of here. This woman is very much affected." *Just imagine how embarrassing! It isn't as if she was the widow! Ever since Elviro died Encarna's been after him,* *nobody can get that idea out of my head.* At last they took her away. Luis went with her and Esther helped him give her a shot of sedative. Then they telephoned for a taxi and took her to Charo's house. Vicente went with them. Little by little, Carmen started to feel like a widow again. "So sorry." "Take care of yourself, Carmen, the little ones need you." "Open up just a crack; you can't even breathe in here." The shapes came in and went out. Carmen shook limp hands and nervous hands. She leaned forward, first on the left side and then on the right and kissed the air, kissed nothing, indiscriminately. "Thanks, darling, you don't know how awfully much I appreciate it."

"Haven't they called?"

Valentina lays one hand over Carmen's hands, which are cold and crossed on her stomach, twitching nervously.

"Don't worry, silly girl. I'll let you know. Rest now. Relax. Try to relax. Vicente hasn't come back yet."

Luis stayed shut up in the room with him for nearly a quarter of an hour. *I felt as if he were confessing him, and I have a notion he was trying to give him mouth-to-mouth resuscitation, what do you think, such a long time, I even got to where I had a few hopes, I said to myself, "Maybe he's not dead," stupid of me, just imagine.* "He doesn't look dead to me. He's just exactly like he was asleep. His color hasn't even gone down." But, finally, Luis came out of the room and said, "A heart attack. It must have happened about five o'clock in the morning. It's strange in an asthenic temperament like Mario's," *I think he said asthenic, eh? don't take me too seriously, you know I'm hopeless about words, but honey, Luis with his eyes all red, like he'd been crying, it really touched me, look, you tell me if a person isn't grateful for a thing like that, because doctors, as a general rule, don't feel and don't suffer, as the saying goes, they're used to it.* "Do you mind opening the window a trifle?" "Health to pray for his soul, Doña Carmen." "You can feel the evening chill now." "Like that, thanks." "So sorry." "Señora, a telegram." Carmen felt the water welling into her nose. Nervously, with one finger, she ripped open the envelope, and sobbed as she read the message. Valentina kissed her on the cheek, directly, effusively, so that she felt the little explosion of the kiss and also its warmth. "Be brave. Don't fall apart now." Carmen held out the blue paper: "It's from Papa. Poor thing, what a terrible time he must be having! I don't even want to think about it." The shapes, their eyes calmer now, were leaving, but some still stayed huddled up to the coffin like flies on flypaper. "So sorry." "What time are they coming for the body tomorrow?" "Health to pray for him." "Do you mind opening the window a trifle? A person can hardly stand it in here." Smoke and murmurs. "Alone again! Alone all my life! What have I done to deserve this punishment?" "Those are conventionalisms, Mother; leave me out of it." "Write it down: 'Pray to God in charity . . .'" For Carmen Sotillo? *I still can't believe it, Valen; I just can't get used to the idea.* "So sorry." Carmen leaned forward, first to the left side, then to the right. Her lips and cheeks hurt from so much kissing. The edges of her right hand hurt too. She could hardly keep from shuddering every time someone shook it. Though she had always hated limp hands, she was glad of them now, gave herself up to them with contemptible pleasure, as in an adultery. "Do you mind closing the window a trifle?" *I have a notion he was giving him mouth-to-mouth resuscitation, what do you think.* "Like that, thanks. I've caught an awful cold." "The good ones die and we bad ones are left." "Good, for whom?" "He didn't just die; he suffocated." *With his eyes all red, like he'd been crying, it really touched me, look, you tell me if a person isn't grateful for a thing like that.* "They dressed up Don Porfirio, the Boss, like a Franciscan, see," *they notice instinctively that they're choking and turn over* . . . "So sorry." "Menchu, sweetie, I'm so glad to see you being so brave." "I promise you it's not the least bit upsetting," *won't even wear mourning for his father, can you beat that?* "Health to pray for his soul . . ." *When all's said and done, books are only good for gathering dust* . . . "The atmosphere's very close in here." "Do you mind . . . ?" *because doctors, as a general rule, don't feel and don't suffer, as the saying goes* . . . "So sorry." *I figure it's like fish when you take them out of the water* . . . "Health to pray for his soul . . ."

Carmen sits bolt upright, so violently that Valentina is frightened.

"Now I know someone's rung the bell, don't tell me they haven't, Valen, I heard it perfectly well."

"All right, dear, calm down. It's probably Vicente. We'll leave you alone very soon. Don't get upset."

Carmen swings her legs down from the bed, and as she does so her skirt bunches up and shows a pair of knees that are too rounded and fleshy. She feels for her shoes without bending over and slips them on her feet. Then she fixes her hair, slipping the fingers of both open hands between the strands and fluffing them out. When she has done that she pulls down the sweater under her armpits, first on the left side and then on the right. She shakes her head violently, protesting:

"I just don't have a widow's breasts, isn't that right, Valen?" she says disconsolately. "Don't fib to me."

A muffled murmur of masculine voices comes from the front hall. Valentina stands up.

"Look, dear, don't be tiresome." She turns back to the night table, to the tube of nose drops and the bottle of tranquilizers and adds, "Can you tell me what this drug store's about?"

Carmen smiles evasively.

"Mario. You know what he was like," she says. "Awfully good, but full of complexes. If he didn't take a pill and put drops in his nose, like I say, over and over, he couldn't get to sleep. Manias of his. If I was to tell you, you're not going to believe it, that once he got up at three o'clock in the morning to try to find an all-night pharmacy, you've heard it all."

Valentina raises her head abruptly, making the white streak in her hair shine for a moment like a shooting star. She smiles too.

"Poor thing," she says. "Mario really was the oddest man."

Carmen has sat up and is looking at herself in the mirror. Furiously she pulls at her sweater under the armpits, first on the left side, then on the right.

"I'm a real mess," she murmurs. "With a black bra or a white bra, these breasts of mine aren't mourning or anything like it."

Valentina is not listening. She has taken the book from the night table and is leafing through it.

"The Bible," she says. "Don't tell me Mario read the Bible too." Her smile returns, and she reads aloud, "And make straight steps with your feet: that no one, halting, may go out of the way; but rather be healed."

Carmen watches her head down, as if she were witnessing a humiliating inspection. Occasionally, with a mechanical movement, she pulls with her fingers at the black sweater, under her breasts. When she speaks, she does so as if excusing herself.

"He used to say that the Bible enriched him and calmed him."

Valentina giggles.

"He said that? How funny! Enriched, I never heard anything so amusing, Menchu, I assure you. And what about the under- lined passages?"

Carmen clears her throat; she feels more and more belittled. She adds, "Manias of his. Mario read over and over, only the underlined parts, understand? Now," her eyes mist over but, paradoxically, her voice grows stronger, "I'll pick up the book and it will be like being with him again. They're his last hours, do you realize that?"

Valentina shuts the book briskly and hands it to Carmen. The murmur of voices in the hall grows louder. Suddenly it stops, and after a few seconds of silence they hear some cautious taps on the bedroom door.

"She's coming," says Carmen. And instinctively, she tugs at the sweater under her armpits.

They hear Mario's voice. "It's Vicente."

"I'm coming," Valentina says. "I'm coming." She goes over to Carmen and puts her arms around her waist. "Really, silly girl, don't you want me to stay with you?"

"Really, Valen, I'd rather be alone, if not I'd tell you just the same, you know me."

Valentina leans forward and both women cross heads, first on the left side, then on the right, and languidly kiss the air, kiss nothing, so that both of them feel the little explosions of the kisses but not their warmth.

In the little hall, Vicente is waiting with his overcoat on. Mario is beside him, crammed into his blue sweater. Carmen helps Valentina put on her coat and then the two of them make a concerted search for her purse. They cross heads again and kiss the air, kiss nothing. "Good-bye, sweetie, I'll be here tomorrow morning first thing. Really, don't you want me to stay with you?" "Really, Valen, thanks for everything." She turns to Vicente. "How about Encarna?"

Vicente clears his throat. Wakes are not his element. He feels out of place.

"She went to sleep," he says. "Finally she went to sleep. Luis says she won't wake up till tomorrow. She was impossible. I've never seen anything like it."

Mario looks first at one of them and then the other as if they were speaking a foreign language and he was having too hard a time translating. As Valentina gives him her hand she says, "You look tired, Mario. You ought to go to bed."

Mario doesn't answer. Carmen answers for him.

"He'll go to bed right away," she says. "Everybody's in bed."

"What about Daddy?"

"I'm going to stay with him."

At last Valentina and Vicente leave, and for quite a long time they can hear Valentina's careful footsteps descending the stairs, and the soothing murmur of Vicente's voice. Carmen turns to face her son and shows him the book.

"Mario," she says, "go to bed, I beg of you. I want to be alone with your father. It's the last time."

Mario hesitates.

"Just as you wish," he says, "but if you need anything, call me; I won't be able to get to sleep."

Spontaneously, he leans forward and unembarrassedly kisses Carmen's right cheek. She feels a warm, sudden moisture at the corners of her eyes. She raises her arms and presses him to her for a few seconds. Finally she says, "Till tomorrow, Mario."

Mario goes down the hall. He has a strange way of walking, half languid and half athletic, as if he had trouble controlling his own strength. Carmen turns and goes into the study. She empties the ashtrays into the wastepaper basket and takes it out into the hall. Even so there is a smell of cigarette butts, but she doesn't mind. She closes the door and sits down in the low armchair. She has turned off all the lights except the floor lamp which floods with light the book she has just opened on her lap, and whose glow reaches to the corpse's feet.

I

....

House and riches are given by parents: but a prudent wife is properly from the Lord and as far as you're concerned, sweetheart, I suppose you're satisfied, you have every reason to be, because here between you and I, life hasn't treated you so badly, you tell me, a woman all to yourself, not bad looking, who's done miracles with practically no money, you don't find one like that around every corner, don't kid yourself. And now when the complications start, whoosh, so long, just like the first night, remember? you go off and leave me all alone pulling the load. And I'm not complaining, understand that, other women are worse off, look at Transi, just imagine with three little ones, but honestly it makes me furious to have you go off without even noticing the worries I have, without a word of appreciation, as if all this was normal and natural. You men, as soon as the knot's tied you take it easy, a faithfulness policy, like I say, of course you don't feel bound by that, you go off on a spree whenever you feel like it and that's that, but us women, you know it all too well, are romantic and stupid. And it isn't that I'm going to say now that you've fooled around, sweetheart, I should say not, I don't want to be unfair, but I wouldn't swear to it on a Bible, see. So I don't trust you? Call it whatever you want to, but the truth is that you people who're so proud of being honorable are the worst kind, the year we went to the beach you certainly got an eyeful, darling, I remember poor Mama, may she rest in peace, with that sharp eye she had, I've never seen anything like it, that the best of men ought to be tied up, so there. Just look at Encarna, I know she's your sister-in-law, but ever since Elviro died she's been after you, nobody can get that out of my head. Encarna has some pretty peculiar ideas about other people's obligations, sweetheart, and she thinks that the younger brother has to take the place of the older brother and things like that, and here, just between the two of us, I'll tell you that when we were going together, every time we went to the movies and I used to hear her whispering to you in the dark, I was madly jealous. And you going on about how she was your sister-in-law, big news, who ever said she wasn't, you always miss the point, trying to defend what can't be defended, you always found excuses for everybody but me and that's the truth. And it's not just for the sake of talking, sweetheart, but sometimes with one excuse and sometimes with another, you still haven't told me what happened between Encarna and you the day you won the competitive exam for your teaching job, I'd like to know what business she had to be there, in your letter you were so careful, my boy, "Encarna went to hear the voting and then we celebrated the victory together." But there are lots of ways of celebrating, it seems to me, and you said you went to Fuima's and had some beer and shrimps, sure, as if a person was stupid, as if I didn't know Encarna, some troublemaker she is, my boy. Do you think I've forgotten, blockhead, the way she used to snuggle up to you in the movies right in front of me? Yes, I know we weren't married then, fine thing if we had been, but if I remember right we'd been going out for more than two years, and that kind of relationship gives any woman some rights, Mario, except for her, I'm telling you the truth, she really drove me wild with her sucking up to you and her silly talk. Do you think that, knowing her, when the two of you were alone, I'm going to swallow the idea that Encarna would be satisfied with a beer and a few shrimps? And that's not what's hardest to bear, mind you, after all we're made of flesh and blood, what hurts me the most is the way you hold back, "Don't be suspicious," "Encarna is a good girl who's been overwhelmed by her misfortune," see, as if a person was an idiot, maybe you could get away with that with a woman who wasn't as smart as I am, but I know better . . . You saw the little scene she put on yesterday, sweetheart, so embarrassing! you're not going to tell me that that was the normal reaction of a sister-in-law, she really called attention to herself, and I was so taken aback, see, it made me look like a woman with no feelings or something, and when Vicente Rojo said, "Take her away, she's very much affected," I was livid, I admit it. In all sincerity, Mario, was that any way to behave? Why, you'd have thought she was the widow! I'll bet anything you please that when what happened to Elviro happened she didn't carry on to that extent, heaven knows what I would have had to do. It's the same as when your father died, Mario, I've always said so, the idea is to put me in a poor light, she did leave me looking bad, don't tell me she didn't. To be truthful with you, I never liked Encarna, Mario, Encarna or women of her kind, of course for you even women of the streets deserve to be pitied, I don't know where we'll wind up with that idea, "Nobody does it because she wants to, victims of society," don't make me laugh, you men are really impossible when you start making excuses, because what I say is, why don't they work? Why don't they go and be maids the way they ought to? It's no news that household help is disappearing, Mario, sweetheart, and even if you do say it's a good sign, fat lot of good your theories have done us, the fact is there's more immorality every day and nowadays even the maids want to be ladies, for your information, the one that doesn't smoke paints her nails or wears pants and I don't know what all. Do you think that's the way it should be? Those women are destroying family life, Mario, just like it sounds, I remember at home, two maids and a housekeeper for just a few of us, that was living, they earned practically nothing, I don't deny it, but they got food and their clothes, can you tell me why they needed anything else? Papa was wonderful about that: "Julia, that's enough; leave a little so they can taste it in the kitchen too." There was family life then, time for everything, and everyone in their own class, everybody happy. Just look at me now, pestered the whole blessed day, when I'm not in the kitchen I'm washing out underwear, you know how it is, a woman can't make two of herself, and no matter how willing she is, with one maid for a family of seven, it's awfully hard to be a lady. But you men just don't realize these things, sweetheart, the day you get married you buy a slave, you make quite a deal, like I say, because everybody knows that men go for the deals, there's no two ways about it. So the woman works like a mule and doesn't have a moment's breathing space? That's her lookout! It's her duty, isn't that lovely, and I'm not reproaching you for anything, darling, but it does hurt that in more than twenty years you haven't spoken a word of appreciation, I know, you haven't exactly been a demanding husband, that's true, but sometimes it isn't enough simply not to be demanding, look at your brother Elviro, and I'm not saying that Elviro was an ideal man, I should say not, but your brother was made of different stuff, oh my yes, he did little things. Do you remember the coin purse he gave me the afternoon we all had a snack together in June of '36? I still have it, mind you, I think it's in the dresser, along with a pile of junk, it seems to me. And the way Encarna behaved! Some scene that was, I thought she was going to eat him up, honestly, and then three months later, when Elviro died, she must've been awfully sorry. Your brother was sensitive, Mario, and any man with a little gumption, simply to be the kind of man he should have been, would have kept his wife on a shorter rein. God forgive me, but ever since I knew them I've got it into my head that Encarna stepped out on him, mind you, I don't know why, she had a lot of temperament for a man like him. And let it be understood that I don't like to make snap judgments, you know that perfectly well, although later, when she became a widow, she went after you, nobody can get that out of my head, and absolutely shameless about it, eh? And I don't care if you swear on a stack of Bibles, I'll never succeed in believing that that day at Fuima's she was satisfied with a beer and some shrimps, and I'm not making it up, you know how I am, I may have other faults but I can't stand to dramatize things. Do you want it spelled out? Do you know that Valentina yesterday, when she took me aside, said to me, exactly like I'm telling you, she said, "Your sister-in-law can't leave him alone even after he's dead." What do you think of that? Are you still going to tell me that it's my imagination? Because no matter what you say about Valen, you're not going to deny that she's a very intelligent woman, I'm not just talking for talk's sake, I'm telling you what she said, "She can't leave him alone even after he's dead." Of course, when you come right down to it, I was the stupid one, or not so stupid, who knows, the fact is that a person has principles and principles are sacred, everybody knows that, if you really look at it there's nothing like principles. And goodness, if I had wanted to! With anybody at all, Mario, mind you, with anybody at all. Take Eliseo San Juan, the one who has the dry-cleaning shop, to give you just one example, he never misses a chance, especially if I'm wearing the blue sweater, to say something to me: "You're terrific, you're terrific, every day you get more terrific." He never lets up, my boy, that man is really persistent, he's been at it for years, it's not something that just started, and there are others I won't mention, you poor fool, I'm still good to look at, I'm no old bag, what did you think. Men still look at me on the street, I'll have you know, Mario, you're always up in the clouds, "A vulgar fellow, that San Juan," don't make me laugh, lots of women wouldn't turn up their noses at him. The thing is that a person has principles even though nowadays principles are nothing but a hindrance, especially when other people don't respect them, and that's another thing. "A vulgar fellow, that San Juan," what do you think of that? And then, at night, not the slightest attention, I never saw such a lukewarm man, my boy, and it isn't that I'm especially interested in all that, I can take it or leave it, you know me, but at least to act like I'm there, you used to let the good days go by and then, all of a sudden, whoosh, you'd take the notion on the very worst days, mind you, "Let's not be stingy with God," "Let's not mix numbers into this," how easy it is to say, and then the one that had all the trouble for nine months, getting sick in the corners, was me, because you, with your classes and your group of friends, had enough, sure, anybody would be happy like that. And do you want to hear some more? Do you think a woman's made of cardboard, and can't feel or suffer? Didn't you realize how humiliated I was every time I got big and you didn't want me? Armando certainly did exactly the right thing, for your information, don't tell me he's a lout, the thing about him is he's absolutely plainspoken, what did you mean by sitting down beside Esther, even if she is such an intellectual,

Armando behaved just exactly right that day, see, "Let everybody take care of his own responsibilities." But just think how embarrassing it was for me, it's all pure whim, because on the good days you didn't want to and the bad days, whoosh, you'd take the notion, you certainly did, and then even my stomach bothered you. Is it a woman's fault if she gets so big, do you want to tell me that? No, Mario darling, nothing unpremeditated about it, now you come out with that excuse, you sat next to Esther willingly and knowingly, let's not go into that again. It's like the business about sleeping with the children, that's right, tell me, how many times have you flung that in my face? And what's so special about it? Isn't it natural that when you had your first class at eleven, and I'd been up and doing since nine, you should have taken charge of the baby? Sure, I know they're a nuisance, what're you going to tell me, just imagine, a pain in the neck, but it's something you have to go through, men can't stand up to anything, they act like martyrs, I'd like to see you having a baby, once and never again after you'd tried it, so there, like your sister-in-law, she didn't know what that's like either, she says that Elviro, well, you guess. But because she doesn't know she has to think something up and run off at the mouth and make trouble between us saying I abuse your patience, look who's talking, and telling me I don't appreciate the kind of husband I have, as if I was leading you to the grave or almost. Encarna has a hide like a rhinoceros, Mario, why should I tell you anything different, though with you men, everybody knows, the better a woman is the worse you treat her, because you're selfish and the day the knot gets tied, a faithfulness policy, you can rest easy. I'd like to see you men with a woman who doesn't have principles, a kind of flighty one, I'm telling you, you'd behave with a little more care, that's logical, because of what's at stake for you, so there.

II

. . . .

But having food, and wherewith to be covered, with these we are
content. For they that will become rich, fall into temptation, and
into the snare of the devil, and into many unprofitable and hurtful
desires, which drown men into destruction and perdition. For the
desire of money is the root of all evils, and that's the selfsame
reason I'll find it very hard to forgive you, sweetheart, if I live
a thousand years, your not letting me have my way about a
car, I know that shortly after we were married it was a luxury,
but nowadays everybody has a little one—a Six Hundred—at
least, Mario, even janitor's wives as far as that goes, it's perfectly obvious. You'll never understand it, but a woman, I
don't know how to tell you, a woman feels humiliated when
all her friends are riding in cars and she's on foot, I'm telling
you the truth, every time Esther or Valentina or even Crescente, the grocer, talked about going for a ride on Sundays I
felt sick, honestly. Though I oughtn't to be the one to say it,
you've had the good luck to happen on a homebody, a woman
who can make two into four, and you've been loved without
loving back, Mario, that's so easy, and you think that with a
cheap brooch or some little trifle for my birthday you've done
your job, far from it, stupid, I'm sick and tired of telling you
that you don't live in the real world, but you, you pay no
attention. And do you know what that is, Mario? Pure selfish-

ness, for your information, of course I know a teacher at the High School isn't a millionaire, if only he were, but there are other things, I think, nowadays nobody's satisfied with only one job. Sure, you're going to tell me you had your books and *El Correo,* but I'm telling you that your books and your miserable rag of a newspaper haven't given us anything but trouble, you know I'm not fibbing, don't come and tell me, my boy, rows with the censorship, rows with people, and what did you get out of it, a pittance. And it's no surprise to me, Mario, because what I say is, who was going to read those wretched things about people who're half dead of hunger and rolling around in the mud like pigs? Come on, use your head, who was going to read that mess about *The Sand Castle* where you don't talk about anything but philosophy? Of course you go on a lot about thesis and impact and all that stuff, but just tell me what earthly good is that? People don't give a damn about theses and impacts, believe me, those friends of yours are the ones who've ruined you, that Aróstegui and that Moyano, the one with the beard, they're a bunch of misfits. And it wasn't that Papa didn't warn you, I should say not, he went over your book with a magnifying glass, Mario, really carefully, I'm telling you, and he said no, that if you were writing to amuse yourself, fine, but if you were aiming for fame or money you'd better try a different tack, do you remember? and well, you kept right on. And I can understand why you wouldn't listen to just anyone, but as far as Papa is concerned, a man as really objective as he is, don't tell me, a man who's written for the illustrated pages of *ABC* for ever so long, I think maybe since the paper was founded, and maybe not in other things, but as far as writing he knows what he's talking about, I should say he does! And me too, Mario, didn't I tell you a thousand times myself to try to find a good plot, for instance the one about

Maximino Conde who married that widow and then fell in love with his stepdaughter? Now those plots are the ones people are interested in, Mario, don't kid yourself, of course I know it was a little bit iffy, well, a teeny bit racy, but you could have made him react decently when she, the girl, offers herself to him, and that way the novel would even set a good example. But you stuck to your guns, in one ear and out the other, and two years later you published that thing, *The Inheritance,* which was really too much, I'm telling you the honest truth, there's just no way to understand it, because do you really think, Mario, that anybody can be interested in a book that takes place in a country that doesn't exist and where the hero is a common soldier whose feet hurt? Valentina laughed her head off telling about it at the Thursday tea; all of them did, of course, only Esther tried to give you a hand, out of habit, see, just to make herself important, you could tell a mile off that she hadn't understood it either. And those soldiers were really weird, Mario, you've got to understand. How can the soldiers of two opposing armies jump out of the trenches and hug each other and say they wouldn't let themselves be pushed around by THAT FORCE any more? In your books you always put words in capital letters or italics, I don't know why, Armando says just because it looks good, heaven knows, but the fact is nobody understood a thing about the book because if the generals saw their soldiers hugging the others they would have shot them then and there and they would have been right besides, mind you. That was weird in the first place, darling, but it was even weirder when the soldier said all of a sudden, completely beside the point, "Where is THAT FORCE? It doesn't have a head, or a shape, and nobody knows where it's hiding," and then, without any more explanation, all the soldiers get scared, go back to their trenches and start shooting at each other again. Honestly, sweetheart, do you think that makes any sense? That silly fool Esther, trying so hard to take your part, that they were symbols, huh, as if she understood what on earth it was all about. Higinio Oyarzun was closer to the mark when he said one night at the Circle, I heard him all right, I went cold all over, that the book was the work of a pacifist and a traitor, and Don Nicolás didn't waste any time coming to you with the tale, I know all about it, that old nuisance of a Don Nicolás, I don't know how they let him edit a newspaper, a man who was in prison, almost a year, back during the war. I don't care how much you laugh at me, Mario, Don Nicolás is a man from the wrong side of the street, I don't know if he was for Lerroux or Alcalá Zamora, but somebody important, and, of course, an awful Red, one of the worst kind, one of those who don't come out in the open. And the people who count are fed up with him, naturally, he's always insinuating things and making trouble, he ought to be ashamed of himself, look, even though a person shouldn't hate, I have a thing about that man, I can't stand him, the harm he's done you. Between him and that Aróstegui and Moyano and the whole bunch, they've really turned your head, darling, you weren't like this to start with, don't come and tell me now. And then that cloud of smoke, my God! Do you mind telling me what you were all doing in there, smoking for so long? Putting the world to rights, that's for sure, every one of you taking the words out of the others' mouths, heavens how you yelled, and what did it all add up to, a few stupid ideas, whether money was smart or money was selfish, look, the only thing you didn't say about money was the gospel truth of it, Mario, that it's necessary, and we would have been a lot better off if instead of talking about money so much you'd set yourself to earning some, like I say. Because you do know how to write, darling, I've told you over and over, the only thing is the plots, I just don't know how you think them up, if you'd gone hunting for them high and low they couldn't have been more obscure, and that was when a person could understand you, and then when you started to talk about structures and things like that, I was really in the dark, I promise you. I would have liked it so much if you'd written love stories! Now there's a subject that gets to people, Mario, because love is an eternal subject, why, just because, because it's very human, because everybody's mind can grasp it. If you'd only listened to me! The story about Maximino Conde, imagine, a mature man, married for the second time to the mother and in love with the daughter, that was a plot for the movies, well, you couldn't even give me that pleasure, you always do the opposite of what I want. I don't want to cry, Mario, but if I look back and think about the few times in my life you've listened to me, I can't help it. Would it have been such a big effort to earn enough for a Six Hundred, you tell me, lazybones? I'm not saying years ago, Mario, but nowadays, they practically give them away, just about everybody, why Paco himself the other day, see, "Do you know how to drive?" and I said, "Not much, hardly at all," what was I going to tell him, "We don't have a car," and then he started to hit himself on the head, "No, no, no!" he didn't believe it, mind you. The children would have gone mad over a Six Hundred, Mario, and as for me, just imagine, it would have changed my life. But no, a car is a luxury, just think, at this stage in the game, anyone who heard you say that, it's just like the set of silverware. Twenty-three years, Mario, wanting a set of silverware, it's so easy to say, twenty-three years waiting to be on a level with our friends, and every time I invited them, see, a cold supper, all canapés, you tell me, a woman can't do miracles. Holy God, it makes me so ashamed! I always hated to be a sponger, I remember Mama, may she rest in peace, was just the opposite, "It's better to sin on the generous side," of course at home it was different, another kind of basis, especially before the thing about Julia with Galli Constantino. But you never cared what my family was like, Mario, let's be truthful, I was brought up for a different type of life, sometimes I think about the expression on poor Mama's face if she'd come back to life, and better off dead, like I'm telling you. I can just hear her: "One maid with five little ones!" "Life evolves, these are different times," sure, don't make me laugh, they're different times for us women, us poor things, because of our good principles, and meanwhile you men go on talking and smoking, you can be sure of that, or writing one of those messes nobody can digest, as if writing were work, Mario, because you can't tell me . . . When you come right down to it, the stupid one was me, when we were going steady I could see already what your weak points were. "One duro a week; as long as I'm not earning it I won't have any more than that," look, how lovely, your father, and I'm not the only one who says so, sweetheart, the whole town gossiped about it, had the reputation of being tight-fisted, and God forbid I should think that you were, but if you, because of your bringing up or for any other reason, didn't need things, that doesn't mean that the rest of us didn't, because to tell you the honest truth I was used to something different, it's not only me that says so, anybody who knows a little bit about me can tell you. Believe me, Mario, the soles of my feet still hurt from tramping the streets, and if it rained, under the archways, and if it was cold, the heat of the air vents in the cafés. Sincerely now, do you think that was any kind of a situation for a girl of the middle class tending toward upper class? Let's not kid ourselves,

Mario, people's habits come from inside them and ever since I've known you, you've had proletarian tastes, because don't tell me that it'd occur to the devil himself to go to the High School on a bicycle. Tell me the truth, was that appropriate for your position? Don't kid yourself, Mario, sweetheart, the bike just isn't for people of your class, every time I saw you I nearly died, believe me, and I don't even mention when you put the little seat on the bar for the child, I could have killed you, you made me cry and everything. Heavens, I was furious! Valen came to see me one day and said so insinuatingly: "I saw Mario with the little boy," I felt like sinking into the ground, I can tell you, "He's taken the notion to do that, see, manias of his," what else could I have said to her. I don't like to think that you did it to humiliate me, Mario, but it does hurt that you never consulted with me, you took the notion and wham, just the same as with the method, a person can't thumb his nose at the whole world, everybody has to live in their place in society, a person's rank carries obligations, you utter fool, and a teacher, I don't say an engineer, but he's somebody, I think, why, Antonio himself, when they made him principal, even if he was smooth as butter about it, came to tell you a word to the wise, that the bike was too much, but you kept right on, no Antonios for you or Antonias either, like I say. And I'll tell you something else, nobody can get it out of my head that when Antonio opened the file on you, apart from other reasons, I won't go into that, it was because he took a dislike to you, see. It's the same as with Bertrán, do you think it's the thing at all for a teacher to be seen in public with an usher? Well, of course not, smarty, it's not as if I was peculiar or anything, it's the same as you and he chatting together, no sir, "Good morning" at most, or "Good afternoon," not for any special reason, simply because it's two different worlds, two different languages. But you, you kept on encouraging him to talk, so did he earn a little or a lot, getting him stirred up, that's all it was, if instead of concerning yourself so much with what other people earned you'd concerned yourself a little bit more about earning it yourself, it'd be an entirely different story, and anyway, when you come right down to it, if Bertrán didn't earn much, how are you going to compare? In his class, he can go to work in bedroom slippers, dressed any old way, while you have to keep up appearances, see, in accordance with your position, though you've often made me despair, too, about the way you wear your clothes.

III

·················

*Thou hast wounded my heart, my sister, my spouse, thou hast
wounded my heart with one of thy eyes, and with one hair of thy
neck,* and yes, that's all very well, Mario, I'm not going to argue
about it, but tell me one thing, come on, please, why didn't
you ever read your poems to me, or even tell me that you
were writing them? If it hadn't been for Elviro, I wouldn't have
known a thing, mind you, why, I hadn't a clue, and then it
turned out that you wrote one to my eyes, how exciting!
Elviro, told me, see, one day, apropos of nothing, he said,
"Does Mario read you his poems?" and I didn't know what he
was talking about, "What poems?" and then he told me, he
told me, I swear he did, "Knowing you, I'm not surprised he
wrote one to your eyes," I blushed and everything, but that
night, when I asked to see them, you wouldn't hear of it, "A
weakness, they're mushy and sentimental," I don't know why
all of you have it in for sentiment these days, my boy, I was
really hurt because you didn't trust me, I'll have you know,
and the more I insisted, that those poems weren't written for
others, what kind of a remark was that, as if a person could
write for nobody at all. You have a lot of stubborn streaks like
that, sweetheart, that's what I say, if you don't speak words to
somebody they aren't anything, smarty, just noises, see, or like
scribbles, you tell me. Miserable words, the trouble words

have given you, and I'm not talking about today, but ever since I've known you! You're not going to believe this, Mario, because I've kept it awfully quiet, but if I went in where you were meeting with your friends sometimes, heavens, what a lot of smoke, my boy, it was to listen to what all of you were saying, you can't put one over on me, you can talk about anything you want to, but nobody can get it out of my head that you were talking about women and every time I showed up you'd change the subject, men are like that, you're all alike. And I don't know if it was coincidence or if you had a password, it's anybody's guess, but every time I'd stick my nose in, it never failed, you were talking about money, if it was smart or it was selfish, and if it wasn't money it was words, every time, and criticizing, of course, weird things, about if God didn't make men bad but words confused them, it's a miracle I didn't burst out at you, you take Señora Felipa's son, deaf and mute from birth, and you say, "So what?" well, look, took an axe to his brother, do you think that's nothing? And you, "Leave that sort of thing alone," I've always been hurt by your poor opinion of me, Mario, as if I was an ignoramus or something. But I can forgive you everything, except not reading me your poems, because here between you and I, I'll tell you that sometimes I think you wrote them for Encarna and then I really lose my head, I realize it, because a word you don't speak to anyone is like going outdoors and yelling at random, see, like you were crazy, and you were perfectly well then, the other thing was lots later, and it's not that I'm saying that the other thing was important, of course not, not the least bit, a spoiled brat's tantrum, because you tell me, if nothing hurt you and you didn't have a fever, what kind of an illness was that? I'm telling you the truth, if I'm sorry about anything it's having spent twenty-three years looking after you, like a martyr, if I'd been a little tougher, it'd be a different story altogether. Transi used to say it even at first, "What do you see in that puny little guy?" and do you know what I saw, do you want to know? Why, a skinny boy, looking starved for affection, see, sad eyes and run-over heels, because you really murder shoes, my boy, there's no shoe that can stand up to you, and then, every time you saw me, you'd look at me fit to break my heart, eh? and you looked all the more miserable when that lout Armando would put his fingers to his temples and bellow like a bull if one of us went walking with Paco Alvarez or anybody else. And Transi, "Don't tell me, honey, he looks like a scarecrow," and you kept right on looking like a poor little fellow because you have deceptive eyes, Mario, I promise you that, and I was seventeen, you tell me, two years younger than Menchu right now, practically a child, and at that age, everybody knows, the thing that makes a woman proudest is to feel she's indispensable to someone. I remember I used to say to myself, "That boy needs me, he might kill himself otherwise," foolishness, of course, romanticizing. Later, of course, I realize it, I made a terrible mistake, like a fool, I ought to have known, you had enough with your teaching and your friends, what did you need me for, let's see? Not for what we did every week, certainly not, any woman would have done for that, maybe better than me; and as for me, you know it full well, on the good days completely indifferent and on the bad days, here between you and I, you acted like a monster, heavens, how you men carry on, go to it like brutes, the things you say, that's assuming you weren't thinking about another woman, it's an obsession, Mario, I can't help it. Because with your friends you talked about other women, Mario, don't you deny it, I heard that Aróstegui plain as plain, and he seems like such a well brought up young man, see, saying that "freedom was a whore in the hands of money," fine way to talk that is, and didn't even apologize when he saw me, of course, naturally, how could it be expected of him, it's the work of Don Nicolás, that's what they think that because they're young they have the right to do anything they want, taking advantage, and you, "A rebellious youth," rebellious about what? because I'd like to know what they have to complain about, you tell me, they've had everything handed to them ready-made, they live in order and peace, more spoiled every day, everybody says so, and you either clam up or talk in code, so as not to lose the knack, "They want a voice," or "They want responsibilities," or "Trying themselves out to see if they can live in society," just phrases, because can you tell me, sweetheart, what you mean by all that? I don't know what they want, but what I can tell you is they ought to have more respect and a little bit more consideration, why even our Mario, you can see for yourself, and I'm well aware that he's very young, but once he gets twisted out of shape, can you tell me who's going to straighten him out? Bad examples, sweetheart, I never get tired of telling you so, and it's not that I'm going to say now that Mario's a lost cause, nowhere near it, because he's affectionate in his way, but don't tell me the way he acts every time he starts talking, why, his eyes pop right out of his head, with this "patriotic gush" and his "Pharisee-isms," and the day I heard him stand up for a lay form of government I almost fainted, Mario, honestly, to think we could come to this. Of course, the University isn't good for these youngsters, don't kid yourself, they stuff them with a lot of weird ideas out there, I don't care what you say about it, now Mama, may she rest in peace, used to really put her finger on it, "Teaching, at school; upbringing, at home," because Mama, and it's not just because I say so, never missed a trick.

But you give the children too much leeway, Mario, and you have to be stern with children, because even if it hurts them at the time they'll thank you for it in the long run. Just look at Mario, twenty-two years old and all the livelong day reading or thinking, and reading and thinking are bad, sweetheart, make sure of that, and his friends more of the same, they scare me and that's the truth. Let's not kid ourselves, Mario, but most of the youngsters today are half Reds, why, I don't know what's wrong with them, they're crazy in the head, full of the wildest ideas about freedom and dialogue and those things they talk about. My God, a few years ago, just remember! Don't talk to a boy about the war nowadays, Mario, and of course I know war is horrible, sweetheart, but after all it's the business of the brave, people can say of us Spaniards that we've always been warlike, but we haven't done so badly it seems to me, there's no country in the world that comes anywhere near us, you've heard Papa say, "Machines, perhaps not; but spiritual values and decency, enough for export." And as for religious values, it's pretty much the same story, Mario, we're the most Catholic people in the world and the best, even the Pope said so, just look at other places, divorce and adultery, they haven't the faintest notion of shame. Here, thank God, except for a few hussies, there's none of that, you know it, just look at me, why, it doesn't even pass through my mind, eh? I don't have to tell you, because I've had chances, take Eliseo San Juan, that man really persecutes me, "You're terrific, you're terrific, every day you get more terrific," it's wicked of him, but he says it just to be saying something, my goodness, he's well aware that he's wasting his time, he won't get anywhere, I should say not! And Eliseo's not bad at all, according to Valen, "As an animal he's got everything," he does have a great build, you can see he's quite something, but I don't pay any attention, as if it wasn't me he was talking about, no Eliseo for me or Saint Eliseo either, I swear. Principles are principles, and Valen, no matter what she says, is more faithful than anybody, she just talks to be talking, for instance you the other night, at their party, you stuck to her like glue, I'd like to know where the two of you went when you left the living room. You oughtn't to drink like that, sweetheart, you drank too much, and it wasn't as if I didn't warn you, "Leave it alone, leave it alone," but you were impossible, and Valentina "tee-hee-hee" and "ha-ha-ha," she's marvelous, Valen is, the way she adjusts, and that I should leave you alone, you were very cute, well! but when you started to pop champagne corks at the streetlights, I could have killed you, mind you, that's no way to behave, as for me, anything but losing my manners, it's a question of upbringing, they really branded that into me at home and look at me now. But even Antonio was annoyed, he said so to Vicente, he didn't even notice I was there, "I think Mario's going too far," I'm telling you, and I know Antonio's no favorite of yours, because of the business about the file, sure, don't say it isn't, that's obvious, but you tell me what he could do, he's a really good person, I don't care what you say, right wing all his life, Mama always said, because Mama, and it's not just because I say so, had some very original and very modern points of view, I don't know how to explain it to you, for instance, I used to tell her, "That boy needs me," about you, of course, and she'd say, "Child, don't confuse love with pity," just think, poor thing, after what happened to Julia with Galli, anything at all, when you come right down to it, the thing about Julia was a terrible blow, just thinking about it I practically die of shame, see. Of course you, right off, with your comprehension, and I don't know why you have so much for some people and so little for others, just look at Antonio and Oyarzun, and as for Antonio, well, that's understandable, but Higinio, you tell me, a fellow who behaved wonderfully during the war, so open and friendly, there's no one like him, well, so "A toady and a tattletale," I'll bet that's what you amuse yourself with when you get together with your friends, probably haven't anything better to do, like I say, what bothers you men is to have somebody come in from outside and take over from the rest of you, that's what it is after all, a man who shows up with the clothes on his back and a few days later he's bought a car, let's be honest, that's what you and your friends can't forgive him for, because you stop to think about it and Oyarzun works like a mule, if he doesn't have five jobs he has six, and at least three of them quite responsible. What does it matter that he arrived here without a cent? Higinio's worth something, and if Fito happened to take to him right from the start, why, so much the better, you had him right in your hands, you poor fool, don't you forget it, and out of stubborness you let everything go smash, because he certainly held out a lifeline to you, and you, playing the fool, paid no attention, neither more nor less, and then as if that wasn't enough you got mad at him and really put the lid on it, because if you'd behaved like you should have and played him along with a little tact, no more than that, God knows where you might have got to with him. But why did you climb on your high horse? After all, didn't Fito mean to do you a favor? But not you, no sir, "Nobody plays around with me," "I don't bet where I can't win," just phrases, for stubbornness you're priceless, my boy, you never had a knack for making friends, admit it, and now that you're alone, what did you expect, a handful of misfits from your little group and that's all. And friends, as poor Mama used to say, may she rest in peace, can do you more good than a university degree, and she's absolutely right, Mario, events have proved me right, you tell me.

IV

....

If one of thy brethren that dwelleth within the gates of thy city in the land which the Lord thy God will give thee, come to poverty: thou shalt not harden thy heart, nor close thy hand, but shalt open it to the poor man, thou shalt lend him, that which thou perceivest he hath need of. Transi was the one who told me, Mario, just think, before we started going steady, what a lot of water has gone under the bridge since then, that your father lent money at interest, of course, I didn't care one way or another about that, banks lend money too and it's legal. And your father didn't seem to be a bad person when I met him, I swear, to be frank with you I expected the worst and then he was just an unhappy man, a little unbalanced maybe, most likely because of Elviro and José María, who knows, do you remember? "I was the one who wouldn't let him go to the office. To be out on the street yesterday was rashness," that's the way he went on the whole time, and your mother was so brave, "Shut up! Don't you hear me, Elviro? Shut up!" but he kept on, hammering away, it was so tiresome, like a parrot, just exactly. After a little while you arrived, and right on your heels Gaudencio Moral, looking terrible, his clothes torn and everything, he'd just escaped from the Reds up in the hills, remember? and he was the one who told us about Elviro, what an afternoon that was, good heavens, grief piled on grief, and I was thinking

"What will Mario do when he sees me?" because even in the middle of all that I had my expectations, what a fool I was, it was all for nothing, you came in and didn't even look at me, only at your mother, "It's been God's will; it's like some natural catastrophe and we happened to get hit, you have to accept it," what kind of a way was that to console her, and during all this I was sitting there in the corner, completely numb, see. After a long time you turned around and I thought "now," but not a bit of it, "Hello" and that was all, always the same, nobody's drier or more detached than you are, sweetheart. And it wasn't as if I expected you to kiss me, I wouldn't have let you or anybody else do that, I should say not, but a little tiny bit more effusive, yes, I even thought, why should I tell you any different, "He'll take my two hands in his and squeeze them. After all it's a terrible misfortune," but sure, sure, just "Hello" and no more. It's the same as after the war ended, you kept staring at me in the movies, and I wondered about it, "Does my face look funny?" but one fine day you started wearing glasses, things would have turned out differently if I'd seen you in them before, and then you didn't even do that any more. And in the park in the mornings, more of the same, don't tell me, "my love" and "sweetheart" over and over, like a broken record, stupid catchwords, you couldn't think up anything more original, dear boy, a lot of poems but for your girlfriend the same old song, sometimes I said to myself, I swear I did, "He doesn't like me, he doesn't like me the least bit," all hot and bothered, that's logical. What a difference with the old guys! I'd have plenty to tell about that. It isn't that Gabriel and Evaristo were so very old, but in comparison, and of course they were both so fresh, the afternoon they took us to the studio, to that attic place, I was so nervous, my heart going pitty-pat, and Transi so cool and collected, you wouldn't believe, who was going to tell her anything, she drank two glasses of peppermint liqueur as if it was nothing at all, and when they showed us the paintings with the naked women in them, she kept commenting, "Yes, that one's very well realized," or "This one's wonderful as to light," the brazen thing, and I, like I'm telling you, never opened my mouth, because I thought the whole thing was so shameless. And when they propped up all the pictures with the naked women in them, the most any of them had on was a necklace or a carnation in their hair, imagine, I didn't know where to look, and suddenly Gabriel put his hand all covered with hair on my leg, and "What do you say, girlie?" I was as stiff as a board, honestly, it took my breath away, I couldn't make a peep or move a finger, and Gabriel "Another drink?" see, and meanwhile Evaristo put his arm around Transi and said he'd like to paint a portrait of her, and Transi, as if it was nothing out of the way, "Like the one of the girl with the carnation in her hair?" and that was all Evaristo needed, "That's the one," he said, and Transi nearly died laughing, "But with a few more clothes on, don't you think?" and Evaristo laughed and laughed too, "What for, girlie? This is art, hadn't you noticed?" But Gabriel wouldn't take his hand away for anything in the world, I was furious when I realized I was starting to blush, take note, and when he said, looking at my bosoms absolutely brazenly, "We'd have to do a bust of this one," what a shameless guy, I thought I was going to burst, I told Transi so on the stairs, "I'd be nuts to go out again with the old guys, I swear; both of them just want to take advantage." But Transi was all excited, you'd be surprised, like she was drunk, "Evaristo has talent, and he's very nice," the stupid thing, the one Evaristo liked was me, you could tell that a mile off, every time they stopped us on the street and told us, "Now, now you're real stunners; last summer you were just kids," he used to look at me and not Transi, but so impudently, you never saw anything like it. Now, she can believe what she wants to, I couldn't care less, after all they were two older guys, just think, their draft call didn't come up till the end of the war, in February of '39 I think it was, and then they got themselves soft jobs in military offices, they didn't go to the front or anything, and that, for me, was final, I never looked at them again, honestly, and then when you and I started going steady, Transi used to spend all day with them, I think she was already involved, mind you, and one day she turned up at home madly excited, "Evaristo's painting a portrait of me," and I was horrified, "Naked?" and she said, "No, honey, not much on, though he'd like it better if I didn't wear anything because he says I have a very pretty figure." Transi was always a little bit like that, not exactly fresh, I don't know, sort of impulsive, I remember her kisses when I wasn't feeling very well, on the mouth, see, and sort of hard, like a man's, strange certainly, "Menchu, you have a fever," she used to say, but affectionately, eh? you men are awfully evil minded. Just between the two of us, I'll tell you that I would have liked for you to kiss me oftener, you disaster you, after we were married, of course, that goes without saying, but ever since we started to go steady you were cold with me, sweetheart, even though every time I saw you in the summer with the newspaper, before I told you yes, on the bench across from our house, just nothing at all, I imagined you'd be much more passionate, honestly, but one fine day I said yes and that was the end of it, all over and done with, like I say. It's true there was still the part about the movies, when you used to stare at me the whole time, so that I'd think, "Does my face look funny?" but all of a sudden you started to wear glasses, heavens, what a disappointment, and then you didn't pay any more attention to me. I think you were like Elviro in that, I've always said so, because, no matter how hard I try, I can't imagine Elviro getting up to anything with Encarna, with that stiff-as-a-board air of his, so skinny that you'd have thought a gust of wind would blow him over, and then so hunched over, so near-sighted . . . Physically your brother Elviro didn't amount to much, honestly, infinitely less than José María, oh my yes, because José María, as a man, wasn't bad at all, by far the best-looking of the three, and if we count girls, the best-looking of the four, because Charo, poor thing, don't tell me, is a pretty miserable-looking specimen, that's perfectly obvious, why kid ourselves, and a lot of it is just sloppiness, like I'm telling you, because if you'd make Charo stand up straight, and put a decent bra on her and take a few layers off her calves, nowadays plastic surgery can work miracles, just look at Bene, she'd be a different person. The voice would be the hardest part, I know, so thin, sort of a whisper, and pronouncing so carefully that you'd think she spent all her time talking to deaf-mutes, and much worse today, just imagine, now that she's hoarse, it's like a man's . . . Your sister's not very attractive, Mario, if the truth be told, and besides that she's stingy, like your father, other faults I can excuse, but stingy people just about kill me, I tell you, I can't stand them. Of course José María was the best one, quite a difference, I laugh just remembering how I used to run away from him every time I happened to meet him on the street, I knew him from the post office, see, a girl's foolishness, you'll say, I used to go and watch him wrapping packages, and Transi would say, "He's fantastic; he has a way of looking at you that makes you dizzy." And she was right, Mario, maybe you won't believe it, I don't know if it was the way he moved, or his eyes, or the way he pursed his lips, sort of in a straight line, but your brother, without being what you'd call good-looking, certainly had something. I don't know how to explain it to you, sometimes I think that it isn't possible that Elviro and José María and you were children of the same father and the same mother, that guy really had a glint in his eyes, it was something special, that you and Elviro never had, I don't know what it was, as if his eyelashes softened the way he looked at you, as if he was caressing you without touching you, I know what I mean. Of course José María had awfully pretty eyes, and it wasn't that they were so light colored, you know, but the rim around his pupils was sort of yellow and that gave him a catlike expression, Transi used to say, I remember as if it was today, twenty-five years, mind you, "They go through you like X-rays," and it was true and every time he looked at me I'd turn red right away, what a power of attraction! till the day when he stopped and said to me all of a sudden, "Little girl, aren't you the one my brother Mario likes?" and you'll never guess, I didn't even answer, I rushed off and didn't stop running till I got to the Plaza, and Transi kept after me, "Aren't you the fool?" but I didn't even know what I was doing, sort of stupefied, an entirely different style from Gabriel and Evaristo, of course, but the minute José María looked at me I lost my head. After that, every time I saw him in the street, I'd manage to run and hide in a doorway, and he didn't even notice, otherwise what a situation, it would have been worse, and Transi, the silly girl, said to me one night, "You know what I think? I think the one you like is José María and not Mario," look, what a ridiculous thing to say. A woman's very complicated, of course, and as a man, it's possible, an attraction, but you were something else again, I don't know how to explain it to you, physically you were nothing special, you know that, but you had something, how do I know, certainly no need to act like Transi, so tiresome, "Throw him over, why don't you, can't you see him? He looks like a scarecrow," nothing like as bad as that, what she wanted was to have Gabriel and Evaristo come up to us, or even Paco, who was quite a clown, he was always joking, and we had a lot of fun with him because he jumbled up his words, I'd like you to see him now, a different man. For me Paco was somebody to pass the time with but nothing else, he was funny all right, I don't deny it, but his family was a little bit you-know, quite humble, you understand what I mean, and if you scratched him the brute showed through right away. And I'm not fussy about other things, but everybody with those of their own class, Mama was wonderful that way, ever since I was a little girl, mind you, same as teaching me to pray, "To marry a first cousin or a man of a lower class is to invite misfortune," take note, and I wasn't about to do that, I don't mean to say you were a marquis or anything, middle class, that's right, a little on the lower-class side if you want, but gentlefolks, with university degrees, I admit that I was scared to death with Mama, fortunately she was still frightened about the business of Julia and Galli Constantino, and I'm not surprised, the thing about Julia was a terrible blow, heavens, what a scandal, but Mama was from a very well-to-do family in Santander and used to the best. Mama was a real lady, Mario, you knew her, and before, what's the use of my telling you! I wish you'd seen her receiving calls before the war, my, what parties, what clothes, a presence like nothing you've ever seen, you only need to think about how she died. I said so to Papa, "She's died just like actresses in the movies go to sleep," but exactly the same, eh? not an ugly facial expression, or even a wheeze, mind you, because a death rattle seems to be the usual thing, well, not even that, just like I'm telling you. I was really shaking when she went to meet your parents, but it was all right, "They seem like decent people," and I could breathe again and took the opportunity to tell her that about your father, Mario, about his being a moneylender and all, that shouldn't bother you, I think, because everybody knows what it's like between mother and daughter, and I was even closer to Mama, and she wrinkled her nose a little bit, that was a very characteristic gesture of hers, Mario, it made her look so cute, "Moneylender?" but right away, in a moment, she pulled herself together, "With that boy, a permanent appointment at the High School already, you can be happy, dear," just like I'm telling you, I was wild with joy, naturally. You were always uneasy with Mama, Mario, don't tell me you weren't, but you're ungrateful, because she was always on your side, and Papa too if you really want my opinion, the only thing that worried Papa was your family's political ideas, and I can understand that very well, I can't imagine what he'd have done if he'd known, my boy. It was bad enough about the moneylending, I think, and then with what happened to José María, I was terribly ashamed about that, if the truth be told, when Gaudencio came with the news about Elviro I was almost glad, mind you, well, not glad, of course, what a silly thing to say, but it did make things up to me, I can assure you, because I was sick and tired, on the street, of "Your future brother-in-law's been taken for a ride because he was a Red," insinuating things, see, but I'd stand right up to them and say, "And they killed the oldest son in Madrid, on the outskirts of the city, just two days apart, think how awful." And all the girls were stopped in their tracks, Mario, I promise you that, and I was almost enjoying it, I give you my word of honor.

V

....

*Come and behold ye the works of the Lord: what wonders he hath
done upon earth, making wars to cease even to the end of the
earth. He shall destroy the bow, and break the weapons: and the
shield he shall burn in the fire,* though, no matter what you say,
I had a marvelous time during the war, listen, I don't know if
I'm overly light-minded or what, but I had some terrific years,
the best ones of my life, don't tell me, everybody sort of on
vacation, the streets full of boys, and all that commotion.
Look, I didn't even mind the bombardments, I wasn't afraid of
them or anything, there were girls who screamed like mad
every time the sirens went. I didn't, honestly, I enjoyed everything, though I never could talk to you about it either before
or after, because every time I started with it you'd say "Be
quiet, please," and shut me up, you stop to think about it,
Mario darling, and serious conversations, really serious conversations, are something we've had very few of. You didn't
care a bit about clothes, let's not even mention the car, parties
the same thing, the war, which was a Crusade, everybody says
so, seemed like a tragedy to you, and all in all, unless we can
talk about smart money or structures and that stuff, you don't
say a word. And with the children practically the same thing,
you should have seen yourself, if I told you about something
cute Borja or Aránzazu said, to start with fine, but then right

away you'd come out with how you worried about that boy or what was going to become of that girl, always the same old song, you used to bore me, sweetheart, with your moaning and groaning. Old Worrywart, as Valen says, and she's absolutely right. If you'd heard Borja yesterday! "I wish Daddy would die every day so I wouldn't have to go to school!" What do you think of that? But right out, just like I'm telling you, in front of everyone, he left me stunned, honestly. I gave him a terrible thrashing, believe me, because if there's anything I can't stand it's a child who doesn't have feelings, he's only six years old, I know, I'm not arguing about that, but if you don't bring them into line at six, would you like to tell me where they're going to wind up? Well, you with your mushiness, leave him alone, life will teach him what it means to suffer, that's a fine thing, letting them get away with everything, laughing at their bright sayings, and that's how what happens later comes about. Because don't come and tell me all that about Alvaro now, the way Alvaro, and even Menchu, act is nothing but childishness, what's so special about having a child ask you if it's true that you and I and Mario and Menchu, and Borja and Aran and Auntie Encarna and Auntie Charo and Doro and everybody are going to die, well, you should have seen yourself, making a big deal of it, most natural thing for a child, "Well, not for many years," what was that all about, after all a good Christian, even if nowadays everything's all stirred up with that business about the Council, ought to be always meditating about death and live thinking that he has to die, we'd be in fine shape if not. Don't come bothering me with fancy arguments and get it into your head, Mario, the only thing that's holding us back is the fear of eternal damnation, that's the way it's always been and always will be, sweetheart, nowadays it seems as if you people don't like preaching about hell, you must not have a very clear conscience, that's what I think, wretched Council that's turning everything upside down, see, the church of the poor, well, all right for the poor, like I say, and the ones who aren't poor, how about us? Well, so you kept going on about how it was abnormal for a child to think those things, see, like his calling soldiers playing-card jacks and going out in the country by himself to build a bonfire, what's so special about that? "We have to take him to the doctor," what an idea, just imagine if you had to take every child to the doctor who gets the idea of making a bonfire, just the same as with Menchu and studying, the child simply doesn't go for the books and I say she's absolutely right, because after all, what's the use of a girl going on with studies, I'd like to know? What does she get out of it, you tell me? Make herself all mannish, that's the size of it, a girl who goes to the university is a girl who isn't feminine, no two ways about it, for me a girl who studies isn't one bit sexy, it's not her thing, come on, admit it. Besides, did I go to the university? Look, you didn't turn up your nose at me, when it comes right down to it, with all your airs of being intellectual, what you and your kind want is a housewife, that's right, and don't tell me you don't, because you sure made dying-sheep's eyes at me, my boy, you looked pitiful, and underneath it all, if you'd met me at the university you'd have spit at me like a cat, see, I can tell where a man's coming from a mile away and if there's anything that hurts your pride it's to run across a girl who's way ahead of you at books and stuff. Look at Paquito Alvarez, to give you just one example, every time he used a word wrong and I corrected him he'd get furious, even though he seemed to take it as a joke, sure, sure, jokes, of course, Paco came from a working-class background and didn't like to be corrected, that's the truth too. You know what Mama used to say about that? She used to say, you'll see, she'd say, "A young lady only needs to know how to walk, how to look, and how to smile, and the best professor in the world can't teach her those things." What do you think of that? She used to make Julia and me walk back and forth in the hall for ten minutes every morning with a big book on our heads, and she'd say jokingly, "Do you see how books are good for something too?" Well, just like I'm telling you, to know how to walk, to look, and to smile, it's not possible, it seems to me, to sum up the ideal of femininity in fewer words, even though you never took Mama seriously, which is one of the things that hurt me most, because Mama, apart from being intelligent, and she was exceptional, Papa says so himself, it's not just a notion of mine, had manners, and a ladylike way about her, that you don't acquire overnight. I used to marvel, I can tell you, at the easy way she had of taking charge of a situation and her knack for placing a person in his social class, and it was all pure intuition, she never really studied, you know, that is, she went to school with the Black Sisters, and spent a year in France, in Dublin I think it was, I'm not sure about that, but she knew French perfectly, she read it fluently, you'd be amazed, exactly like it was Spanish. And that's what I ask myself, Mario, why can't Menchu take after Mama? But there aren't any excuses as far as you're concerned, Mario, every flunking grade's a catastrophe, "And with me teaching in the boys' section too," you go on about it so, when you know perfectly well that today things aren't like they used to be, why, even letting a friend copy from you is disappearing, nowadays to pass a course you have to know more than the professor, and if Menchu passes the lower-level certificate next time, that'll do, there are plenty of girls who at eighteen haven't even started, for your information, there's Mercedes

Villar, and she's no fool. And when Menchu gets through, if God helps me to do it, that's another problem, I'll bring her out, once she's stopped wearing mourning, mind you, mustn't waste her best years, but no working, that's another mania of yours that God's pardoned you for I hope, Mario, because since when have nice girls worked? If you had your way, we people who count would go tumbling down and down until you couldn't tell us from working class, the child will have no need of that, sweetheart, we'll live modestly, of course, but a dignified modesty is better than comfort bought at any price. That French fellow, that Perret or whatever his name is, put some freakish ideas into your head, Mario, because you and that Aróstegui and Moyano and even Don Nicolás himself always look at everything that comes from abroad with your mouths hanging open, you're a bunch of jerks, and of course I know that girls work in other countries, but that's a mistake, no principles or anything, we have to defend our own customs tooth and nail if need be. Those disgusting foreigners, with all their progress, don't have anything to teach us, if they come here, as Papa says, it's to eat well and nothing else, why, the beaches are a disgrace, and that Perret would turn back the clock in his own country if he could, and bring back the times of ladies and gentlemen, you can tell a mile off that he comes from a good family, but since he can't, the easiest thing is for everybody to be in a mess together. Remember Papa's article, I cut it out and saved it, it's wonderful, every time I read it I get goose-pimples, mind you, and what he says at the end, "Machines, perhaps not; but spiritual values and decency, enough for export," and that's the simple truth, and as for religious values let's not even mention them, Mario, sweetheart, what's happening is that all of you have fallen for this monomania of culture, and you go around stirring up heaven and earth to let poor people study, that's another mistake, you take poor people out of their element and they're no good either for coarse or fine, you ruin them, make sure of that, right away they want to be ladies and gentlemen and that just can't be, everybody has to shift for themselves within their own class the way it's always been, you really amuse me with that campaign of yours in *El Correo*, I don't know why they don't close it down and have done with it, honestly, to have all the kids, rich and poor, go to the university, heavens, what a mess, that's idiotic, and excuse my frankness, someday you'll admit I'm right, that Don Nicolás of yours, may God confound him, is getting you all involved, and secretly he's playing his own game, because, if you want to know, he's of extremely humble extraction, his mother was a washerwoman or something worse, just imagine, and even though in the newspaper, because it's to his advantage, he seems to present both sides of a question, Don Nicolás is a real twister, politically he's unreliable, I'm telling you, it doesn't matter that he goes to mass, it's to cover up, see, but during the war, in case you want to know, he was in prison, and if they didn't shoot him it was out of pity, and instead of being grateful, which is what he ought to be, he's looking out for his own interests, setting people against each other with his rag of a newspaper, and as if that wasn't enough, now Oyarzun says he's a freethinker, that's just what you'd expect of him, mind you, all these things are a plot by freethinkers, Mario, don't kid yourself, of course, when he was dismissed from his job it was for being a freethinker, that's for sure, although later Moyano, instead of shaving off those disgusting whiskers, came out with one of his jokes, which I didn't think was the least bit funny, about how could a man who pissed holy water be a freethinker, what a vulgar thing to say. That's precisely how you can tell

freethinkers, because they don't seem to be, they burrow in
before you know it and trick you, if they went around yelling
at the tops of their voices "I'm a freethinker," everybody would
close their doors to them, that's logical, like the Communists,
they go after what they want, they burrow in and burrow in
and before you know it they've taken over. And for that
reason, and only for that reason, it hurt me, sweetheart, to
have you write that way in *El Correo*, because you were stupidly, stupidly playing into the hands of the forces of evil, it
might pass if they paid you, but look, twenty duros for an
article, a pittance, it's not worth it, and then every time I saw
you take communion, I was scared to death thinking that you
might be committing a sacrilege, mind you, I never told you
so, because there are things that can't be reconciled, Mario, for
instance God and *El Correo*, why, that's like lighting one
candle to God and another to the devil. And you can be sure
that every time Don Nicolás takes communion he does it in
mortal sin, because Don Nicolás is a wicked person and if you
think so highly of him it's simply because he defended you
that night when the thing happened with the policeman, and
even if he did hit you, see, which I don't believe, the law is
the law and if you can't cross the park on a bicycle, well,
everybody knows it, any way you look at it, the policeman
was doing his duty, and if he'd killed you, why it would have
been in the course of his duty, mind you, what do you want
me to tell you, just because, because that's the way things are,
because things have been fixed that way, and what you did
wasn't serious if you like, but you did break the law, and the
other fellow, with his uniform and all, see, has to defend it,
that's what he gets paid for, you men think that after you stop
being a child you have a right to anything, and I should say
not, you're ever so mistaken, when you've grown up you still

have to keep on obeying just like when you were children, not your father or mother of course but authority, yes, authority, takes their place, we'd be in fine shape if it didn't! And I don't care what you say, Ramón Filgueira was a perfect gentleman when he received you in his office, but he was absolutely right, heavens, my boy, if a mayor doesn't believe in his policemen who's going to believe them? And what he told you, a policeman at two in the morning, and especially with that below-freezing temperature, is just the same as the Minister of the Interior, see, and if he's not who is? And as for the Civil Guard barracks and the police station, that's logical, after all they weren't going to greet you with rose petals, you have the strangest ideas, think what you'd do if a student came to bother you at that hour, why, you'd throw him down the stairs! Naturally, we're only human, and especially if you hadn't set to work to grade papers at that hour, or taken the notion to ride a bicycle, which isn't suitable for a person of your class, we wouldn't have anything to be sorry about. That wretched bike, every time I saw you riding it I nearly died of shame, and I don't even mention when you put the seat on it for the child, I could have killed you, you made me cry and everything, smarty, you've never had the slightest consideration for me, see if you have. Of course things come from inside a person and you always did have working-class tastes, that's no novelty, but it makes me furious that Don Nicolás got into the act, I can't stand him, who asked him after all, and if it was abuse of authority and assault on human dignity, he ought to know, the fine was exactly what he deserved, and if I'd had anything to do with it the punishment would have been worse. Castor oil, just like during the war, I'm telling you the truth, to see if he'd learn his lesson once and for all, or that nine-tails thing, whatever it's called, I know what I mean, that foreigners use to crack down on disturbers of the peace.

VI

· · · · · · · · · · · · · · · ·

In this we have known the charity of God, because he hath laid down his life for us: and we ought to lay down our lives for the brethren. He that hath the substance of this world, and shall see his brother in need, and shall shut up his bowels from him: how doth the charity of God abide in him? . . . If any man say, I love God, and hateth his brother; he is a liar. For he that loveth not his brother, whom he seeth, how can he love God, whom he seeth not? which is precisely what I've always maintained, sweetheart, your ideas about charity are fit to be collected in a book, and don't get angry, I still remember your lecture, what an awful experience! my boy, you stop to think about it and nobody can understand you, you scolded me every time I went to the slums to hand out oranges and chocolate as if the children there had more than they could eat, for heaven's sake, and let's not even mention the afternoon I got the idea of going to the thrift shop with Valen. Do you mind letting a person know what's the matter with you? There have always been poor people and rich people, Mario, and the obligation of those of us who, thanks be to God, have enough, is to help those who don't, but you start out right away to improve things, you find defects even in the gospels, my boy, I'd like to know if your theories are yours or that Perret's, I can't stand him, or Don Nicolás', or anybody else's in your gang, each one of them is more twisted than the rest, don't come and tell me. "To accept that means accepting that the distribution of wealth is fair," who ever heard of such a thing, every time you gave me a speech, sweetheart, about how charity only ought to fill the cracks in justice but not the abysses of injustice, what Armando said was "That's a good phrase for a Communist representative," look, you're stirring up the poor too much, and the day they listen to you and all of them study and get to be civil engineers, you tell me where we'll exercise charity, darling, that's another story, and without charity, so long, gospel! Don't you understand? Everything will come tumbling down, that's only common sense. From top to bottom, you're all poisoned, like I say, I get the shivers every time I think you've gone without being reconciled to the Church, and it isn't that I think you're bad, because you're not, but you are credulous, that's right, credulous and a little bit stupid, Mario, why not say so, because, on the other hand, what Caritas does seemed, just fine to you, I don't understand it, honestly, because if Caritas has done anything in that way it's to keep us from having direct contact with the poor and to do away with the prayer before receiving alms, that is, leading the really poor astray, I'll have you understand, and as if that wasn't enough, to take away the prayers, why, I remember ages ago with Mama, they couldn't thank her enough, my God! what beautiful sights! They'd pray with such devotion and kiss the hand that helped them. Try to do that nowadays, goodness, the way they act! And do you know who's been just as much at fault as you? Caritas, for your information! because it hands things out at random, without finding out beforehand who's deserving, why, good-for-nothings stick out their hands to you same as the Protestants, just the same, it's a mess, and that's what simply can't be, I'm tired of saying it. And a fine showing they make, I've never seen the poor so spoiled, and I don't like to think about the day when the coin comes up on the other side, we'll get a few bullets for our pains, that's right, evil for good, as far as I'm concerned you can go on with your meetings, my boy, you'll see how much it does for you, saying that Caritas is necessary as long as the structures aren't changed, heaven knows what you and your friends mean by that, all the livelong day discussing structures and you yourselves don't know what earthly good it is. And meanwhile Don Nicolás is rubbing his hands, that's the thing that makes me the maddest, you're playing his game without realizing it. You know lots of other things, I'm not arguing about that, but what you know about charity is zero, Mario, make sure of that, it's the same as when you used to spend your afternoons with the prisoners, listening to their stories, you tell me what kind of benefit you could get out of those down-and-outers, if society draws away from them there has to be a reason, that goes without saying. What's happening is that nowadays everybody wants to start at the top instead of the bottom, everybody wants to be a general, like I say, but Mario, if there aren't any common soldiers, can you tell me what we need generals for? And don't come and tell me that you can exercise charity by talking and listening and that charity doesn't consist in giving but in giving oneself, you're capable of selling your soul to the devil for a phrase, like I say, your miserable showing off, like that about putting sentences in your books in italics or with capital letters when they're not proper names or anything, that makes no sense even if Armando does say it always looks good, he says it as a joke, just kidding, see, he's always cracking jokes, you know what he's like. It's the same as that business about Hernando de Miguel and the lamb, the most natural thing, a favor, look, his boy simply wasn't prepared, and besides that he came all the way from Trascastro carrying it on his back and you yelled at him, those are no kind of manners, it seems to me, and you wound up throwing the lamb down the stairwell, you hit him in the middle of the back, you might have killed him, it was an animal that weighed at least four kilos, a real shame. Why do you have those outbursts, Mario, sweetheart? Charity begins at home, and the children, you know it, don't get all that much meat, with wages going up the way they are you can imagine the price of it, when you and your friends write you don't realize what you're doing, you stubborn thing, just look at Armando in the factory, the wage bases, and what he says is "I'm not going to be more papist than the Pope," all right then, four kilos down the stairwell, for no reason, I'd like to see what harm we'd have done to anybody by accepting that lamb. It's like your not accepting bottles and cakes, if people want to make you a gift, let them! Don't pay any attention to that fool Esther, just because she reads books she thinks she's somebody, quite an oracle you've taken on there, my boy, "Men like Mario are the conscience of the world today," don't make me laugh, I wish she'd seen the conscience of the world tied in knots about whether refusing the lamb was offending his neighbor and accepting it was opening the door to corruption, and to tell the truth I don't know why you have to think so much if everything is so simple, and if you thought that and the children needed vitamins, why did you throw the lamb at Hernando de Miguel, I'd like to know? Then, when you had that, the prostration or depression or whatever it's called, you cried for every foolish little thing, remember, my boy, what sessions! and that the anguish was caused by your not knowing what the road was, or whether you were doing harm or not, when even the littlest child knows that a blow in the ribs with a four-kilo lamb could be fatal, you could have killed him, Mario, don't kid yourself, and that you envied me and all those like me who were so sure of everything and know where we're going, and if that were true, praise be to God, why haven't you followed my example and left Don Nicolás and his whole circle of fakers alone? But no indeed, at bottom that humility of yours is pride, Mario, and bring on the pills, pills for arrogance, like I call them, and, after all, they're nothing but drugs, they even take away your willpower. And Luis listened to me, you bet he listened, doctors think they can play around with sick people, and, right at the start, he said that about the depression so meaningfully, and that was when I got angry, what else could I have done, "Mario doesn't have any reason to be depressed; he eats well and I do more for him than I can afford the time for," I really told him off, of course I told him off, just like I told him off about the pills, I really got it off my chest, Mario, and I'm not sorry, I swear I'm not. But, if the truth be told, when you were like that, believe me, that was when the house went smoothly, you didn't interfere in anything, and everybody knows that men, in these matters, are more of a hindrance than anything else. The only thing was your crying spells, you really broke my heart, eh? You cried as if you were being murdered, my heavens, what sobs! you were amazing, Mario, as if you'd never cried before, not even when your parents died or anything, and then that came out, see, and I got scared, Mario, honestly I did, and I told Luis, and Luis agreed with me, Mario, I'll have you know, "Excessive emotional control and lack of satisfaction," why, I remember like it was yesterday that I said "What?" and he very kindly explained it to me, this psychiatry stuff is fascinating, mind you, even though nobody can get it out of my head that when you men act like that, without a fever and without anything hurting you, it's just being spoiled and silly. Don't you think that's so, Mario, you've always been just like a little boy, even if you did study so much later on and write those things, I don't know, maybe they're all right, I'm not arguing about it, but of course they were an awful bore, frankly, why should I lie to you and tell you something I don't feel. Ordinarily, people who think a lot are infantile, Mario, haven't you noticed? look at Don Lucas Sarmiento, simple tastes and some absurd theories about life, sort of philosophical or something. And that was what happened to you, sweetheart, and it'll happen to Mario if God doesn't prevent it, because that boy, with so many big books and all that seriousness he has, is going to come to a bad end. I keep telling him so, but since you don't back me up, "Leave him alone, he has to grow up," just exactly as if I was talking to the walls, he doesn't even listen, look, the other afternoon, to give you just one example, I'd made a milkshake for Alvaro, with an egg beaten up in it and all, and the other one goes and stretches out his hand and drinks it, but never even looking up from his book, it really put me in a temper, honestly, prices are so high and Mario has plenty to eat already, goodness, if we had our way we'd all drink milkshakes every hour of the day, mind you. But Alvaro's something else again, understand, it's not that I'm saying that because he goes off in the hills to light bonfires we've got to give him extra food, but he's so thin, he's nothing but skin and bones, Mario, that boy worries me, why, if anything came along it would catch him without any defenses and that would be the end of him. Mama used to say, "Prevention is better than cure, " get it, Mario? And it isn't that I have a special fondness for Alvarito, the rest of you are so malicious, he tickles me, that's all, maybe because of his name, who knows, remember that way back when we were going steady I used to say, "I'd love to have a son so I could call him Alvaro"? It's a mania I've always had, I think ever since I was born, mind you, Alvaro's a name I'm crazy about, which isn't to say that I don't like Mario, I think it's a very masculine name and all, but the other's a weakness, I understand that myself. It makes me laugh to think what this house would have been like if I'd left it to you to choose names, heaven only knows, a Salustiano, a Eufemiano and a Gabina, anything at all, heaven only knows, like your wanting to give the children names in your family, was there ever a less civilized custom. Would you like to tell me what I would have done with an Elviro and a José María in the house, the most vulgar thing, I don't care if they did get killed? I accepted Mario and Menchu, which after all were our names, but why go on? When there are names as pretty as Alvaro, Borja, and Aránzazu, the other thing doesn't make sense, admit it, what happens is that all you people are living in the Middle Ages, my boy, and pardon my frankness, just look at the people who count, and it's natural, Mario, sweetheart, that a name gives a person character, it's for his whole life, and that's saying a lot. Look, there's something they ought to take up in the Council, they'd all be names of saints, I'm not saying they wouldn't, but instead of rowing with each other all the time and then coming out and saying that Jews and Protestants are good, that's all we needed, why, they ought to revise the list of saints, a really thorough job, no arguments about it, this name's all right and this one isn't, so people would know what was the proper thing to do on this point. When you come right down to it everything's topsy-turvy, Mario, at this rate any day now they're going to come out and say we're the bad ones, after what we've seen, anything could happen . . . And that's the pass we've come to, you look around you and even the negroes in Africa want to give us lessons when they're nothing but cannibals. I don't care how often you say that we don't teach them anything else, just look at Papa, he certainly set forth the problem on TV the other night, you ought to have heard Valen. One thing, Mario, here between you and I, that I haven't dared to tell you before, listen; I won't even try to find out if it's true what Higinio Oyarzun says, that you used to meet on Thursdays with a group of Protestants to pray together, but if someone could prove to me that it was true without my trying to find out, even though it would make me feel terrible, you'd have to accept the idea that we never met, that our children will never again hear me say a word about you, mind what I say, I'd rather they thought they were illegitimate, I'd swallow even that with pleasure before I'd tell them their father had gone back on his faith. Yes, Mario, yes, I'm crying, but enough's enough, I can put up with anything, you know that, not many women are as understanding and generous as I am, but I'd rather die, mind what I say, die, than have anything to do with a Jew or a Protestant. Are we going to forget, sweetheart, that the Jews crucified Our Lord? Where will we wind up if we take that road, can you tell me that? And please, don't come to me with tales about how we all crucify Christ every day, fairy stories, if Christ came back to life you can be sure he wouldn't come to pray with Protestants, or say that poor people ought to go to the university, or buy jumping jacks off all the good-for-nothings in Madrid, or let other people go ahead of him in shops, or, that's for certain, throw lambs down the stairwell at Hernando de Miguel. You have a very poor idea of Christ from what I can see, darling, I'm no softy, Mario, I should say not, and if Christ did return, you can be sure I'd stand up for him even if the whole world was against me, I wouldn't do what Saint Peter did, that I can assure you of, because, though I'm a woman, I'm no softy, just look at the end of the war, the year of hunger, don't think I hung back, I should say not, I went to the filthiest villages in Uncle Eduardo's car, with a charcoal-burning fuel tank and everything, looking for food for my parents. I don't give that impression, Mario, I've told you ever so many times, but I've got more backbone than I seem to.

VII

....

For every violent taking of spoils, with tumult, and garment min-
gled with blood, shall be burnt, and be fuel for the fire. For a child
is born to us, and a son is given to us, and the government is upon
his shoulder: and his name shall be called . . . the Prince of Peace,
and I don't know if it's a terrible thing to say, because with
you men a person never knows, but I had a perfectly marvelous time during the war, why should I say anything different,
with the demonstrations and the boys and everything topsy-
turvy, I wasn't even afraid of the sirens or anything, other
girls, see, went crazy in the bomb shelters when they started
to go, but I loved it. I remember Mama used to make Julia and
me put on stockings and comb our hair before we went down
to Doña Casilda's basement, just imagine, sometimes the explosions and machine-gun fire would catch us halfway down
the stairs, and it was so funny, to see people jostling each
other. Then, in the bomb shelter, it was a barrel of fun,
imagine what it was like with all the people in the apartment
house together, there was a woman named Espe, the one who
lived up on the top floor, the widow of a railwayman, who
was an awful Red, I only have to tell you that in the first days
of the war they shaved every bit of her hair off, who didn't do
anything but say over and over, "This is the end," and she'd
cross herself, take note of that, but with her eyes rolled up,

and I remember Papa used to say to her ever so slyly, "What are you afraid of, Esperanza? It's your side that's bringing you greetings." You'd have to have seen her, Mario, it was a scream! with a horrible black kerchief over her head, writhing with fear, "Oh, don't say any more, for God's sake, Don Ramón, this war is a horrible thing!" and Papa, intentionally, of course, "You seem to think a lot about God these days, Esperanza," imagine, in normal times she never even went to mass, I should say not, a Socialist, but one of the most conspicuous ones, and Papa, you know what he's like, would keep talking to her about defensive wars, a whole treatise on the subject, and poor Espe, at the end, "Oh, Don Ramón, if you say so, you have such a lot of knowledge, it must be true." And all this time, Teresita Abril's children, who were just little brats then and now, mind you, they're grown men, all of them married, goodness, how time passes! Miguel, the smallest one, seven children, why, it doesn't seem possible, but then if you'd only seen them, making a terrible noise among the bottles and jars, and good old Timoteo Setién, Doña Casilda's husband, didn't do anything but walk up and down, with his gray apron on and his hands to his head, "Careful, be very careful, there are inflammable materials here," and what a laugh! to keep them quiet, you can imagine, ham, chocolate, dried chestnuts and that was all. But old Timoteo was one of those tightwads, my heavens what a stingy man, I remember that every time Mama paid the bill, it was always a big one, and Julia and I were still little girls, Doña Casilda would give us a candy behind his back, "Put it in your pocket, don't let him see it," really terrified, there's nothing that repels me more than a tightfisted man, they scare me, I promise you, and when Transi told me that about your father, about his moneylending and all, I started to shake, Mario, like I'm telling you. And then, to tell the truth, you hardly noticed it in him, I don't know if it was because of what happened to Elviro and José María, but nothing about money, only his saying that it was his fault, that he was the one who didn't let him go to the office, that it was madness to go out on the street that day, obsessed, and it was stupid, see, because your brother was on the hit list a long time before that, Mario, admit it. Oyarzun, who seems to know everything, I don't know where he finds the time, told me that the part about the office was the least of it, that there were witnesses who'd seen José María at Azaña's meeting in the bullring, and in April of '31 shouting approval of the Republic, waving the tricolor flag like a madman, Mario, which is even worse. The things that happen in life, like I say, at our house on April 14 it was like a funeral, Papa was on the point of tears and I'm still not quite sure he didn't cry, all day long pacing back and forth, from his armchair to the study, from his study to the armchair, like he was stunned. Poor Papa aged ten years that day, for him the king was the greatest thing in the world, more than any of us, mind you, more than the whole family put together, veneration was what Papa had for the monarchy, worship. And when it was confirmed about the Republic, he stood up, very pale, very solemn, I don't know how to explain it to you, he went to the bathroom and came back with a black necktie on: "I won't take off this necktie until the king returns to Madrid," he said, and all of us were as quiet as if someone had died. And then you, what a joke, you thought that the tie was for Mama, may she rest in peace, I should say not, Mario, for the king, men who are faithful to a clearcut ideal make me feel very sentimental, because the monarchy is lovely, Mario, I don't care what you say, and it isn't that I'm as impassioned about it as Papa, but just think, a king in a palace and a beautiful queen and some blond princes and princesses and the carriages, and the etiquette and the protocol and all that. You used to say that monarchy and republic, in themselves, didn't mean a lot, that the important thing is what there is underneath, whatever you mean by that, but what I can tell you right away is that they can't be compared. A monarchy is something else, the republic, I don't know, is sort of more ordinary, don't deny it, I remember when it was established, poor folks and drunks all over the place, disgusting, my boy, every day I understand Papa better, I assure you, Mario, his blind spot about the king. What does seem absurd is that he should have fallen out with Uncle Eduardo, he was such a monarchist too, but goodness, argue like two furies, you wouldn't believe, once Papa had a fainting fit and we had to call the doctor in a big hurry, and when he came to, shouting, "Of course, if Eduardo's king comes I won't take the necktie off!" I don't think that's any way to behave, see, two kings, as if kings could be twins or triplets either, I don't understand it. And the other evening Higinio Oyarzun, at Valentina's party, gave me a big piece of news, I assure you, I hadn't finished telling him about it and he took the attitude that Papa could take off his black necktie because Spain was in fact a monarchy, just imagine what a strange thing, and I didn't have the faintest idea, honestly, with so many kids I don't even have time to read the newspaper, you know that, and it was what I told him, I thought about writing a little note to Papa, but no, Papa said perfectly clearly that when the king was in Madrid, which is something else. I'd adore to see Papa, mind you, all of a sudden, in a colored necktie! It wouldn't look like him, for sure, it's been so many years. That's faithfulness to an idea, don't tell me, and all the rest is foolishness, just look at you, with your father, do you remember? you were in a great hurry to take off mourning, you just couldn't wait, eh? and even with your father, the least sign you could show, with your mother not even that, it makes me ashamed to think that I, who after all didn't belong to them, a year and a half and you not the slightest thing. You're a real case, with you a person doesn't know whether to laugh or cry, at first everything was just fine, but when you crossed your legs and saw your socks and shoes, God help us! "It makes me sad to see my calves all black, and I have enough sadness inside." And no sooner said than done, that was the end of the mourning. You men are real cases, Mario, of course it's going to make you feel sad to see your black calves, naturally, that's what mourning is for, blockhead, to remind you that you have to be sad and if you're about to sing, to shut up, and if you're about applaud, to keep quiet and resist the temptation. It's for that and so that other people can know that you've had a very great misfortune in the family, understand? and I, right now, I'll even wear crepe, sweetheart, I should hope so, but it isn't as if it suits me, understand that, black on black looks perfectly dreadful, but a person has to keep up appearances and, after all, you're my husband, aren't you? Well, of course I will, even though your son doesn't seem to understand it either, now it's time for you to reap what you sowed, he and I had a fine set-to, that boy drives me wild with his exaggerated ideas, see, his father laid out in the study and he with his tweedy sweater on, as if nothing had happened. And when I told him about the black necktie, you should have seen how angry he got, "Those are conventionalisms, Mother; leave me out of it," just like it sounds, but so impolitely, eh? you wouldn't want to believe it of Mario, just think, he's always been so quiet, I spent a quarter of an hour in the bathroom, so angry that you can't imagine it. To have children for this! Well, now you're hearing it, he told me leave him alone, same as with the first-class funeral, how could you do less for a father! "Vanities," he said, what do you think of that? Leave him alone, see, what more could all of us want than to be left alone, what a miserable experience, my God! that boy is the spit and image of you, since he was just a toddler, ever since you carried him in the little seat on your bike, Mario, he even uses strange words, "conventionalisms," take note, just to throw me off balance. I don't want to make myself sadder than I am already, Mario, sweetheart, but youth today is hopeless, some with the twist and some for books, they're all a lost cause, I can remember before, how are you going to compare? Don't talk to these kids today about the war, they'd call you crazy and yes, war's as horrible as you like, but after all, it's the business of the brave, when all's said and done it's not so bad, because, I don't care what you say, I had a really good time during the war, all right, maybe it was out of stupidity, but don't tell me why, that was like an endless holiday, every day something differ- ent, if it wasn't the legionnaires it was the Italians, whether this or that place had been captured, and everybody, even the old folks, singing "The Volunteers," which has such pretty words, or "Death's Sweetheart," that song is absolutely the best of all. And then I didn't even mind the bombardments, or One Course at Table Day, because Mama, with that special clever- ness of hers, put everything on one plate and we never went hungry, I swear, like the No Dessert Day, Transi and I would buy candy and we didn't even notice. The ones who were a little bit you-know, sort of fresh, I realize it now, were the boys from the little towns, see, boys without any manners, I remember when we used to stick the medal that was meant to stop bullets on them, but running the pin right into their flesh, eh? all the time touching us and saying "Wish us luck," and Transi and I never said a word, see, they were so brave. Did you know that, even though I was going steady with you, I sponsored one of them? Pablo, Pablo Haza I think his name was, he used to write me the most hilarious letters, full of spelling mistakes, he was a brute from head to foot, but don't be jealous, because something had to be done for those poor people and I used to answer him, one time he turned up on leave and was determined to go out with me, imagine, I told him there was no question of that, and then would I go to the movies, and I said even less likely, imagine, with all the people around, and he began to dramatize, that maybe he'd get killed the next day, and I said what could I do about that, that I'd feel terribly sorry about it, and then he stuck one finger, dirty nail and all, into his mouth and put a gold tooth in my hand, and I was horrified, "Why are you doing that?" because I always talked to him very formally, Mario, don't think I didn't, Mama was right about that: "It's fine to help them, but keeping your distance; soldiers are lower-class people," and he said the Moorish troops split open dead soldiers' heads, imagine how awful, to take their gold teeth, and that I should keep it for him till the end of the war, it must have been a premonition, because nothing more was ever heard of the good Pablo Haza, Mama and I had to go one day to give the tooth to the Treasury. There was a lot of that during the war, unfortunately, look at Juan Ignacio Cuevas to give just one example, I think I told you about it before, Transi's brother, who was sort of retarded, kind of abnormal, but they called him up and took him to a barracks, for auxiliary services and that, but you know what happens in wars, they must have needed people or whatever, the fact is that one morning Transi's parents found a paper all full of spelling mistakes under the door: "They're takin me." just imagine. without a g. "to the warr," with an extra r, "I'm awful scared, Good By," and down at the bottom, "Juanito." Well, from that day to this, and a lot of water's gone under the bridge, they moved heaven and earth don't think they didn't, people like them, but not a trace. Of course what I say is, the way the boy was, better for God to take him, a burden, imagine what a future, mason's helper or something of that kind, better off dead, but Transi, my boy, went all sentimental. "No, no, honey, a brother's a brother," well, that depends on how you look at it, but if she felt like that, it's ridiculous that she paid any attention to Evaristo, a draft dodger, she even let him paint her nude or however he did it, in other things maybe not, Mario, sweetheart, but on that point you can have an easy mind, I never did anything like that, certainly not, you know it, and not for lack of opportunities, Mario, because men, in case you didn't know, still look at me on the street and there are all kinds of looks and Eliseo San Juan, every time he catches sight of me, you ought to hear him, a regular cyclone, he doesn't draw the line at anything, "You're terrific, you're terrific, every day you get more terrific," if I gave him the chance I don't know what would happen, I don't even look at him, I just go on and ignore him, until he gets tired, I promise you, as if it was nothing to do with me, but goodness, if I gave him the chance . . .

VIII

Thou shalt not deliver to his master the servant that is fled to thee. He shall dwell with thee in the place that shall please him, and shall rest in one of thy cities: give him no trouble, like that simpleton Doro, "A person could serve the master for nothing," talk for talk's sake, you know it, Mario, I serve the master too and she doesn't realize it, life's like that, look, for hardly as much as a glass of water, it's really amusing, and then at Christmas or for my birthday you give me some absurd thing, like a tip, honestly, especially when you see me every day practically barefoot and scraping every cent, but you're like that, my boy, I'm well aware, for some things you can spend on a grand scale. You ought to have heard Valen, Mario, she laughs her head off at Doro's devotion to you, the way she carries on about "our master," as if she was referring to Jesus Christ or almost, and here between you and I, poor Doro is awfully stupid, faithful and affectionate in her own way, but awfully stupid, I can't understand how foreign countries let people like her in, Mario, they go by the hundreds, mind you, more every day, I'd like to know what they do there, according to Valen the roughest jobs, the ones that animals do here, for instance, see, pulling carts and that, it's hard to believe, of course, though I could believe anything of those wretched foreigners. They're tricked into going, because those crude people, who've never bothered to learn to read or anything, you talk to them about foreign countries and they all but go into a trance, mind you, there's still a lot of stupid ignorance, Mario, and anything for a change, all that glitters isn't gold, and then they're furious and wanting to go home, so there! nobody's better off than in Spain. Because, after all, what do they go to foreign countries to look for, like I say? All they want is to have a change and act like fools, learn what they shouldn't, that's right, these are terrible times and even if you laugh, Mario, some day Spain will save the world, and it won't be the first time. I have lots of fun with Valen, she's a wonderful girl, the other day she stopped me on the street and said, "I'm going to Germany; it's the only way I can have a cook, a housekeeper, and a maid," see how cute, you admit yourself that she has a sense of humor and to judge from the other night she must have a good one, the two of you made me nervous with such a lot of whispering and so much "tee-hee-hee" and "ha-ha-ha," and that could still pass, but when you started to pop champagne corks at the streetlights, I could have killed you, what a spectacle! and it isn't as if it was any old group, Mario, the best people were there. You drank too much, darling, and I just hate that and it wasn't as if I didn't warn you, I spent the evening saying "Don't drink any more, don't drink any more," but you, not the slightest attention, once you get going nobody can stop you, thank goodness Valen can be trusted. Of course, I'm crazy about Valen, don't you like her, sweetheart? She probably spends a lot on face glop, I don't deny it, Bene is always taking potshots at her for that, but it shows, she's not like other women, Valen is awfully skillful about makeup, especially her eyes. Did you know that Valen has her skin cleaned in Madrid every week? Take note, Mario, how I'd love to do that, and it leaves her looking marvelous, that's the truth, it doesn't seem possible that a thing like a person's skin could respond that much. Then that dyed lock of hair suits her so well, there are lots of people it doesn't suit at all, me for instance, dreadful, remember, and then with that height of hers, it doesn't surprise me one bit that people turn to look at her, she draws attention on the street, I like to go with her because of that. Admit it, Mario, of all the teachers' wives at the High School she's the only one, just look at those little parties at the end of the school year, no sense of manners, they don't even know how to use fish forks, if it wasn't for Valentina lord knows what they'd be like. And she must be filthy rich, because you go down the street with her and she buys whatever she takes a fancy to, anything, like I'm telling you, doesn't even look at the prices, and then she's so generous . . . She's a treasure, Valen is, I love her so much! And Bene says she's the one with the money, really I can't understand how Vicente got so lucky, what a terrific match! It isn't that he's so bad, you understand, but a girl with Valen's looks and with money too, it's like winning the lottery. Bene, the principal's wife, says Vicente had a hard time persuading her, and I'm not surprised, that when they met in Madrid, Valen was going out with an Italian, and you can't trust an Italian an inch either, my word, the successes they have, I don't understand it, honestly, they're more or less like us, Latins after all's said and done, and as far as that goes less manly. Do you remember when they arrived here during the war? What excitement, heavenly days, I don't even want to think about it! All the girls were beside themselves, see, the novelty, and then they fooled you, look what happened later in Guadalajara, Valen says that Mussolini chose the tallest ones and all, the best-looking ones, for propaganda, I don't know. Of course, the batallion or whatever it was that came here really started a revolution, what well-set-up guys they were, everybody throwing flowers at them when they had a parade, quite a welcome that was, they couldn't have complained, and then later, after the disaster at Guadalajara, the scene changed, heavens, how people jeered, and yet now, that baby of an Aróstegui, who never saw the war at all, no matter how much of a young rebel he pretends to be, can come out and say that what happened in Guadalajara showed that the Italians are civilized because they're not warlike no matter how much Mussolini dressed them up as soldiers. And that stupid Moyano, who'd get ahead faster if he shaved off those disgusting whiskers, saying that the Italians are the greatest thing in the world, wherever they go they hit the mark, that they've even taken over Paris with their sweaters and their shoes, anybody could take over with things like that, see, how ridiculous, it's the same as with the Italian girls' good looks, there must be all kinds, I suppose, just like everywhere else, now it's natural that in the movies they show the best they've got, they're not going to be stupid, but the attraction about Italian movies, you can't fool me, is what those girls show, Mario, those Italian girls are filthy, don't tell me, because if not just look at those awful pictures they made after the war, how terrible, children that were lousy and dying of hunger, all of them just alike, for me, frankly, the movies are to have a good time, life has enough problems as it is. And I'm telling you and demonstrating to you, that nobody can beat them for shameless behavior, we're all well aware of that aspect, I'd like to know what knack it is they have, but here, during the war, what a swath they cut, if the truth be told, of course they billeted them in private houses and that's dangerous if a girl doesn't have good solid principles. Just look at the case of Galli Constantino, and there were hundreds like him, and I'm not exaggerating. Galli came to our house like it was conquered territory, smiling, very tanned, with his little thread of a mustache and his eyes so blue . . . Handsome, he was very handsome, give him his due, a medal, and then, so charming, "bambina" here, "bambina" there, I was very young then, see, in '37, a mere child, but I loved to hear him say it. Galli smoked all the time and because back then girls never thought of doing it, that seemed very manly to Julia and me, it was childish, you'll say, but between that and the uniform, and the medals he'd won in Abyssinia, just imagine, against the negroes, now that must have been a horrible war, well, we were bowled over, see, naturally. I remember that lots of afternoons I'd stay home alone with Galli, because Papa and Mama would go out for a walk and Julia had her violin class, and I loved it, and he used to take hold of my hands, not with bad intentions, of course, don't get jealous, but it used to make my heart race, and he'd tell me things about Pisa and Abyssinia, and about his children, Romano and Ana Maria, as "los figlios" of the Duce, and he'd call me "bambina," and I was thrilled, and Transi, I don't need to tell you, was dying of envy: "Introduce me to him, honey, don't be selfish." The only thing I didn't like about Galli, see, before what happened happened, was the creams and cosmetic jars in the bathroom, Mama kept going on about it, poor thing, saying "Who ever saw a man with so much cosmetic stuff?" and Julia never said a word, and Papa, mind you, avoided him, what made Papa furious with him was that Galli used to make him give the Roman salute after the news broadcast, when they played the hymns, imagine Papa, the least martial man in the world, and when it was over, Galli, "Long live Spain!" and "Long live Italy!" and all of us saying it, but very low, practically dying of shame, it was too funny. And one night when Galli wasn't there, because lots of nights he didn't even come for supper, who knows where he went, he was a real sneak, Papa said that he "found him a bit theatrical," and you should have seen Julia, I don't know if she was angry about something else, she got so mad, and said why theatrical, "either a person is or he isn't," I don't know exactly what she meant but she left Papa speechless, honestly, he didn't even open his mouth. The fact is that Julia and I used to go out with Galli practically every afternoon in his Fiat convertible and then Transi would pester me, "He's so cute; come on, honey, don't be like that, introduce me to him; don't be selfish," but I didn't pay the slightest attention, mind you, the way Transi was about things like that. And Galli would buy us ice cream and pastries, and one afternoon he took us to a bookshop and bought an Italian grammar for the two of us, I don't know how much he spent, because Galli, apart from being generous, had a good quality, rare in a man, mind you, I never saw him angry, even when I'd laugh because he pronounced things wrong, and he'd be so persistent, "Per che ride, bambina? Per che?" and then he'd squint his eyes in ways that drove me crazy, don't get mad, Mario, I don't mean anything bad by it. It was a marvelous time, honestly, we went everywhere in the Fiat convertible, everybody else sweating, that was when I thought, when I get married a car first thing, you can see it goes back a long way, because Papa was very unwilling, and even though he could have, he never took the notion, I don't know why, it was a mania like any other, but I said to myself, "When I get married, a car first thing," you can see how foolish I was, with what was in store for me, and all so that Encarna can come along and say that I nag you about it, for the one thing I've wanted in my life, you stop and think about it and nothing's ever been done in this house except exactly the way you wanted it, neither more nor less. Outside of the children's names, the housekeeping, the children's schools and things like that, I don't count for a thing, don't come and tell me now, and what hurts me the most, Mario, is that for a few lousy thousands of pesetas, you've taken the greatest pleasure of my life away from me, I'm not saying a Mercedes, I know all too well we can't run to that, with all our expenses, but what's less than a Six Hundred, Mario, why even janitors' wives have a Six Hundred nowadays, why, they call them navels, sweetheart, didn't you know? because everybody has one. What would it have been like, Mario! Would've changed my life, mind you; I don't even want to think about it. But no, no, an automobile is a luxury, a teacher's job doesn't pay well enough for that, don't make me laugh, as if I didn't know that the ones who were holding you back were those friends of yours, but look at Don Nicolás, doesn't follow his own advice, he has a big car, a Fifteen Hundred, that's what I say, it's one thing to preach and another to practice, a lot of equality and all that jazz, but just look at him, it's the same old story, if you'd asked him for it he'd have given you a little Gordini, so there, and I won't go back on what I've said, because you've had no lack of opportunities, just look at Fito, he had the best intentions in the world, and even without going as far as that, Mario, because you do write well, everybody says so, but about things that nobody understands and when they do understand it's even worse, about miserable people that actually smell bad, their clothes in rags and dying of hunger. And people don't like that, no, Mario, people are very smart and they don't like to be presented with problems, they have enough of those already, I'm sick and tired of telling you so. If you knew how excited I was when I suggested that about Maximino Conde! When Oyarzun told me about it I couldn't wait to rush home, I got here out of breath, you saw me, and

all for nothing, though you won't deny that it was a tremen-
dous plot, very human and all, maybe a teeny bit racy, but
then there wasn't any need to carry things to extremes, I think,
no ugly situations, it was enough to have him fall in love with
the stepdaughter, understand? And once she surrendered and,
so to speak, gave herself to him, to Maximino, or however he
was going to be called in the novel, then you'd make him react
decently and that way the book would even set a good example. But with you, sweetheart, no use arguing, just exactly
like talking to a wall, "yes," "no," "all right," no notes, no
interest, didn't even listen to me, that's what I find hardest to
bear, you men are so full of pride, you think you've got the
truth by the tail and not the slightest attention to us women.
And whether you like it or not, we women understand an
awful lot about life, Mario, why, I don't know how many
books my friends read, you always say, "They can't be many,"
with that contempt, it isn't that I'm going to say that we read
a lot of them, we don't even have time to read the newspaper,
but if you don't count Esther, the books they read aren't about
wars, certainly not, or social problems or stuff, but about
passions and love, it never fails. And furthermore it's logical,
darling, because love is an eternal subject, get that into your
head, look at Don Juan Tenorio, that doesn't go out of date,
it's not a passing fad, you tell me what the world would be
like without love, it wouldn't even exist, so there, naturally it
would all have come to nothing.

IX

....

The kingdom of heaven is likened to a king . . . king, that's a hot
one, something I've asked myself a thousand times, Mario,
sweetheart, if you didn't care about the monarchy one way or
the other, for heaven's sake why did you pick the quarrel you
picked with Josechu Prados? Because don't tell me, there's
nobody better than Josechu, from a local family, all his life,
just think about the Prados, very well known, he spent the
war in the front lines, absolutely honorable, what on earth
came over you? Why provoke him? After all, he was the
presiding officer or whatever it's called, it was nothing to do
with you, let him take the consequences, he was the one
responsible, wasn't he? But you, no indeed, they had to count,
one by one and take a count, I don't know how you had the
nerve after they'd showed confidence in you, you tell me, if
they chose you it was as a representative person, but you went
there very, very reluctantly, Mario, and with the idea of making trouble, nobody can get that out of my head. And if
Josechu took the notion to say that ninety percent yes, four
percent no, and six percent abstentions, blank votes or whatever that's called, well, he was presiding, wasn't he? he can do
anything he pleases, what did it matter to you, after all? But
no, it was the same as with Hernando de Miguel's lamb,
or the row with Fito, the spirit of contradiction, sweetheart,

that's your fate, because, actually, if you didn't like that, and it seems to me it wasn't important enough to matter, you could have said so with good manners, politely, but never letting things get out of hand, standing up to them, if you'd said, "I don't like it but I accept the majority decision," why, everybody would be happy, that's for sure, when all's said and done that's democracy if I haven't misunderstood you, "I can't lend myself to that," sure, right out, in capital letters, my boy, like in your books, so they could all hear you, till the very last one could hear you, if you can't say things at the top of your voice you'll burst, like I say, and then insisting on counting and recounting, and if we don't count the minutes aren't valid, blackmail, how lovely, you've always been a ridiculous person, Mario, and what you like to do in life is stir up trouble, challenge the whole city, here I stand, and if everyone says white, I say black, just because, because I take the notion, I can see right through you. And that's not the way, Mario, you disaster you, to live in the world you have to be more flexible, loosen up a little bit, you and your kind do such a lot of preaching tolerance and then you do as you damn well please, because, after all, if you'd been a republican all your life, a republican a hundred percent, for goodness' sake, I'd understand it, but you've spent your whole life saying that republic and monarchy are only words, and that one was just as good as the other and that the important thing is what was underneath, then why call attention to yourself by not signing the minutes? Why hand such a snub to Josechu Prados when he's never done us anything but favors? It doesn't make sense, you can be sure of that, it was a first-class blunder, why, Vicente Rojo says that Josechu arrived at the Circle all shaken up, white as a sheet, and that he stammered when he talked and everything, something might have happened to him, how awful, remember his father, a stroke, he spent half his life in a wheelchair, poor man, all because a maid talked back to him. You have to be more careful, Mario, you poor fool, you don't get anywhere by climbing up on your high horse, make sure of that, and you have to live in the world, Josechu's a very good person, but he has his pride too, so there, we're human, and he got a grudge against you, remember the business about the apartment, if you treat him right he's gentle as a lamb, but don't get the idea of opposing him, that's common knowledge. Do you know what Higinio Oyarzun said the other night, and look, a lot of water's gone under the bridge since then? Well, he says that he, Josechu, said, understand? that you were a puritan but that day he didn't smash your face in, like I'm telling you, because of the friendship his parents had with mine, take note of that, how embarrassing, I don't know how you manage it but, with one excuse or another, you've quarreled with the whole city, sweetheart, that's the inheritance you're leaving me, you tell me now, if it weren't for Papa, a pension, sure, the widow's pension won't even pay the rent on the apartment, that's another thing that's not right, I understand it myself. You really amuse me with that idea of yours that if you put the truth first you can accomplish anything, don't make me laugh, no use arguing with you, because would you like to tell me what you've accomplished, sweetheart? everybody with a car and your wife on shank's mare, that's right, you don't have a red cent, for God's sake! a set of nickel silver at the very most, it even makes me ashamed to say it. Do you think that's living? Tell me the honest truth, Mario, do you think there are many women who would have put up with this misery? I'm telling you the truth, but the fact that you don't recognize it is what's hardest to bear, that in twenty-three years of marriage, that's so easy to say, you've never spoken a single word of gratitude, because there were other men, Mario, and you know it, I didn't have any lack of chances, and there still are if you want to know the truth, even after I was married I wouldn't have had any lack of opportunities, and if I was to tell you, that's the joke of it, because a person's a homebody, the kind of woman she ought to be, you men can take it easy, that's what you exploit: once the knot's tied, a faithfulness policy, like I say, you've bought a scrubwoman, a woman who does wonders with practically no money, what more can you ask? Things are very comfortable that way, and meanwhile, you men, I'm off! the grass is greener on the other side of the fence, you do whatever you want. Like that tale about how you came to marriage as virgin as I was, look, pretty-boy, go tell it to the judge, a fib like that, and you said, "Don't thank me for it; it was out of timidity more than anything else," timidity, my foot! As if I didn't know you men, all alike, everybody knows, and you insisting that your awkwardness was the best proof, what a lot of malarkey! the fact is that there's still a great distance between a fallen woman and a decent one, and, deep down, there's always something honorable in you men and that's what comes to the surface when you get married, neither more nor less, less nor more. You a virgin! But do you think I'm an idiot, Mario, sweetheart? And it isn't that I'm going to say that you were immoral, you weren't that either, but, goodness, a little fling once in a while . . . And then the business about Madrid, the wedding trip, you humiliated me to a point you wouldn't believe, a slap like that, of course I admit that I was scared, I knew something strange had to happen, because of having babies, see, but I thought it was only once, I swear I did, and I was resigned, I swear to you, to anything it might be, but you lay down and "good night," as if you'd climbed into bed with a sergeant of the guard, mind you, so much control, so much control, why, I haven't even told it to Valen, and I tell things to Valen, you can just imagine, she's not the same as Esther, because Esther, though she's been my friend all my life, is different, much less understanding, oh my yes, and there are subjects like that, a little bit daring, that are taboo with her, she prides herself on being so modern and well read and she's nothing but a fuddy-duddy, lots of times I think you and she would have done well together, see, you're exactly alike, my boy, as if you'd been turned out of the same mold. To begin with, Esther thinks you're intelligent and she reads those strange kinds of books, big boring things nobody can stand, I remember *The Inheritance,* Valen was laughing her head off, and Esther, that know-it-all, saying that it was a symbolic book, take note, what does she know, and when you had the depression or whatever, same old story, when you were such a bore, going on about frivolity and violence, and then Valen said, "Heavens, what a pessimistic way of looking at things!" and then Esther, my boy, said that she knew you very well, yes indeed, and that we ought to open a magazine to see what things it talked about besides princesses on vacation or massacres in the Congo. She certainly has a golden tongue, sweetheart, she may not talk very much but every time she opens her mouth it's to say the last word, goodness, such airs! you'd think she was a preacher. "Mario's got things inside him, but among all of you you keep him from letting them show," that was it, the last word, as far as I'm concerned, look, I certainly hurried to tell you the story about Maximino Conde and I might as well never have said a word, if I'd known how to write, Mario, what a novel! The thing about Esther is that she's never seen you in bedroom slippers, that's the way men have to be looked at, when you put on your bedroom slippers you

take off the mask, like I say. Every time that subject comes up,
I remember Mama, may she rest in peace, Mario, she used to
say that before getting married a woman ought to see her
fiancé in bedroom slippers for a few months and a lot of
disillusionments would be avoided that way. Take note, it's
not just because I say so, Mario, but Mama knew it all, that's
what experience does, at seventeen a girl thinks she knows
everything, and all that seems like old folks' dodderings, and
then what happens happens, all of us stub our toes on the
same pebble, it isn't that I'm complaining, let's see if we
understand each other, but, the first time, when you turned
over and said good night, I felt as cold as ice, nobody ever
snubbed me like that before, I may not be a Sophia Loren, I
realize that, but not bad enough for a slap of that magnitude.
Paquito Alvarez, I can tell you, would never have done that to
me, and not to mention Eliseo San Juan, or even Evaristo to
give you just one example, he may be as degenerate as you
please, they even say that he has a suitcaseful of chicken
feathers and dresses up with mirrors and weird things, but
just exactly because of that. And it wasn't as if it was news to
me, certainly not, I've always heard that night is really all out,
that it's no fun, something you have to put up with, but I
don't know of anybody, no one, who turned over and said
good night. And don't come and tell me it was out of respect
and there are times when we have to control the brute, because whether we like it or not we're animals, Mario, and
what's worse, animals with habits, and a woman, no matter
how sound her principles are, in a situation like that, can
accept brutality rather than contempt, you know what I'm
like. What happened on our wedding night, Mario, I don't
care what you say, is something I won't forget if I live a
thousand years, heavens, to do that to me, and Father Fando

can still say it was out of consideration, I won't confess with him again, these young priests are certainly acting funny, they don't think anything is important, only whether workers earn a little or a lot, I'll bet you anything they think it's worse for a boss to refuse paying a bonus than to make love to a woman who's not his wife, this is the pass we've come to, Mario, though it's sad to have to admit it, we're losing our sense of morality and that's why we're in such a fix, that wretched Council, when we were so happy as we were. And aren't they talking now about how the Protestants are going to open a chapel here, right on the corner? Why, are we in our right minds, just imagine, with five kids? What kind of peace of mind can a person have about letting them go out? I don't even want to think about it, Mario, this is happening to us because you and your kind aren't the way they ought to be, people don't meditate about the Beyond any more, or don't have principles or anything like them. But we had an example at home, Mario, remember, "Tell me about your little escapades before we were married, even if it does hurt me. I forgive you in advance," I think with the best of intentions, because I was ready to drink the cup to the dregs, I promise you that, maybe I'm silly, but I can't help it, I fly off the handle and suddenly, one fine day, I feel like forgiving the whole world, and I was going to do it, I swear I was, let you talk and then, a kiss and "What's past is past," but you, not a word, reserved even to your little wifie, that's the thing that's hardest to bear, and when I insisted, capital letters, my boy, just like in your books: "I WAS AS MUCH A VIRGIN AS YOU WERE, BUT DON'T THANK ME FOR IT; IT WAS OUT OF TIMIDITY MORE THAN ANYTHING ELSE." What do you think of that? If there's anything that drives me wild, Mario, it's your lack of confidence in me, get that through your head once and for all, because if you'd told me the truth that night I would have forgiven you just the same, even if it was hard for me, I swear by whatever you hold most dear. The same thing with that business of Encarna in Madrid, a person doesn't have to be dirty minded, and I'm not saying it would have happened nowadays, but look, twenty-five years ago, with the euphoria, a beer and some shrimps, no, Mario, tell me another, it's as not as if I was stupid, do you think I don't know Encarna? And then, having won and all that, what more did you need for things to get out of hand, sure, I understand it, but no matter how you look at it, it was such an indecent thing, between in-laws, even if only out of respect for Elviro's sacred memory. Now with José María's widow, if he'd been married, it would have seemed the same but it wouldn't have been the same, it's different, see, a man with no beliefs. No matter how much we keep quiet about things, Mario, it all comes out in the end, the world's a very small place as poor Mama used to say, and with Encarna, up to about fifteen years ago, there have been things that weren't very clear, sweetheart, according to you it's all compassion, but I'd like to know, I'm not saying she has more money than she needs or that she ought to go to work, heaven forbid, but I know you gave her money and she took it, and I can even tell you the place and the date if you want it any clearer, a person keeps her mouth shut and finds out everything in the end.

X

....

Amen I say to you, as long as you did it to one of these my least brethren, you did it to me. Listen to something, Mario, do you know that I liked it every time you used to say, "What a little reactionary you are"? I suppose you said it because of the things I used to come out with, see, what other reason would you have? but even so. I remember when we were kids, Paco, when he used to chase after me, always calling me "little one," over and over, there was a time when I liked Paco, like I'm telling you, I was a child, of course, at the time I hardly noticed that he didn't even know how to talk right, because Paco's family was a little bit you-know, how can I say it, well, a little bit, a working-class family actually, and when you scratched him the brute showed through, but as he was always cracking jokes you had a good time with him, I've never seen a man so taken with anybody in my life, I'm telling you the truth. I remember when we used to meet you and your bunch, and that lout Armando would put his fingers to his forehead and bellow, Paco used to say, "If they bring out another bull I'll jump into the ring, little one, just to show you what bravery's like," and Transi used to die laughing, I don't know why Paco appealed to her but she always preferred him, and if not him the old guys, and as for you, she wouldn't have had you as a gift, if the truth be told, and really she had no reason to be so against you, "Throw him over, just look at that Adam's apple, he looks like a scarecrow," you tell me, in the early days, as soon as you'd gone, she used to kiss me on the mouth, pressing hard, I must say they were strange, like a vise, "Menchu, you have a fever, you oughtn't to go out tomorrow," I don't know if she was jealous or what, understand? Frankly, Transi hasn't been lucky, she may have her little faults, and who doesn't, but she also has some very good qualities, see, like about the fever, at that age, concern like that can't be repaid. I don't know why, or why not, but she was crazy about Paco Alvarez, she nearly died laughing with him, see? correcting him, because Paco used to say "relation" for "reaction" and "perceptive" for "perspective," he mixed all his words up, Transi used to call him The Workingman, between ourselves, of course, without making a big thing of it, and that's what I think is the strangest, although, when you come right down to it, it wasn't the important thing, the worst of it was that you saw he was a man without any polish, I don't know exactly in what respect, in every way, he didn't even worry about whether he walked on the outside of me, and he always said "my mama," just imagine, at his age. But if you don't count that, Paco, as a man, was really very handsome, not to mention nowadays, he's so tanned, with a little gray in his hair, he looks like an actor, but it seems like it's always been my fate to attract lower-class people, Eliseo, Evaristo, Paco, and so on. Valen says that happens when a woman's a little bit on the plump side, but except for my bosom, I always had a little too much there, I never was fat, do you think? And that's not to mention now, naturally, you ought to see Eliseo San Juan, he goes all squinty, listen, and if I have the blue sweater on it's ever so much worse, "You're terrific, you're terrific, every day you get more terrific," it's a wicked thing, Mario, he just won't leave me alone, an obsession. And then, with that jawline, and that deep voice and those shoulders he has on him, he's a knockout, honestly, well, as I was saying, Paco Alvarez was always something different, I'm not going to say more refined, but, I don't know! less overpowering, sort of more polite, different, even his eyes, I've never seen anything like them, I give you my word, it's a strange green for eyes, admit it, like cats' eyes or the water in swimming pools. And he did little things, I certainly noticed that, Paco may have been unrefined and so on but it was always a struggle between his humble background and a polite nature. You should see him now, a gentleman, a real gentleman, I remember when we were kids, going up or down a curb, he always used to take my arm, as if it were accidental, you know, carelessly, but for a woman it's nice to notice that a man recognizes her weakness. And something I haven't told you, Mario, the other day, about two weeks ago, the second of last month to be exact, Paco took me downtown in his Citroën, a huge car that long, you never saw anything like it, I was standing in line for the bus and all of a sudden, wham! he put on the brakes, just like in the movies, eh? like I'm telling you, I hadn't seen Paquito for about a thousand years, you'll never believe it, I blushed and everything, just think how infuriating, if there's anything that makes me really angry it's to notice that the blood's rushing to my face and not be able to do anything about it. And he acted as if he hadn't noticed, and my goodness, such a voice, such poise, such manners, a different Paco, Mario, just like I'm telling you, "Going downtown?" "Why, yes," what could I have answered after all, but I didn't budge, and right there, next to me, was Crescente with his delivery cart, snooping of course, so as not to get out of practice, but Paco never hesitated, "I'll take you," and I got in without even thinking what I was doing. And what a car, Mario, a dream, honestly! I only need to tell you that I got all dizzy, why, I didn't even notice the bumps in the road, and then Paco drives with such assurance, like he'd never done anything else all his life, and I, what a fool I am, my heart going pitty-pat the whole time, not for any real reason, just for being shut up in a car with another man who wasn't you, but Paco certainly isn't the person he was, what a way of expressing himself, Mario, few words but just the right ones, in a level tone, without twisting up his features or anything, just like the right sort of people. You men are lucky, like I say, you improve with age, and the man who doesn't look good at twenty only has to wait twenty more years, take Paco for example, talking like a book, sort of very manly, when he was a youngster, so blond, he looked a little bit namby-pamby for my taste, a teeny bit soft, I don't know, but now you can tell a mile off that he's somebody, "Time doesn't pass for you, little one; you're just the same as when we used to go walking on the promenade," see, and I said, "Aren't you foolish," what else could I say to him, we hadn't spoken for twenty-five years, silver anniversary, imagine, in point of fact ever since I was a mere child, and then I, to change the subject, "What a marvelous car," and he said it looked even better with me inside, an empty compliment, you'll say, couldn't have been cheaper, it caught me by surprise and then I was sorry about it, if the truth be told, but that doesn't take away from it, a compliment's always a pleasure. And when we didn't say anything more, he kept looking at me sideways, a little bit iffy, I'm not saying like a man making a conquest, but anyway, he went the long way round to take me to the Plaza, but I didn't say a word, I know perfectly well he's married and has a bunch of kids, and me too, of course, so I played dumb, and then, when we said good-bye, he kept looking into my eyes, and he held my hand for quite a while, I thought he was going to burst out with something, because you look at Paco now and it's like he was a different man, Mario, a control, an assurance, it doesn't seem possible he could change so much. Apparently, after the war he spent several years in Madrid, establishing commercial connections, you know? he told me so, and now with this new industrial park he's interested in things here, as a sales representative and I don't know what kind of real estate business or whatever it's called. Of course, he always was hardworking and he behaved wonderfully during the war, goodness, what a record, a brother of his was killed and he took shrapnel in the chest and a whole lot of other wounds, distinguished himself ever so much, who could have told him, that insignificant little kid, the world certainly has its changes, if I'd married him, see, by this time I could have had anything I wanted. Because you'll laugh, Mario, but nowadays people spend a lot of money, that's what makes me the maddest, you're very far from stupid but look at you, I'm not saying a Citroën, but a Six Hundred . . . Even janitor's wives have one of those nowadays, sweetheart, I'm not exaggerating, on Sundays who do you see on the street, a few poor people half dead of hunger and us. Not for any special reason, Mario, but seeing Paco has made me think, and it's actually sinful not to take advantage of the talents God has given us, it really is, and by writing those things you write in *El Correo,* you don't get anywhere and you don't do anyone any good, it's wasting your time, like I say, look at Paco, I realize myself that meeting him left me a little bit stunned, that's logical, after so long, it isn't that there could be any men for me except you, you understand, but for a woman it's always flattering to know that somebody likes her. Do you know how he looked at me, Mario? When I left him I didn't know what attitude to take, I swear, he didn't start the car and he must have been looking after me, it made me cross to have gone out looking like that, as if I didn't have anything else to wear, but just this one time, of course, if I'd known. Fortunately you men don't even notice, when he took hold of my hand I was thinking the whole time, "Let him not look at my buttons, let him not realize my coat's been turned," but nowadays he doesn't sweat or anything, I remember when he was young, of course nowadays there are products for everything, but when he was a youngster every time he'd take my arm to help me up the curb, I'd say under my breath to Transi, "He's soaked me already," and she'd die laughing, and poor Paco, "What are you laughing about, little one, if it's not a bad question to ask?" he used to leave my arm all damp, like I'm telling you. And I'm not going to say now that it bowled me over to have Paco hold on to my hand, but you have to admit it was an attention, something you never did with me, sweetheart, you were always colder than anything, and I'm not saying to kiss me, I wouldn't have permitted that to you or anybody on earth, that would have been a fine thing, but a little bit more passion, you disaster you, because you were always such a lukewarm person, a lot of "my love" and "my own," and then, nothing solid. Just look at our wedding night! Consideration, don't make me laugh, you certainly do put me in embarrassing situations, Valen, for instance, she even bled, and I have to tell her I did too, out of pure shame, look, how do you expect me to tell her that you turned over and acted like you'd never seen me? What more do you want? Well, you take Armando and Esther, my boy, and very intellectual she is, don't tell me, well, they got engaged, in case you'd like to know, by his holding her hand, neither more or less, he didn't propose or anything and that's the joke of it, she noticed it because he didn't let go, only because of that, and that's the way they began, so there. I wouldn't have put up with that system, that's something else, I like things done right, Mario, and the proposal is like the benediction to be husband and wife, the same thing, I remember poor Mama, "Things need a beginning," take note, she was absolutely right. An engagement's a very important commitment, Mario, it's a lifelong step, a lot of people don't even realize, I like you, you like me, well, on with it! why, people even make a joke of it, and it isn't, that's the reason things turn out the way they do. Now, a little bit of passion, no matter what you say, is fundamental. Look at Armando, fifteen years married, a lot of experience behind him, but don't let anybody look at his wife, I remember the other night at the Atrium, in the bar, what a scene he made, and I don't think poor Esther has much to look at, well, that's another story, but it doesn't matter to him, he really shoved the other fellow, acting very much the man, the way a man has to be, they had a big argument, and all because he winked at her, you'll see how they won't try that again, that's for sure. And that time at the movies when they were engaged? I saw it and he got exactly what he deserved, what a scene, Armando gave that fellow a punch in the jaw that actually broke the movie posters and everything, only because he blew smoke on her as he went by, only because of that, take note, that's why I'm crazy about Armando, he may be all the brute you please, but he's healthy minded, sort of old-fashioned, with principles, you understand me. We women like men with a little bit more gumption, darling, men who defend what's theirs, who kill each other for us, if necessary. Don't they do it for their country? Well, more of the same, Mario, for your information, the wife or the fiancée have to be sacred, like I say, no touching them or letting them be touched, though with you it doesn't even register, "I have confidence in you," "You know already how you ought to behave," how comfortable! And suppose I forget? And suppose that someday I just plain don't feel like doing what I ought to? That's just lovely, you men, once the knot's tied you can sleep easy, a faithfulness policy, like I say, always the same story, but get this into your head, Mario, there are times when a man has to earn that faithfulness the hard way, and with his fists if need be, you take Armando, follow his example, nobody's going to look at his little wifie because he's capable of anything. And most men are like Armando, make sure of that, I don't know about Paco, it's been a long time since I lost track of him, but it's the most likely thing, you only have to see him, to begin with he demonstrated it during the war, just imagine what his body's like, like a sieve, so many shrapnel scars. I know I get boring about it, but I'll never tire of telling you, stupid, that you have to put some spirit into things that are really worthwhile instead of wasting your time writing foolish stuff that doesn't even make money for you or interest anybody, you heard Papa, and Papa on other subjects maybe not, but when it comes to writing he's not just anybody, you know it full well, it makes me absolutely furious to see you acting like a fool.

XI

How beautiful thou art, my love, how beautiful art thou! thy eyes are doves' eyes, and excuse me for insisting, Mario, maybe I'm even being tiresome, but it isn't unimportant, for me, the declaration of love, it's fundamental, absolutely necessary, mind you, no matter how often you insist that it's all foolishness. Well, it isn't, it's not foolishness, see, you stop to think about it, getting engaged is the most important step in the life of a man and a woman, I'm not just talking for talk's sake, and, logically, that step has to be solemn, even, if you really want my opinion, expressed in ritual words, remember what poor Mama, may she rest in peace, used to say. That's why, no matter how much he defends her and no matter how much he yells, I'm not crazy about Armando's method of going out together for a few afternoons and holding her hand for a good while and then considering themselves engaged. That may be a tacit engagement if you like, but if anyone was to ask me, I wouldn't have any hesitation about speaking up, I assure you, I'd stick to my guns, Esther and Armando got married practically without being engaged, all in a rush, just like it sounds, a thing that, when you come right down to it, I don't think is even moral. It's the same as if a man wanted to be a woman's husband just because he'd put his hand on her, just exactly, marriage may be a sacrament and anything else you please, but an engagement, darling, is the gateway to that sacrament, it isn't unimportant, and it has to be formalized too, I know there are lots of formulas, heaps of them, what are you going to tell me, from "I love you" to "I'd like you to be the mother of my children," corny as it is, mind you, like a soldier and a nursemaid, but in spite of everything it's a formula, and I accept it as such. That's why I insisted so much, Mario, sweetheart, understand, I like to do things right and you've always been a little bit inhibited, ever since I've known you, even now you are, unless you have a couple of drinks and then you go too far, you spoil the party, so there, and if you're alone you start to look miserable and don't say a word, and ready to turn up your toes. Like the other night at Valentina's, see, you were unbearable, I'm telling you the way I feel it, Mario, why should I say anything else, the whole time firing champagne corks at the streetlights, I'd like to know what the help thought, because to lose your manners is something only lower-class people can get away with, Mario, fortunately we still have classes, smarty, you've always taken the attitude that all this business of good manners was a trifle, and it isn't. Like your greeting people on the street without paying any attention to who they were, you used to make me feel sick, and you said you were thinking about your concerns, well and good, Mario, but as poor Mama used to say, "Every hour has its responsibilities," because people oughtn't to feel as if they have to guess whether you're absentminded, or bad mannered, or just disagreeable. The number of enemies you've acquired because of that, and so stupidly! Between that and your books and your insistence on going against the grain, you've annoyed the whole city, sweetheart, and that just can't be done, I'll have you know, we live among civilized people and among civilized people you have to behave like a civilized person, and if you don't greet someone you know, then why in the world, if you can tell me that, are you going to greet some stranger, I remember how embarrassed you made me feel, right next to Arronde's pharmacy, with that impertinent shabby fellow, "Excuse me, can you tell me where we've met before?" and then you were mortified, naturally, and said you'd mistaken him for someone else and this and that and the other thing, words, and he, the fresh thing, "Don't worry, from today on we know each other," right on the main street, I didn't know where to look, and on top of that, slapping each other on the back, what do you think of that, a streetsweeper or heaven knows what, what could the people who saw us have thought. You simply can't do that, Mario, if only for your own self-esteem, and as if that wasn't enough, "Friends, then, and anything I can do for you," to some raggedy stranger, you have to realize, it's a way of attracting attention to yourself too, all the more knowing that it bothers me, it's not out of pride, but birds of a feather flock together, you disaster you, as far as keeping up appearances, you rate zero. That's why I'm happier every day that I made you jump through the hoop, I should say so, if it had been left to you, "I want to go out with you, but just the two of us," how about that, and I playing dumb, "What ever for?" "Why, as sweethearts," "But we're not, don't you know that?" and you trying to back out of it, but not a chance. These things, Mario, sweetheart, need solemnity, it's not just an idea of mine, the world knows what it's doing, and when things have always been done like that, that's the way it has to be, make sure of it, if not everything would be a mess, so to speak, and if some fine day you'd decided to take off for pastures new, what hold would I have had on you, nothing at all, see? While the other way, I'm not saying that it's actually legal, but you'd always be thought of as a louse, from the social standpoint, I mean. And so I waited one day after another, holding on, and you've certainly blamed me for it since, but you had to jump through the hoop, you rascal, I should say so, and here between you and I, I'm telling you that I had no lack of choices, just look at Paquito . . . I had proposals to burn, every day of the week practically, and I kept saying no, see, and Transi nearly crazy, "You're not going to tell me that you like that puny little guy even a teeny bit?" I wouldn't go as far as that, but physically, sweetheart, you certainly didn't have very much to like, frankly, and I was sort of romantic, I'm nothing but a romantic and a fool, "That boy needs me," you can see at that age, I went all emotional about feeling indispensable, stupid of me, Mama with that sharp eye she had, I've never seen anything like it, "Child, don't confuse love with pity," just think how clever she was. But I was blind, I realize it, at that age, because I'm not going to say for sure, but maybe if that lout Armando hadn't put his fingers to his temples and bellowed like a bull, it made me so ashamed, I wouldn't even have noticed you, there are times when the future depends on something absolutely foolish, mind you, a little detail like that, the way things are. The fact is that I felt terribly sorry for you, I don't know, because I just hated that brown suit, I admit it, and the heels of your shoes sort of run over, and you like that, so sad, but of course you never know, and, all of a sudden, one day I noticed that you were starting to appeal to me, it was stupid, if you'd seen Transi, "Throw him over, do you mind letting me know what you're thinking of?" it was torture, sweetheart, you can't imagine, against the wishes of everyone, Mama would never have consented, you can thank the business about Galli, on the rebound from that, see. Mama, though I'm not the one to say it, was the most even-tempered woman I've ever known, always smiling, so neat and clean, never raised her voice to anyone, one of those people who soothe you, Mario, just look at how she died, didn't even lose her composure, don't tell me, I think of it lots of times, that Mama, before she got to where your father was, would have died of hunger, I'll bet you anything, I should say so, she was cleanliness in person, before she would have done it in bed, anything, I'm absolutely sure of it, what they say about "from the cradle to the grave" is true and more than true, people die the way they live, careful people die careful and the ones who let themselves go die that way too, now take your mother, to give you just one example, "Take care of him; Mario's a fine boy, my dear," always satisfied with what she had, it never failed, admit it, she probably had other virtues, I don't say she didn't, but her children, even José María, see, fine one he was, were saints, and Charo, I don't need to tell you, perfect, and the furniture in her house, all of it put together wasn't worth a thing and yet she could say that what wasn't walnut was mahogany. Your mother was funny, Mario, the most stuck-up person in the world, how wonderful to be like that, I wish I could be, I remember the day she showed me the cooler outside the bathroom window, I got nauseous, I swear, I wanted to throw up, "The best refrigerator in the world wouldn't keep milk the way this cooler does, my dear. The milk doesn't turn sour here even in August," imagine, and then, when I was pregnant, every time I went to your house I couldn't swallow a mouthful, it was just impossible, such disgust. I believe, I think about it lots of times, that if you never had any ambition, you understand, in the good sense, it was because you were raised in such a stingy atmosphere. Why, you were even grudging about saying you loved me, darling! You certainly gave me a lot of trouble, but I'd promised it to myself, "Do you want to be engaged?" what a way to put it, "What for?" "Why, just because," so stubborn, "So two people get engaged just because?" and you, like a child with no manners, you really are something, "I like being with you," and I had to try not to laugh, I give you my word, "If you like to be with me there must be some reason, don't you think?" and finally you jumped through the hoop, you rascal, or don't you remember any more? "Because I love you," and I said to you, I remember like I was seeing it now, by the angel fountain, on the second bench, as you come into the park from the right past the aviary, "Well, that's better." But a lot of good it did me, my boy, accepting you was a piece of bad luck, after that nothing but walking through the strangest streets, no people, at first I was a little bit suspicious, see, a person never knows, and since you talk so little, I really don't understand how you men get along without talking, I didn't know a thing, honestly, the day that Armando told me, "Mario's an enemy of the multitudes," I breathed easier, but I don't know, if you're an enemy of the multitudes why do you concern yourself so much with workingmen, there are certainly plenty of them, millions and millions, and then the country people, Valen laughs her head off with your mania for yokels, what she says is, "Hunger, not a bit of it, honey, they butcher pigs I'd like to have for myself." One of two things, Mario, nobody can understand you, either you're an enemy or a friend, but if you're a friend, then associate with your equals, you rascal, that's what your place in society calls for, and leave the workingmen alone, and the yokels who know perfectly well how to take care of themselves, just listen to Paco, fine ones they are, and then the maids too, nowadays everybody wants the moon. I've said to Valen lots of times that it seems like you and your kind go out of your way to be inconsistent, sweetheart, lots of God, lots of love-your-neighbor, but if poor people study and stop being poor, can you tell me who's going to be left to exercise charity on? Go on, tell me, you always have an answer ready! And the fact is that you don't realize, because if you only thought all these things, well, it would be bad but it would pass, but no, you've got to write it and write it in capital letters, there, in big letters, so nobody can miss seeing it, that's the way you like it. If *El Correo* would burn down some day how happy I'd be, Mario, believe me, what you and your friends are doing in that rag of a newspaper is the devil's work, confusing the unfortunate and filling their heads with fantasies, admit it, you stubborn thing, you're so hardheaded and you've never listened to reason, you're eaten up with arrogance, sweetheart, your own self before anything else, and don't say it's not true, it was arrogance that made you stand up to Solórzano, no less, the man holds out his hand to you, "No, sir, I have no reason to bow my head," it's pride and nothing but pride, look at Higinio Oyarzun, I don't think he's done so badly, and after all that fuss about the minutes with Josechu, the fact that Fito Solórzano proposed you for the City Council was raising the flag of truce, wasn't it? let bygones be bygones, wipe out the past and start over, Papa said it perfectly clearly in his letter, but you, no sir, you were proud of it, "They want to compromise me," "The price of silence," what poppycock, when what they were offering you was a platform, you blockhead, a responsible position, you heard Antonio, "To get into City Hall as a cultural representative is to go in through the front door," and it's not just me that says it, Antonio says it, get that into your head, you stubborn thing. Well, you didn't pay the slightest attention, "My name's there for the sound of it, not for real," you always come out with these things, my boy, you're the strangest person, complexes, that's what you've got, you and your friends are full of complexes, you tell me, always talking in code, "For the sound of it, not for real," nobody can understand you, a bore, what a bore you are, and the worst of it is that your son comes along with the very same tricks, you heard him yesterday, "Mother, those are stupid conventionalisms," get that, and sulky to boot, I was so embarrassed, crying in the bathroom for half an hour, I'm telling you, and not being able to come out. And then you can say . . . I prefer Menchu a thousand times, with all her laziness, to these young fellows, I don't know if it's the university or what, but all of them come out halfway to being Reds, haven't the slightest consideration, and Menchu, whether she studies or not, at least she's easy to manage, and she'll pass the exam for the lower-level certificate somehow or other, you can be sure of it, and that's enough, a girl ought not to know any more, Mario, she has to be given time to be a woman, when all's said and done that's her role in life. After all, the lower-level course is just the same as the higher one in our time, Mario, oh my yes, and after she's through wearing mourning, the child will be able to dress well, and since she's cute and clever about handling boys, she'll soon have a crowd around her, and if not, let a little time pass, my experience is good for something and I'll take care of her making a good choice, she's easy to manage and ever since she was a little girl she hasn't bought so much as a pin without consulting me. I know, you're going to say that I'm strangling her personality, you make me sick, you big dummy, because if personality means refusing to wear mourning for a father or having no respect for a mother, then I don't want children with personality, I'll have you know, I've had enough trouble with your personality, my ideas aren't so bad, after all, and either I'm good for nothing or my ideas are going to be my children's ideas, I'm even going to crack down on that insolent Mario, you can be sure of it, and if he wants to think for himself let him earn his way and go off and think somewhere else, because as long as he lives under my roof, the ones who depend on me will have to think the way I tell them to. Don't laugh, Mario, but a strong authority is a guarantee of order, just remember the Republic, and it's not that I'm inventing it, here in Spain and everywhere, and order has to be maintained by fair means or foul. "Either a thing's so or it isn't," as poor Mama would say.

XII

He is proud, knowing nothing, but sick about questions and strifes
of words; from which arise envies, contentions, blasphemies, evil
suspicions, conflicts of men corrupted in mind, and who are desti-
tute of the truth, supposing gain to be godliness, and don't try and
fool me, Mario, what bothers you and your friends about
Higinio Oyarzun is the car, let's speak frankly, and that fifteen
years after arriving here he's gone into society, something that
neither you nor any of your gang have succeeded in doing,
nor will you ever succeed, for the simple reason that you're all
so standoffish, why kid ourselves, you haven't any manners
and don't even know how to straighten a tie. Yes, I know,
you're going to tell me that you're not interested, like the fox,
they're not ripe, same as always, you're really something, but
with Valen the other night, you tell me, tickled to death, what
a time you had! and don't forget that the Rojos are among the
best people in town, for your information, what happens is
that because he's a teacher at the High School, they have to
act like they had less than they do, so there. But if Vicente
weren't a teacher, I can tell you right now, we wouldn't put a
foot inside their house! even though it makes Valen look good
to entertain writers and all, what she does is laugh at you, like
I'm telling you, because Valen has a great sense of humor even
if she doesn't seem to, she'll laugh at absolutely anything,

don't think she doesn't. And what a supper she gave us, the kind you dream about, oodles of everything, even lobster and caviar, and what lobster, Mario, and everything so well served, why, not even the wedding in Canaan, like I say, and if you hadn't gone too far, one of the happiest nights of my life, mind you, what a supper, and because she says, "Come and have a drink on Saturday," she underplays it, you think it's going to be something else. But you were on the point of spoiling everything, sweetheart, you're really something, and I'm telling you that I felt it coming, you're not going to believe it, I swear, the minute we got there, when we went in and I saw Solórzano and Higinio, I thought, like I'm telling you, "Either Mario sulks in a corner or he makes a spectacle of himself," how well I know you, as soon as I caught a glimpse of Oyarzun, I don't know why you have such a thing about him, he seems like a polite young man to me, and I'm not talking with no basis, because you saw me, and I had a very nice time with him, that doesn't mean I'm going to say he has such good looks, because he doesn't, he doesn't have, he's no Adonis if that's what you want to know, but considering that he's a small man, with that smell of pipe tobacco and those lovely ties he wears, in the end you find him attractive, funny the way things are. Higinio is one of those men who fool you, because at first he doesn't seem like much, I agree, but as you see more of him you begin to recognize that he has something, you ask me what and I haven't a clue, I'll start by telling you that I don't know if it's because he dresses well or knows how to wear clothes, which are two very different things, even though that's Greek to you. But for your information, sweetheart, and I'm not insinuating anything, there are people who're so gussied up when they dress for a party that they sort of get on your nerves, as if they'd just taken off their country corduroys to go to a wedding, you understand me, and there are others who don't, and that's what Higinio's like, he has an ease and a special kind of charm, why, you put that boy, short and thin as he is, into a formal outfit and he'd be like a fish in water, I'll bet you anything. You can tell a mile off that he's a man about town, not a bit of the upstart about him, and if somebody tells you that he's a gossip, certainly not, the absolute opposite, he always has a pleasant word for everyone, and look, he has plenty of reasons to be stuck up, but nothing like that, so simple, even to me, take note, I see him on the street and hello and hello, and then, right away, about your books, what were you writing and if anything new was going to come out this year, really interested. And don't tell me, as for you about him, better not to speak of it, saying that he's a tattletale and a gossip, you tell me, anybody else, after the campaigns in *El Correo* and the thing about Fito Solórzano, the least he could have done was ignore you, but not he, like I'm telling you, like you were the best writer in Spain, now I'm not saying that you write badly, understand, the only thing is the plots, but he's all praises, the only thing was that sometimes you went a teeny bit too far, see, a teeny bit, a really good person, that's what he is, maybe not in other things, but nobody can beat me for a sharp eye. And the same with the thing about Papa, you wouldn't believe it, about the necktie, "He can take it off tomorrow, little girl; Spain is in fact a monarchy," listen, I didn't have the faintest idea, I admit it, but he didn't think it was strange, "It's an established thing; that's been the case since the year one, but then you young ladies hadn't been born yet," a compliment, mind you, because whether I look them or not I've got a few years behind me, even if Paco the other day did say that I looked exactly like when we used to walk up and down the promenade, I only wish I did. Because

I don't know if I've told you that Paco took me in his car twice, Mario, a week apart, at the same time and the same bus stop, which is certainly a coincidence. I was embarrassed, don't think I wasn't, a long line and then I saw a red Citroën coming and wham! braking hard, but just like in the movies. "Are you going downtown?" and I was upset, why, it's Paco, imagine, hadn't seen him for ages, and Crescente snooping all the time out of his delivery cart and I was so abashed, naturally, "Why, yes," what else was I going to say to him, he didn't even give me time to think about it, he opened the door and in I went. What a change in Paco, darling, no matter how much I told you, you just can't imagine! A different man, really a different man. He still has those eyes that are so ideal according to my taste, prettier, if that's possible, a greenish blue, halfway between cats' eyes and the water in a swimming pool, and over the years, I don't know how to explain it to you, he's taken on poise, I remember when he was a boy, a little shrimp, and now he has presence, he looks like somebody, and he speaks correctly, he was a scream before. Well, there he was, with his Citroën, piling up millions, I don't quite remember where he told me he worked, of course it has something to do with the industrial park, don't take what I say for gospel even though I was really impressed when he talked about the apartments. And yet I didn't dare say a word to Higinio, I was stupid, I realize it myself, because after all he belonged to the commission that administered them, but, mind you, after all the time that's passed, at the time, I realize it, I had an awful fit, but I wasn't going to go to him with the tale again, it seems to me it wasn't the place, besides, they were absolutely right, some day you'll have to admit, you disaster you, that in this world friends are better than university degrees. But if you go and stand up against them, criticizing them night and day, not wanting to be on the Council, refusing to sign their minutes, do you think they're going to give you an apartment on top if it? They'd have to be crazy, Mario, don't kid yourself, and I'm the first to recognize that it's not your fault, if they'd given that Don Nicolás, may God confound him, what he deserved at the right time, it'd be a different story, because that Don Nicolás and that Aróstegui and that Moyano, who'd get along faster if he'd shave off that disgusting beard, like I say, and the whole gang of you, Father Fando included, I used to think before that he was made of different stuff, have done you a lot of harm, and that's the truth. I already know Don Nicolás' theory, "In today's world, a writer is either a critic or he's nothing," words, just words, the idea is to bamboozle the young people, cannon fodder, neither more nor less. I don't know why on earth youngsters are so stirred up nowadays, I just can't stand that Don Nicolás of yours, mind you, he may be as intelligent as you please but nobody's worse than he is, and besides you can see right through him, that's another thing. Take away his little group, and I don't know of a single person he speaks well of, heavens, what a tongue! look at those verses he wrote about poor Canido. Of course, Canido was just an excuse, he doesn't fool me, and besides, I'm not ashamed of saying so, I just love Canido's poems, you can all say whatever you want, he may be as old-fashioned as you please, but they rhyme divinely and they're wonderfully easy to understand, it's not like poetry nowadays, just look at the poets too, my boy, they write in code, I can't abide them, and he running around saying that "Canido's verses aren't verses but versicles, and Solórzano's texts aren't texts but testicles," and Moyano, I heard him all right, saying that "Fito was one of those that were pure balls," see, what manners! he doesn't know himself what he means by that. And I'm not going to come out now and say that Solórzano speaks well, that would be stupid of me, but not badly either, he speaks normally, doesn't call attention to himself one way or the other, and anyway, if he felt like printing his speeches in the House of Culture, if he took the notion to do that, well, others have other notions, he's not doing anyone any harm it seems to me, if he paid for the printing himself, the name of the publisher was the least important part, goodness, how you all reacted, you'd have thought they wanted to shoot you, not only did you say no and that you'd rather stop printing anything at all, it wasn't worth making such a fuss, but then, on top if it, you and your friends had to go running around saying that printing one speech would be sufficient, that in the others it was enough to substitute "trough" for "telephone" or for "fountain" or for "cemetery," I've never seen such ill will in my life, I'll have you know. Though you pretend to be high-minded, you're trying to make trouble, sweetheart, and you got way out of line, criticizing and causing trouble all day long, and then, see, nobody can stand you, that's logical, look at the people who came to the house yesterday, outside of half a dozen people who count, youngsters and shabby folks, that's the pass we've come to. If I tell you the truth, I don't understand why they haven't cracked down on you yet, believe me, because after the business about José María you ought to have been more careful, all the more so in view of your father's reputation, he managed to keep out of trouble but he was a Red too, I don't know whether of Lerroux's party or Alcalá Zamora's, but Red of course, quite a nest of sedition your house was, my boy, you'd have to look high and low to find another like it. Fortunately there was the thing about Elviro in Madrid and the war, and, willingly or not, in the end you did serve, that's true, but the business about José María was a great big black mark, don't tell me, a man of importance, enough to put your whole family in quarantine, mind you, your father used to make me laugh, so tiresome, saying it was he who wouldn't let him go to the office, that was the least of it, you can be sure of that, when the Republic was proclaimed he went out on the street with the flag and he was at Azaña's meeting in the bullring, there are witnesses, it's not something I made up. You cover up with Elviro, Mario, but that's not enough, he was one of the Fallen and everything you please, but there's also the thing about the other one, why, I don't know how you dare to talk about tolerance and understanding and that we can't be like Cain and Abel forever and ever, tell it to them, José María and people like him are Cains, worse than Cains, you make a fool of yourself every time you say in public that your two brothers thought the same, who ever heard of such a thing, that José María went too far one way and Elviro didn't go far enough the other, always with your riddles, you disaster you, you drive a person out of her head with them, instead of speaking plain. Just the same with the heroes of the two sides, or that without an act of collective expiation it would be very difficult to start over, or that clear-eyed boys who wanted a different Spain, the ones on one side and the other, but that politics and money made it all fail. How are you going to compare, are you a fool? why, they didn't even go to mass, dear boy, you certainly have it in for money, money is something you have or don't have but it can't think, it isn't as if it was a person, you and your friends would sell your souls to the devil to make a phrase. It's like the thing about José María, when Charo comes out and says that before they killed him he said it wasn't the first time a just man was dying for others, that's just talk, who knows what José María said if he said anything, that is, he was probably half dead of fright and praying My Lord Jesus Christ, like everybody in that kind of a fix, naturally. People on the wrong side of the street, because it's to their advantage, are awfully fond of coming out with phrases and polishing them like brass doorknobs, there are people who feed on phrases, like I say, what a bore, words certainly give you a lot of trouble, sweetheart, what Valen says is, by turning them over in your brain so many times you don't know where to put your feet, and then all of you want to set the world to rights and you don't know a single thing, that's the joke of it, and you think that you know it all. Listen, Mario, here between you and I, every time Borja went to sleep listening to the Fifth Symphony and you'd say, "This is the intellectual of the family," I got frantic, I can tell you, because not for anything in the world would I want to have an intellectual child, a misfortune like that, I'd rather God took him instead, mind you. Recognize once and for all, Mario, intellectuals with their wild ideas, they're the ones who tangle everything up, all of them are half crazy, because they think they know things but the only thing they know how to do is make trouble, the only thing, mind you, and drive poor people out of their minds, and the one who doesn't wind up a Red winds up a Protestant or something worse. I'd give half my life to get that into your head, darling, I don't know how to put it to you any more, there are people who stop me right on the street, and it's not just one or two, always the same thing, asking if you've become a Red, imagine what a situation, how can I possibly answer them, and then, every time I saw you take communion, I'd get a chill down my spine you can't imagine, because however much I tried to excuse you in my heart of hearts, there are things that can't be reconciled, sweetheart, for instance, God and *El Correo*, but just like that, no need to think about it, it's something so obvious. The Lord doesn't like halfway measures, sweetheart, and may he forgive me, but I think this John XXIII, may he be in glory, placed the church in a dead-end street, it's not that I'm saying he was a bad man, God forbid, but as far as I'm concerned the office of Pope was a little too big for him, or maybe it came when he was too old, anything's possible, I'm not sanctimonious or a last-ditcher, Mario, you know me, but that fine gentleman has done and said things that are enough to scare anybody, don't tell me, because if at this stage in the game it's also going to turn out that Protestants are good people, we'll wind up not knowing our right hand from our left.

XIII
....

Behold the inheritance of the Lord are children: the reward, the fruit of the womb. As arrows in the hand of the mighty, so the children of them that have been shaken. Blessed is the man that hath filled the desire with them. How lovely! But then the one who had to be on the go all day was me. It's not for any special reason, Mario, but some day you'll realize how little you've helped me in bringing up the children, Antonio, who's a great teacher, says so too, see, that when the father holds back, the children feel it, isn't that interesting, that they can be sort of lame but inside themselves, understand? scarred or something. Of course on that score it's no novelty, the bad times are always for the mother; you men are all a bunch of egotists, everybody knows that, they're not all cut to the same pattern, but if there's one man who takes the prize in that respect it's you, Mario, sweetheart, and pardon my frankness. For heaven's sake! You got it into your head that girls should go to the university and there they are, come hell or high water, poor Menchu, and don't try to play dumb, because you know that girls who study, in the end, turn out to be mannish. And then, with the boys, how lovely, a different standard, just look how delightful, and if they don't want to study let them work with their hands. But are you in your right mind, Mario? Can you imagine a Sotillo in workman's coveralls? I'll be darned if I can understand you, my boy, but the truth is you have some tastes that ought to be beaten out of you, I agree that a vocation deserves respect, but there are vocations for poor people and vocations for people of the better kind, each in his own class, I think, why, at this rate, in a couple of years the world will be topsy-turvy, poor folks will be engineers and the rich fixing fuses, imagine how amusing. But for girls there's no vocation worthy of the name, there's nothing in it for them, like I say, it doesn't work, and if they have a vocation to be mothers, it's the noblest one there could be, let them put up with the situation and go to the High School, for the simple reason that girls oughtn't to be ignorant, they oughtn't to have less than secondary studies, but you hurt me where it did the most harm, Mario, if you care to know it, I don't have the secondary certificate and you're well aware of it, but what you were doing was to deprive me of authority in front of my children, and that's something I can't forgive you for, sweetheart, if I live a thousand years, because if there's anything hateful in this life it's that, to set children against their mother, it's the devil's work, just like it sounds, and that's what you've been doing day after day and year after year, with a persistence that's worthy of a better cause. And then, instead of standing up for me when I'd tell them to clean their shoes when they came into the house and learn to manage fish forks, you came out with the bright idea that what they ought to do was read and that Alvarito was a very strange boy and that going off to the country by himself to light a bonfire was abnormal and that his obsession with death and the stars was another abnormality, what nonsense, what it is about Alvaro is that he has a vocation to be a boyscoot or whatever that's called, I'm hopeless with languages, as you know, but why in the world to the doctor? Alvaro's just an ordinary boy, Mario, anyone who heard you, and when you stop to think about it there are other things that worry me more, look at Borja, what a remark to come out with, do you know what he said to me yesterday and he was perfectly sincere, it wasn't that it was a joke? Well, he comes and says to me, but right out, eh? "I wish Daddy would die every day so I wouldn't have to go to school," what do you think of that? I gave him a terrible thrashing, believe me, I know he's only six, I realize that, but at that age I felt such veneration for Papa, see, that if they'd told me that something had happened to him I'd have died, why, the first thing I did, as soon as I learned to read, was to look for his byline in *ABC,* but every day, eh? sort of a habit, and every time I found it, not very often, naturally, Mama would say, "Papa is a great writer, child," and I'd be pleased as Punch, so proud, but a healthy pride, nothing sinful about it, don't think things that aren't true, and I'd get to school and dumbfound my girlfriends with it the minute I could, and they'd be furious because their fathers didn't write in the newspapers, and I, well, just imagine, happy as a lark. Respect and admiration for parents is the first thing you have to implant in children, Mario, and you don't accomplish that except with authority, you think you're doing them a favor by being soft with them, and in the long run it's just the opposite, take the case of Borja, your saying he wasn't thriving and that he stiffened up when he cried, well, he'll get unstiffened soon, you absolutely drooled over him, my, how you spoiled him, even Doro was surprised about it, see, "His papa is crazy about that child," the minute she came to work for us, you can't make differences between children, treat them all the same, just look at me, I don't favor one or the other, I should say not! but the thing about Aran is different, that child isn't growing, I know she's the youngest but she's very short for her age, Mario, she takes after her Auntie Charo, and I hate that, I'm telling you the way I feel about it, because your sister's shaped like a little jug, nothing attractive about her, as for being good, good as gold, I know that, but if an unattractive girl isn't good, can you tell me what she's got left? "There's no virtue in ugly saints, and so they're not saints," Mama used to say, she was so amusing, and it's true, Mario, nobody was wittier than Mama, I remember when I was little, the ladies who came to visit with their mouths open, she was always the one they listened to, Valen reminds me of her a little bit, there's something similar about them, mind you, though Mama, if you want, a little bit plumper, those were different times. Tears come to my eyes just thinking about what a bad time she had with the thing about Julia, if there was anybody who didn't seem as if something like that could happen to her it was Mama, I'm telling you seriously, so upright, so fair-minded, she must have suffered horribly, I only have to tell you that she never touched sweets again! It's not just because I say so, but there are fewer real ladies like Mama every day, of course I understand that at that time domestic help was easier to find, no comparison, for a hundred pesetas, and I'm stretching it, you had all you wanted, with everything taken care of. That's another victory of *El Correo* you can all be proud of, that miserable *Correo*, that only knows how to stir up the poor and you can already see the results, fifteen hundred pesetas for a maid, I don't know what we're coming to, Mario, those women are destroying family life, there are practically none left and the ones there are, God help us! you tell me how they're different from young ladies, the bars, the pants, and if they go to the movies the most expensive seats, my boy, like ladies, sometimes I get the notion that these are signs of the end of the world and it makes me shiver, I promise you it does, nowadays everything's upside down, Mario, and us ladies have to put our shoulders to the wheel and never stop working. And you still say that I complain; I don't complain nearly enough, you rascal, you just don't realize, you men amuse me, "We have to simplify," and one day you pick up a broom or take the children out for a walk and you think you've done something great, you're heroes, see, I remember that you, when you had the depression or whatever, at the time they opened the file on you and the business about Solórzano, those fusses, how you kept crying, but for nothing at all, and what sobs, my heavens, "Does something hurt?" "Do you have a fever?" I was worried, see, and you "I only feel disgust and fear," what kind of a thing is that to come out with, and "What are you afraid of, sweetheart?" "I don't know, that's the bad part," what do you think of that? While if I complained it was a bad habit, my disgust didn't count, egotists, that's what you men are, and to top it off Moyano encouraging you, asking if you were crazy enough to put on your pyjama jacket as if it were the pants, what a ridiculous thing, you tell me, and you said yes, and he started to laugh, nothing neurotic about you then. What I think is that you were trying to keep me from getting mad at you about the file, the point was to make yourself important, as if you hadn't tried that before, my boy, when you criticized the Inquisition they certainly called you on the carpet and Antonio himself, in his office, told you a thing or two, because what you can't do, Mario, is try to improve on God, if you're not taking the skin off someone or something it seems like you aren't happy, what a mania you have, you drive me wild. Are you telling me the Inquisition was bad, smarty? In all sincerity, now don't you think that a little bit of Inquisition is just what we need in the present circumstances? Stop kidding yourself, Mario, the world needs authority and a firm hand, some of you men think that just because of that, of the mere fact that you're grown men, school discipline is over, and you're so very mistaken, you have to shut up and obey, always, all your life, blindly, you've become so enthused about dialogue, holy Virgin! you don't talk about anything else, it seems like there isn't a bigger problem in the world, and so, if before you couldn't ask and now you ask but they don't answer, which amounts to the same thing, dialogue can go hang. Like the other one, that baby of an Aróstegui, who'd be better off playing with a hoop, like I say, freedom of expression, do you mind letting a person know what he wants if for? Do you want to tell me what would happen if they let all of us yell and everybody yelled what he wanted to? No, Mario, you're asking for the impossible, it would be a mad-house, that's right, an insane asylum, no matter how you look at it, the Inquisition was really good because it forced all of us to think right, that is like Christians, you can see how it is in Spain, all Catholics and Catholics to the nth degree, why, just look at the devotion, not like those foreigners who don't even kneel to take communion or anything, if I were a priest, and I'm not talking for talk's sake, I'd ask the government to kick them out of Spain, see, they only come here to show their legs and scandalize people. All this about the beaches and the tourists, I don't care what you say, is organized by the Masons and the Communists, Mario, to weaken our moral reserves and then, whoosh! finish us off in one fell swoop, and you, criticizing the Inquisition and all the good things, you really amuse me, why, with those tales of yours that the Inquisition's methods were unchristian you're playing right into their hands, and I don't say you do it in bad faith, I don't go as far as that, but out of simple-mindedness, Mario, because you were on very shaky ground when you said it's unchristian to kill a man because he doesn't want to deny his conscience, because when all's said and done, can you tell me if we'd gather a single grain of wheat unless we'd previously eliminated the weeds? Go on, answer me, it's very easy to talk, darling, but let's get to the practical angle, because, make sure of it, weeds have to be cut off at the root, be exterminated, because we'd be in fine shape if not. Love, love, always going on about love, what does a man know about love who turns over on his wedding night and acts like he'd never seen you, I won't forget a humiliation like that if I live a thousand years, sweetheart, and excuse my frankness, because now what you and your kind are going to say is that for love of the weeds we have to lose the wheat, when what we have to love is the wheat, smarty, and for love of it we have to tear up the weeds and then burn them, even if it hurts us. We certainly need a little bit of Inquisition, believe me, and lots of times I think that if they'd improve that atomic bomb to the point that it could distinguish, I know it's a stupid thing to say, but anyway, and it'd kill only the people who don't have principles, the world would be a very peaceful place, no two ways about it. But I know already that it goes in one ear and out the other, imagine how well I know you, why, you've never listened to me, Mario, sweetheart, never in this world, not even when I reminded you about the bad days, you went after what you wanted, "Let's not mix numbers into this," "Let's not be stingy with God," well, naturally, I'd be stiff as a board, I'd like to know what you expected, and on top of everything else, to have you say that God's been watching over us, I'm not one to have lots of kids, for whatever reason, because if I was one of those working-class rabbits who turn them out by pairs, I need hardly tell you. You were always out for yourself, you disaster you, yourself and only yourself, see, didn't even listen to Antonio when he had you on the carpet, which isn't to say that you had one good reason or another, it was all stubbornness, you earned that file by your own unaided effort, my boy, and if they didn't fire you out of hand it was a real miracle, my knees still hurt from the praying I did, don't think it's a lie, they got all swollen and everything. And don't come and tell me that Antonio, because Antonio, no matter how you look at it, couldn't have done anything else, Mario, because, even though you hate to admit it, he'd had you on the carpet before, you can't deny it, and if a student went and complained, something which here between you and I doesn't surprise me at all, then he couldn't do anything else but inform Madrid. The whole thing is, I've told you so a thousand times, that you and your kind think this is a circus where everybody can do exactly as he pleases and you're very much mistaken, it's the same here as in a home, the very same thing, except that instead of parents it's authority, but there always has to be someone who says this has to be done and this can't be done and now everybody shut up and obey, that's the only way things can work. You've heard Papa, at the time of the Republic, a total mess, nobody could understand anybody else, and why? don't be closed-minded, my boy, it was because there was no authority, why, to give you an idea, it's as if one day we said to Mario, Menchu, Alvaro, Borja, and Aran, go on, eat whatever you please, yell your heads off, go to bed whenever you take the notion, you're the masters of the house, you give orders just as much as Mother and Daddy, can you imagine the confusion? It's just common sense, Mario, you don't have to be especially intelligent to understand it, you take Higinio Oyarzun the other day "To make a country work well, military discipline," I know you're not a bit fond of Oyarzun, but Antonio himself, no matter how often you say that you think he enjoyed it, certainly not, he went through several very bad days, I know he did, from Valen, if you want to know, why he even came to see me, "It hurts me more than doing it to myself, Carmen," he said to me, tell me if a person oughtn't to be grateful for a thing like that, and then on the other hand, you stop to think about it, and he was absolutely right that what you said was serious enough to make it necessary, why, it wouldn't have occurred to the devil himself, and if it wasn't a sacrilege it wasn't far from it, see, you and your kind get yourselves warmed up and you don't know what you're saying any more. And you can still give thanks to Vicente, because if you'd ask Valen to do anything for us she would, you know her, because if they'd assigned you a different file compiler or whatever it's called, you'd have been in the soup, but Valen is a darling, I just love her! . . . And she's a woman who knows a lot about everything, don't tell me, she even understands algebra, it doesn't seem to go with her, mind you, does it, and she goes to Madrid once a week to have her skin cleaned, that's why she has the complexion she has, it's a marvel! I'm ever so crazy about her, you'll say, of course you can notice it! nobody knows the kind of filth that can get into your skin until it's been cleaned once, you can hardly believe it!

XIV

When brethren dwell together, and one of them dieth without children, the wife of the deceased shall not marry to another: but his brother shall take her, and raise up seed for his brother. That's just what I said! From the very day they killed Elviro, Encarna was after you, Mario, nobody can get that out of my head, your sister-in-law may be anything you please, I won't go into that, but she has some pretty peculiar ideas, I'd like to know what she was thinking of, because how she pursued you, dear boy, no excuse for it, and here between you and I, I'll tell you that even when we were going together, every time I heard her whispering to you at the movies, I was madly jealous, and you could still make excuses for her, that she was your sister-in-law, that she'd suffered a lot, sentimentality, and then later, Encarna's in our hair all the time, my, such a lot of little visits, and as if that wasn't enough, you giving her money in Madrid, everything comes out in the end, Mario, the devil knows more because he's old than because he's the devil, and I'm not going to tell you that she ought to go to work, that would be the last straw, but she has parents it seems to me. There's Julia, she lives with my father and nothing's happened to her because of it, she hasn't exactly started a boarding house, I should say not, but renting rooms to American students is quite a fashion-able thing to do, it's quite in style nowadays, I know wonderful families who do it, and don't come and tell me that Encarna's father is paralyzed, that's another reason for her to look after him. Because it doesn't make sense, Mario, that when your father was so sick, and did everything in bed, remember? it was really disgusting, Encarna looked after him, and now she's so finicky about taking care of her own father. No matter how you look at it, it's inconsistent, and I'm not convinced by that about her mother being a strange person and not liking anyone else to interfere, those are just an old woman's drivelings, we know that, if Encarna would just go there without asking permission of anyone and pitch in, I can tell you right now that there wouldn't be a peep out of anybody, she's a fine one. But no, since no one can see her there, she's not interested, so there! with your father the only thing she wanted was to have you see her and teach me a lesson, just like it sounds, Mario, teach me a lesson, and that's foolishness, mind you, because she would hardly let me put an oar in, and your mother still less, but we all knew perfectly well that she was stronger than the two of us put together. It's just like now, whenever she comes, going on about polishing the brass and washing the children's clothes, she's so tiresome, and if she can just put these things through the washing machine, mind you, it doesn't do them as well as by hand, but you have no choice but to obey, your sister-in-law adores teaching lessons, and if you don't thank her five times for everything she does you're in for it, my boy, that miserable Encarna, I can't wait for the day I don't have to see her any more. The thing about your sister-in-law, sweetheart, is that she's so mannish, as for femininity, zero, like I say, just think about Elviro, you could hardly see him beside her, he was so little and skinny, the weaker sex, don't make me laugh, I don't like to think evil, God forgive me, but I think Encarna stepped out on him, see,

Elviro wasn't enough of a man for her. You should have seen the way she used to toss your father around! Just like a little child, Mario, don't tell me, she'd shift him from one place to another and then, since he didn't even know when he had to, what smells, my boy, you couldn't get rid of them with disinfectant, the house smelled like a pigsty, I've never had a worse time in my life, didn't bother your mother one bit, in the best of all possible worlds, I don't know whether it's that in those cases a person loses the sense of smell or what, and if even you didn't go very often, why should I have gone, I'd like to know? They had enough and more than enough with Encarna, Mario, and I had enough to do with two babies at home, and furthermore, in case you're interested in knowing, between being pregnant with Alvaro and the cooler in the bathroom, I don't know how in the world that occurred to your mother, I just couldn't stay, I swear to you, or eat so much as a crust of bread, and that's saying a lot. But I went, Mario, I went because I had to, it was certainly no pleasure, of course that type of sick people who aren't continent make me nauseous, Mario, I can't help it, I'd love to feel compassion but I can't, it's too much for me, I only wish I could, and then, your father, so tiresome, the part about being a moneylender didn't show, if the truth be told, but he'd lost his mind, my boy, don't tell me, what a nuisance, every night the same thing, "Tell that lady to go home; it's time for supper," about your mother, you tell me, I've never seen such a thing in my life, like when he'd start with, "Did you realize, my dear?" "What?" just to go along with him, see, and he, "This woman doesn't know it, but it's very funny, my dear; it's the only thing we talk about," every day the same old song, "Why, I don't know a word, " "Listen," and then he'd nearly die laughing, half coughing, "This woman doesn't know a thing," I think your father would have been a thousand times better off in a home, and then suddenly he'd get very serious, sort of sad, "Now I can't remember. I've forgotten it, my dear, but it was something very funny," what do you think of that, hopelessly gaga, ought to have been shut up, Mario, even though it's a hard thing to say, he probably did suffer a lot over the business of your brothers, I'm not denying that, but your father's last year was really tough, and after all, who knows, lots of times these things are left over from a person's youth, from excesses, you know what I mean? strange diseases, you ask Luis. And as if that wasn't enough, it was so long, a year, Mario, when he didn't get better and didn't die, so tiresome, imagine what I was going to go there for, to get in the way, that's all, because he was well taken care of. What a difference with Mama! Do you remember, Mario? And even when it's more difficult in a hospital, but it never failed, a clean nightie every day and the flowers, in that kind of a situation it seems like a person can't do anything about it, but you could see, it was a pleasure to be there, and what I say is, if Mama, may she rest in peace, had reached the point your father did, she would have stopped eating, I'll bet you anything, she would have died of hunger before she did it in bed, take note of that. I agree, good breeding isn't a thing of the moment, you're born with it or not born with it, it's one of the things you have from the cradle, though if you really think about it upbringing, manners, can do miracles too, now take the case of Paquito Alvarez to give you just one example, nothing but a workingman, may as well admit it, who as a boy mixed up all his words, it was a scream, well, you see him now and he's a different man, what poise, what manners, I don't know how he's done it, but you men are lucky, if you're not much at twenty you only have to wait another twenty years. And then, those eyes. You have to admit that Paco always had ideal eyes, a greenish blue, halfway between cats' eyes and the water in a swimming pool, but now he's put on weight and has more of a presence, he has a different way of looking at you, sort of more intentionally, I don't know if I'm saying it right, and furthermore, since he doesn't get flustered when he talks, he speaks just enough and in a level tone, with that smell of good tobacco, that's a smell I just adore, he's attractive, he's one of those men who really stir you up, mind you, who would ever have said it of him. I'd give anything to have you smoke good tobacco, Mario, though it probably seems foolish to you, or at least with a filter, it makes a difference, and not that tobacco of yours, my boy, the kind nobody smokes any more, I've never been able to stand it, every time you start to roll one in a group of people I get sick, like I'm telling you, and then that smell, of straw or whatever it is, I'd like to know what pleasure you can get out of that junk, if it were even elegant or something like that, it'd pass, but rolling a cigarette, really rolling one, you've never seen anyone but louts, not even janitor's children, if you really want my opinion, and they burn holes in your clothes and then you look terrible, like I say. Of course, you'll say what do clothes matter to you, that's another thing, you never cared about that, you've embarrassed me more times than you can imagine, my boy, you always look awful, I don't know how you manage but two days after you've put on a suit for the first time, it's ready for the garbage, why, I don't even know how I fell in love with you, frankly, I just hated that brown suit, the one with the stripes, and I dreamed about changing you, but, my goodness, people don't change, at that age, everybody knows, romanticism, but not a bit of it, Mario, you disaster, I've had very little luck with you in that regard, you've made me suffer a lot. And it isn't a question of having more or less, I should say not, why, I remember Evaristo, the old guy, wash it and wear it, that was all, but what he had was ironed and pressed to a fare-thee-well, he was a real picture, you should have seen him, and don't think he was ashamed to say so, "I stand on a chair to put on or take off my trousers; it's the only way," he was just careful, that's all, and then, at night, nicely folded, under the mattress, and a crease in them, Mario, it's not just idle talk, that you couldn't have put in with an iron, think of it! Of course, as far as you're concerned what Don Nicolás says to you is more important, or that pig with the beard, than what your little wifie tells you, I know, I don't have any influence on you, but he isn't the one either to ask me whether rascals can be known or not by the crease in their pants, and you, instead of laughing, should have stopped him in his tracks, Mario, I don't know what we're coming to, like your other friend said, that freedom is a whore in the hands of money, how lovely, right out loud, too, in front of me, and that's not to say he didn't see me, he'd said hello and everything, fine rascal he is, that's what I say, Mario, is that any way to behave, and if you talk about those women in our house, and I'm not saying that it's all right, at least you should be more careful, and if that spoiled baby wants to be a rebel he can go to his own house, the least he can do in someone else's is have some consideration for a lady. That Don Nicolás, how I hate him, he certainly sowed a fine crop! I'm telling you the truth, Mario, and don't repeat it, but I prefer Gabriel and Evaristo, for all they've been so shameless all their lives, to this gang of intellectuals or whatever you want to call them. After all, Gabriel and Evaristo went after what they wanted, and it's very human, God put that instinct into men and women and a person can explain a lot of weaknesses that way, and it isn't that I'm going to tell you that it's right, understand, because I know instinct has to be channeled and all that stuff, but it's easier for me to pardon those excesses than yours, you and your friends, even so. Because, after all, the woman who'd give in to Gabriel and Evaristo was just as shameless as they were, they certainly took me to their studio, all full of pictures of naked women, and here I am, Mario, it never even passed through my imagination, you know that, well, it just didn't, because I'm the way a woman ought to be, that's the reason, I can say it loud and clear, if I went to the altar a virgin, I've been faithful in marriage, even though you, sweetheart, haven't contributed much on your side, there's nobody more indifferent or colder than you are, just the same as for eating, I'd try to take such care, and then, "It doesn't matter," you wouldn't even look at it, the only thing was to kill your hunger, that's all. Pay no attention to me, I'm laughing to think about Valen, the things she says, but every time she tells me that it's always different, that there's always something new, I agree with her just to shut her up, see, I'm not about to tell her that for my husband it's just routine, and that's the simple truth, Mario, for you it's over right away and you leave a person high and dry, I don't even enjoy it, and it's not that I'm saying that all that's fundamental for me, heavens no, but goodness, at bottom, I don't care who you are, nobody minds having a treat. Yes, I'm not denying it, maybe it's just frivolity . . . frivolity, do you remember? "Everything in the word is frivolity or violence," I know it by heart, how you sulked, sweetheart, didn't even read the paper, "I can't, it makes me want to throw up," "Take an antacid tablet," "It's not a question of that," I knew that all too well, "Everything makes me feel disgust and fear," my, how amusing, but I couldn't feel disgust about the cooler in your house, that was taboo, that's what you men are like. Your illness makes me laugh! Nerves, nerves . . . when doctors don't know what to say they blame it all on nerves, because you tell me, if nothing hurts you, and you don't have a fever, what do you have to complain about? Well, you kept on crying, sounded as if you were being murdered, heavens, such carrying on, and that you couldn't sleep and every time you tried to you felt as if the mattress was collapsing on you, some news that is, that's happened to me ever since I was a little girl, since I was so high, mind you, it's like those dreams where they're chasing you and you can't run, or when you're flying by moving your arms and legs very fast, and things like that. Sickness my foot, Mario! You men complain out of bad habit and it's our fault, we women are fools, all the livelong day taking care of you, first there's the meals, then there's your clothes, because if you were afraid that we'd go off and do it with somebody else, then, I'm telling you, you wouldn't even remember you had nerves, the fact is that when you don't lack anything at all, you have to invent something to make yourselves seem more important. You men are arrogant, just arrogant, that's what you are, I'd like to see you with one of my sick headaches, sweetheart, now that's suffering and all the rest is moonshine, it feels like my head was going to split in pieces, I promise you, and you, "Go to bed, with a couple of aspirins; tomorrow you'll be fine," how easy that is, right? and so sure of yourself, my boy, you'd think you were a doctor. But none of my prescriptions did you any good, you just kept stuffing yourself with pills, and the most expensive ones too, I don't even like to think about the fortune we've spent on medicine for your miserable nerves. I'll bet you anything you please that if they'd give me back that money, bill for bill, I'd have a Six Hundred tomorrow, like I'm telling you, but it seemed that if the medicines weren't expensive they didn't do you any good, stupid, that's how dumb you men are! I'd like to have seen you with one of my sick headaches, for no other reason, Mario, just once, just for the pleasure of having you know what it is to suffer.

XV

....

The keepers that go about the city found me: they struck me: and wounded me, but first of all I want to tell you something, sweetheart, even if you do get angry, of course I know you don't like to talk about it, but, just between the two of us, I'll tell you that I never swallowed the story about the policeman hitting you, how you went on about it, I didn't even dare to tell you so at the time, but I was absolutely in agreement with Ramón Filgueira, why in the world would a policeman hit you for crossing the park on your bicycle? Don't get excited, please think about it, don't you understand that it's absurd? Tell me the truth, you fell, the policeman said so and a policeman doesn't lie just to be lying, when you come right down to it a policeman at three o'clock in the morning is like the Minister of the Interior, he must have told you to stop and you were startled and fell, that's logical, that's how you got that bruise on your face. The thing is that you have a weakness for the bicycle, always have, you've embarrassed me so many times, and rather than admitting that you'd fallen, after so much bragging in front of the children about how you were the Eagle of Toledo and stupid things like that, well, see, you made up the part about his hitting you and all that tale about the pistol, when you struggled; just fibs, look, if you'd said you were tired from correcting papers, that certainly must be a big bore, I understand it, all of them alike and so on, but why take it out on the poor policeman who, after all, was only doing his duty? It can't be very pleasant either, I'd say, to have to stand on a corner at three in the morning, and stay there all night, Mario, it's easy to say, and worse still with the below-freezing temperature there was. And especially, sweetheart, you're too old to be riding a bicycle, you're not a child, even though you insist on hanging onto your childhood the years don't pass in vain, see, it's the way life is, nobody can struggle against that, just remember Mama, may she rest in peace, "There's a cure for everything but death," that's quite something for a woman to say . . . If you want me to tell you the truth, I can't understand that stupid hankering you have to stay in shape, to ride your bicycle for fifty kilometers at random, without going anywhere or anything, there are tastes that ought to be stamped out, don't tell me, if you'd applied the same effort to a better purpose, which is what I say, how could you have gained weight? It would be different if you were an athlete, but physically you certainly didn't have much to lose, sweetheart, you weren't worth a thing, so long and skinny, I remember at the beach, so white, it's something that, no matter how often I think about it, I'll never manage to understand, because, if you didn't have anything, what were you trying to preserve, if you can tell me that? I don't know if you write well or not, I won't go into that, but as for being the sporting type, not a bit of it, tell the truth and shame the devil, not even the physique, the absolute opposite, mind you, everybody ought to do what he's good at. And if Ramón Filgueira received you in his office like a father, which you admit yourself, what made you climb on your high horse and blame it all on the policeman, when you've never been a liar? It hurts me that out of the stupid vanity of not wanting to admit that you fell off your bicycle, you'd lie like that, in cold blood, you're really something, it's a thing that surprises me in you, see, that out of misplaced pride you'd get a poor devil into trouble, that's not your style. But you, it seems like you're proud of it, my boy, because if at the start you'd gone straight to Filgueira and simply told him, "You're right, I was mistaken," everything would have changed, of course, and neither he nor Josechu Prados, or Oyarzun, would have refused to let us have the apartment, I'd stake my head on it, the fact is that you've always wanted to make a big fuss about things, and you mistake good manners for servility. Heavens, you and your wretched servility, hasn't it just given you trouble! Servility and structures are two words that have hardly been out of your mouth ever since I've known you and, no matter how you look at it, it's a mania like any other, for you to be pleasant to someone in authority seems like backing down or something, is that true or isn't it? Why, listening to you, my boy, you'd think I was a freak, and that's what I mind the most, that because of the mere fact of having common sense a woman's made to look bad, heavens, it's so tiresome. But listen, I'll tell you some more, even accepting the fact that that policeman hit you, which I very much doubt, don't you think that a fist in the face is a fair exchange for a six-room apartment, elevator, central hot water, and a mere seven hundred pesetas rent? Let's forget about romanticisms and think with your head, sweetheart, you take pride in swimming against the current, we live in a practical age and that's behaving like a fool, not to call it something worse, because I'm not saying you have to agree with him, simply act tolerant, without being humble about it, with the mayor as well as with Oyarzun and Josechu Prados, it wouldn't have occurred to the devil himself to demand a count, do you believe that either one of them

would have refused us his vote about the apartment? Don't
kid yourself, Mario, you don't reap unless you sow, Mama
used to say, may she rest in peace, "A firm friendship does
more good in life than a university degree," and events have
proved her right, just look, and I'll never tire of repeating it to
you, my boy, you've tried to be good and you've only succeeded in being stupid, just like it sounds. "If you put truth
first, you can accomplish anything," what do you think of
that? but you can see what a fat lot of good your theories have
done us, because, no matter how much you think about it,
you can't be on good terms with everyone in life and if you
take sides with some, you make the others mad at you, no two
ways about that, but if things have to be that way because they
always have been, why not get on the side of those who can
do something for you? But no sir, you keep on with the
shabby ones and the country yokels, as if raggedy people and
yokels were even going to thank you for it, you've really
outdone yourself, sweetheart, every time I think that because
of a policeman, or some minutes, or one of those things, we're
still living in this hole, I get frantic, believe me, if that's all I'm
to have life's hardly worth living. And furthermore, didn't you
have it in for the poor policemen! You took a grudge against
them, like I say, you ought to have seen Solórzano's face when
you signed that protest because a policeman had taken his
nightstick to somebody who jumped onto the football field,
fine thing that was, he must not have liked it one bit, that's for
sure, why, I couldn't believe it myself, I promise you, when
they called from the police station, I kept saying over and
over, "But my husband doesn't go to football games," and then
you came home and goodness, how angry you got with me,
after all it wasn't so very important, I think, heavens, anybody
would have agreed, "And who told you to say anything, tell

me that?" fine, my boy, don't carry on so! They asked questions and I answered, neither more nor less, right away I realized, if you'd like to know, that the same ones as always were behind it, that Don Nicolás and his gang, see, as if a person was an idiot, that character may have other defects but at least you can see where he's coming from, and what I say is, that if they'd finished him off when they should have, instead of handling him with kid gloves, we would have been spared a lot of bad moments. Others got killed for less, after all, and don't come and tell me about José María, because what happened to your brother was a case of justice, and look, I don't care one way or the other, the fact that he didn't go to the office was the least of it, see, even if your father was so tiresome about it, there were witnesses that he was at the bullring, at Azaña's meeting, and the day the Republic was proclaimed he went along the street yelling like a fanatic, with the tricolor flag across his shoulder, it's not like Elviro's case, José María thought that his charm would save him, but no, maybe with women, but that does no good with men. Furthermore, what does this whole story have to do with policemen? The thing you have about policemen is a ridiculous phobia, darling, why, even Valen every time she sees a pair of them, squeezes my arm, honestly, and laughs, "If Mario should come along," she says, see, but what I say is, at bottom what bothers you and your kind is authority, you think that just because you've finished school you have a right to everything, and that's not true, Mario, fine shape we'd be in, you have to obey in life and submit to discipline from the time you're born, first with your parents and then with authority, it's the same thing in the end. And even more, if once in a month of Sundays we catch a stray punch, instead of getting angry about it we ought to humbly accept it because the person who gives it to us, you can be sure he doesn't do it because he wants to but for our own good, so we don't go off the track. You used to say that you wanted things clean, and that righting a wrong made life worth living, pure pride, let's not kid ourselves, Mario, because can you tell me what you've righted, what you've lived for, tell me, if you haven't been able to buy your wife a miserable Six Hundred? Love and comprehension, don't make me laugh, I'm very outspoken, you know that already, and you're nothing but a professional naysayer, you always were, you'd fly off the handle for some foolish reason and then, you'd let the cars pass when you were on a zebra crossing, or you'd buy a jumping jack from every good-for-nothing in Madrid, or give up your turn in shops, if there's anything in the world that annoys me it's exactly that, I'll have you know, the person who wants to buy early has to get up early, Mario, that's what standing in line is for, I should hope so. Nobody can understand you, Mario, that's the gospel truth, you stop to think about it and you don't even understand yourself, just look at that business about Hernando de Miguel's lamb, you throw it down the stairwell, you almost kill him, and then you spend the afternoon sitting and doing nothing, "These conflicts between charity and corruption can't be solved by anyone," heavens, what a problem, I wish they'd give me no harder ones, you get simply impossible, dear boy, because it's one thing to write boring stuff like that for the person who wants to read it, and another for you to come out with it to me, face to face, you used to drive me wild, I promise you, and if I took advantage of the opportunity to talk to you about money or the Six Hundred or something important you'd say, "Be quiet," as if it was nothing to do with you, there's nothing that makes me more furious than to have you talk about what you want to and then shut up when it suits you. That's your usual pattern, Mario, stand up to those in authority and give in to the raggedy ones, see how lovely, because what I say is, either you give in to everyone or don't give in to anyone, either you fly off the handle or you don't fly off the handle, but to want to always have your own way, sometimes going against the current and other times crawling to people, seems to me a terrible way to behave, I'll have you know. Valen laughs, all my friends laugh, because they don't have to put up with you, I'd like to see them in my place, sweetheart, wouldn't last two weeks, listen to what I'm saying, Valen says that you can't stand either neckties or old people and she's not so far off with that, if the truth be told, because if it's not so, why on earth this mania of yours for men less than forty years old, saying they're not allowed to talk and maybe they'd understand each other? Can you tell me who doesn't allow them to talk, dear boy, why, they're the ones who make the most noise, nowadays you can't walk down the street for the shouting and those motor scooters, and there's no more respect, or consideration, or anything? The spirit of contradiction, that's what you are, everything at the wrong time, just look at you with your parents, you didn't so much as wet an eyelash, as the saying goes, and then out of pure whim, all the livelong day crying, my heavens, you looked like a paid mourner at a funeral. Nerves, don't make me laugh, saying you felt anguish for fear of not finding the honorable path, and that you envied me, me, take note of that, last thing I expected to hear, and those who like me were sure of everything. Well now, my boy, what did you think? When a person has a clear conscience, then let people rave, that's what you ought to do, you rascal, if you envy me so much, look in my mirror, and leave that Aróstegui and that Moyano and the whole gang alone, fine examples they are, sometimes I get to thinking that the only time you were all right was when you got sick, take note of that, maybe you'll think it's a joke, because what's always mortified you is to obey and shut up, just like those young fellows you defend so much, and, if you really look at them, they're junk, that's right, garbage, even though you come out with the ridiculous statement that they're "not at fault," phrases, Mario, I tell you and I repeat, because if we're going to take that attitude, do you mind letting a person know what fault it is of mine that we don't have a car when all my friends have one? And Mama? Was it Mama's fault, may she rest in peace? and yet she went through the war and the war was worse for her than for others even though she didn't advertise it, because the thing about Julia was worse than death itself, Mario, get that through your head once and for all, you always bring up your parents and your brothers, you're a great big egotist and nothing but an egotist, but it never occurred to you to think about my family. No two ways about it, sweetheart, obeying is what you can't stand, obeying and shutting up, after all, it's in the blood, look at Charo, why do you think your sister left the convent? why, for the same reason, darling, more of the same, because she doesn't know how to obey or shut up, because she got on her high horse, because neither you or her, or her or you, can resign yourselves to submitting to a rule, and what happens is, now she's out of place, see, she's neither in or out, she's queerer every day, I assure you that if I keep sending the children to her on Sundays it's out of charity, heavens, what a house, Mario, it's no better than a tomb, you've heard Alvaro, "I'd rather not eat than eat at Auntie Charo's house," that's logical, I understand it perfectly, because she, your sister, that dull little thing, she really gets my goat, mind you, keeps bringing up the grandparents and the uncles, what a bright idea that is, talk to the children about dead people, just because she happens to feel like it. And Charo's not an exception, I should say not, she's your spit and image, she'll never be happy anywhere, just like José María, all cut from the same pattern, even though you say that your sister's efficient, but you only say that to annoy me, I know you, because she doesn't have a maid, but the time has come when I just can't stand her, I swear to you, she's so insipid, it seems as if she's about to faint, and then her face is scrubbed so, that's something else, at seventeen it could pass, but at her age it's not halfway nice, Mario, even out of respect for other people, it's actually disagreeable to look at a skin that's so muddy and dry. If you say it to annoy me you're wasting your time, Mario, as far as I'm concerned you can say anything you please, I'm telling you, you're not going to belittle me by saying that, but, I'll have you know, I'm not one of those useless women or the kind that don't care, why, the year of hunger, when I had to, I certainly went with Uncle Eduardo to the most disgusting little towns looking for chick-peas and lentils so my parents could eat. And don't think that cars then were like the ones now, we went with a charcoal-burning fuel tank, my boy, what did you think? but I didn't care, and if it had to be done over, I'd pitch in again, because maybe not in other ways, but nobody can put up with more than I can, you know that, I can say it loud and clear.

XVI

Go then, and eat thy bread with joy, and drink thy wine with gladness: because thy works please God. At all times let thy garments be white, and let not oil depart from thy head. Live joyfully with the wife whom thou lovest, all the days of thy unsteady life, which are given to thee under the sun. But the fact is that I start to think about it and having a good time, a really good time, Mario, I've never seen you in your life, not even on our wedding trip, which is saying a lot. According to Valen that night is a real ordeal and I agree with her, that's logical, I'm not going to tell her that you turned your back on me, but on the other hand, in the daytime, everybody seems to have a great time except us, I remember, in Madrid, "Shall we sit in this café?" "Whatever you want," "Shall we go to the theater?" "Whatever you want," didn't you know how to say anything else, you poor fool? A woman is a defenseless being, Mario, she needs to be guided, you disaster you, that's why I would have just hated to marry a short man, authority ought to show itself even in stature, mind you, you probably think it's stupid. But you didn't seem to care about anything; you didn't even glance at the shop windows; no attention to the crowds; the movies, not a bit of it! you didn't like bullfights. Sincerely, Mario, do you think that's a wedding trip? And if it had only been that! but, as if that wasn't enough, always with a long face, like you were thinking about something else, it's the same as when you came back from the war, my boy, I'll never forget it as long as I live, look, everyone was wild with joy at that time, but you, no sir, and that when you'd been on the winning side, imagine if you'd lost . . . Nobody can understand you, Mario, sweetheart, and no one knows how much I suffer to see that you're not normal, I'm not saying that life doesn't have setbacks, if only it didn't, but you have to rise above them, life has to be enjoyed, I think, you take Mama, all day long, "Child, we only live once," you hear it like that and it seems it's not so, seems like foolishness, but you stop to think about it and there's a lot of philosophy in that saying, it has a lot of content, Mario, more than it seems, well, but you, no sir, first of all the things that are wrong. And it isn't that I'm going to say that there aren't injustices, or corruption, or those things that you say, but they've always been there, haven't they? just like there have always been poor people and rich people, Mario, it's the way life is, don't kid yourself. I laugh my head off with you, sweetheart, "Our obligation is to denounce those things," just like that, over and done with, period, but who laid that obligation on you, I'd like to know? Your obligation is to teach, Mario, that's what you became a teacher for, judges are there to denounce injustice and to relieve suffering there's charity, you and your kind are unbearable with the airs you put on, that wretched Don Nicolás, I don't know why people read *El Correo,* it falls out of people's hands, my boy, doesn't carry anything but miseries and calamities, that there are thousands of children with no schools to go to, that it's cold in the prisons, that laborers are dying of hunger, that country yokels live in subhuman conditions, but what are you trying to do? If you'd say what you meant once and for all! Because if you gave yokels an elevator and central heating, they'd stop being yokels, wouldn't they? goodness, it seems to me, I don't understand anything about that, but it's just like the poor, we'll always have them with us, I say, because that's what life is like, and if life's like that there's no point in putting on a long face, funny, what you'd call funny, I've never seen you except when you've had a couple of drinks, look at the embarrassment you put me through the other night at Valentina's house, firing champagne corks at the streetlights. And I can tell you that I saw it coming, eh? I swear I did, as soon as we came in, as soon as I saw Fito Solórzano and Oyarzun, I said to myself, "Either Mario sulks in a corner or he makes a scene." Oh, I know you, darling, I haven't spent more than twenty years with you for nothing. The same as with Encarna in Madrid, when you won the competition, of course you drank, sure you did! I'll bet anything you please that the celebration didn't end with the beer and the shrimps. Where did you go afterward? What I wouldn't give to find out, Mario, you can't even imagine, of course at that time you probably laughed more than you do now, for sure, that's what makes me the maddest, that you have one face for outsiders and another different one for your wife. Look, you tell me if it isn't a cause for irritation, you haven't caught that from Don Nicolás, see, only the bad things, he must be an awfully twisted person, but you can see where he's coming from, that's the advantage. He laughs at absolutely anything, but you can see where he's coming from, you certainly can, although as far as I'm concerned, I promise you, his little ways don't amuse me in the least, you take the other night, when he was telling about when he was a prisoner during the war. Do you believe a word of the story about that fellow who lined them up and said to the corporal, "I'm supposed to have 367, count 'em, if there are 366 go out on the street and pull in the first man that passes by, and if there are 368 take the last man in this row and shoot him." All lies. Naturally, the last man in the row was him, if not it wouldn't have been funny, but do you believe a word of all that? I might possibly go as far as to say that the fellow said it as a joke, just for the fun of it, to pass the time, see, it can't have been very enjoyable spending hours and hours without anything to do, shut up with more than three hundred Reds, without being able to talk to anyone or anything. I can't stand him, believe me, I can't help myself, he may have a way with words and write as well as you please, I'm not arguing about that, but he's a troublemaker and a bad person, he can't think what to invent next and put it in the paper and make trouble. Now I can tell you, Mario, I've never been happier than the day *El Correo* published that note saying that he was leaving, when they appointed his brother Benjamín as assistant editor, remember? and they told him, "If your brother Nicolás gets out of line, you're fired," which seemed just perfectly fine to me, legitimate defense, as far as Don Nicolás was concerned it was nothing, naturally, he has plenty of money, but for his brother's sake he'd be a little bit more careful. And the end of it all was nothing solid, that big sneak is still there, underhandedly, just the same as before, a little care at the beginning and then more of the same, just like always. It's funny how uppity that man Don Nicolás has become, Papa remembers him, a man of very, very humble origin, you'll hardly believe it, his mother a laundress or something worse, what seems strange to me is that the people who count pay any attention to him, because no matter how clever he is, what can the son of a laundress accomplish, intellectually I mean, Mario, can you tell me that? Papa's always saying, every time he sees one of those types who come up in the world fast, he says, "It takes at least four generations to turn out a good mind." And now don't come and tell me, Mario, you may like Papa more or less, but he's not just anybody, you know it, been in *ABC* since the year one, it isn't just recently. And you saw yourself what a Pedagogical Report he made for you when you had the examination for your teaching job, first-rate, goodness, and afterward you certainly weren't very grateful to him, you could tell that the poor man was hurt about it, although, of course, he didn't say a word. Poor thing! You can't imagine how many hours he spent on your report, my boy, why, he even spoke twice with Don Lucas Sarmiento, the dean, who was at our house, I was so nervous I couldn't stay still, I remember like it was yesterday, twitching like a lizard's tail, thinking all the time, "Will those two be able to do it for him?" imagine what was riding on it. And if you stop to think about it Papa didn't have the slightest obligation because, after all, it was carelessness on your part, as usual, it seems like you live on the moon. Just imagine, after such a long time, to turn up without the report, which was an absolute requirement! It just doesn't enter a human head, my goodness, and even then, you insisting that you thought it was a research project, and for that you needed six months going from archive to archive, a loss of time, you tell me, you really are something, my boy, same as the time you talked to that raggedy fellow on the street, right next to Arronde's pharmacy, I really felt like giving you a good slap, you made a person look like a fool. Well, poor Papa got you out of a tight place, but once the examination was over you forgot all about it, a little letter of appreciation and that was all. Poor Papa! I think he didn't sleep for a week, honestly, I remember that he said, "I'm not a historian, but I'll try, I'll try," and he never raised his head, I swear, for a week he never raised his head. Of course if a man's good at something he's good at everything, Mario, and it's not just because I'm saying it, but he did something for you that was as good as a book, Mario, the least thing you could have done for him, and don't tell me I didn't let you know about it, was to have had it printed in the House of Culture, it would have made him happy, mind you, because the poor man, and it's not because I'm his daughter, is satisfied with very little. But you never did have the knack of doing things for people, that's the truth, Mario, a little letter of appreciation and that was the end of it. And it's not that I'm going to say now that Papa's report was anything long or complicated, it wasn't, I agree, but it was very well written, don't tell me, even though I don't go in much for reading, but because it was something to do with you I read it, three times, imagine! and I just loved it, you may not believe it, all that about the regressive method, or whatever it's called, that about studying history backward, like crabs, because wars and those things don't happen for nothing, they have a cause, and as Papa said, I still have a copy in the dresser, see, with that ease he had in writing, "You go back from the consequences to the causes." I'm absolutely sure, see, that if you passed it was because of Papa, of course you never know but in this particular case, it was lucky that you overlooked it, because you're probably terribly careful and anything you please, but you never would have done a paper as lovely as Papa's, because Papa is awfully good, Mario, I could say that all day and all night and I still wouldn't have begun to say how good he is, and you can be sure he would have come yesterday if he weren't so old, the poor thing isn't good for anything any more, that's the gospel truth, Julia says he doesn't even go out of the house, just imagine in Madrid with so much traffic, it's natural, but what a telegram he sent me, Mario, so full of feeling, and then so well expressed, it made me cry, and I was trying to be brave, I couldn't restrain myself, mind you, it must be an awful shock for the poor dear. As for Constantino, he'd better stay at home, because, when you stop to think about it, he didn't even know you. And besides, I'm not a bit pleased with the idea of his being in contact with Mario, it's suspicious of me if you want, but I can't look upon that boy as a normal nephew, I can't help it, it seems to me as if he has it written on his face that he's the child of sin, see. How disgusting it was, Mario, the way I found them, if you'd seen it! It was the same day that Santander was taken, I'll never forget it as long as I live, in each other's arms, rolling around on the rug, what an awful thing, I don't even like to think about it! And then the nerve of him, "We were playing, bambina," the brazen fellow, I nearly fainted dead away, I was within a hair of doing it. And the fact is that I could have sworn I was the one Galli liked, but if Julia gave him the chance, well, he wasn't stupid, see, he knew what he wanted, he might have tried it with me, it made me raving mad, but I didn't say a word, out of shame, see, and Mama didn't even find out until Julia started to get big and then she took her to Burgos and later to Madrid. But imagine what that was like for Mama, may she rest in peace, an awful blow, she was so correct, so well connected in society, because the thing about Julia was the talk of the town, you must have been on the moon, my boy, I can't understand it, absolutely everyone found out, those things can't be hidden no matter how hard you try. Poor Mama, what she went through! When I tell you that she even wrote to Rome I've said it all, she was trying to dissolve Galli's first marriage, understand? but he, apparently, had two children with the other one and that's the bad part, the children in these matters, according to what people say, hopeless, it's terribly difficult. And in the middle of it all, Papa could make a joke about it, "And to think that that scalawag made me raise my arm in the Fascist salute," imagine, as monarchist as he is, he was furious, well, furious isn't strong enough, it's understandable, if he'd caught Galli at that time I think he would have strangled him. I admit I was dying to get married so I could tell you all about it, do you remember that when we were engaged you asked me about Julia and I told you, fine, in Madrid studying fine arts? Do you remember? Well, it was because of that, as soon as the war was over she went there with her little boy and didn't come back again, and when Mama, may she rest in peace, died, Papa went to live with her, he forgave her, I'm telling you, because it had been at least seven years since he'd talked to her. And Mama, it was almost worse, when she'd always had such a sweet tooth, stopped eating sweets, mind you, but forever, quite a sacrifice it was, too. But before we were married I thought about the expression on your face when I'd tell you about it, I was so anxious I could hardly wait, and in the train I sprang it on you, remember? you can't imagine how angry I was, you were so cool, you must have ice water in your veins, my boy, "God is merciful; wars upset a lot of things," what do wars have to do with shame, I could have killed you, because if there was anything that made it up to me for the thing about Julia, well, not made it up to me, you know what I mean, it was telling you about it, I said to myself, "He's going to be frozen with horror," and then you didn't even pay attention, just the same as when I came running to tell you about Maximino Conde for a novel, you didn't even look at me, "He has trouble enough," what kind of a remark was that? And what makes me angry is that if that doesn't have any importance for you, you haven't appreciated the fact that I've been different, because, in case you'd like to know, I could have done the same with

Evaristo, or with Paco, or with that legionnaire I sponsored, or even with Galli, or with anyone at all, whenever I'd wanted to, mind you, and if I didn't do it, it was out of respect for principles, but nowadays it seems as if it's ridiculous to have principles, I don't know what we're coming to, and if a girl is good and pure it's by sheer chance. Because tell me one thing, Mario, would you have liked to marry me after I'd slept with Galli Constantino? No, right? Well then, smarty, how come so much indulgence for my sister? We have to be impartial, sweetheart, and Julia, to speak the honest truth, was a hussy, what in the name of heaven did the war have to do with it? You people, with all this blaming things on the war, are capable of saying that night is day, neither more nor less, you excuse the thing about Galli and then you, when you could, that's another story, the union had been blessed and everything, you turn over and "Until tomorrow," that's something, mind what I say, that I won't be able to forget if I live a thousand years, I don't have to tell you, an insult like that, why, I don't even dare tell Valen about it, take note of that, as close as I am to Valen.

XVII

A foolish woman and clamorous, and full of allurements, and knowing nothing at all, sat at the door of her house, upon a seat, in a high place of the city, to call them that pass by the way, and go on their journey, but he didn't take me straight downtown, the second time I mean, I said to him, "I'm crazy about your car, it doesn't make a noise or anything," and then he turned around and started off like a flash on the highway to the pine grove. I said to him, "Go back, Paco, are you out of your mind? What are people going to say?" and he laughed and said, do you know what he said? he said, "Tell them to mind their own business," that he wasn't in the least concerned about gossip. What a change there's been in Paco, Mario, no matter how much I told you about it you can't even imagine! He always had ideal eyes for my taste, a strange sort of green, between cats' eyes and the water in a swimming pool, but the fact is that now he's acquired a kind of air, sort of a poise, a gentlemanly quality he didn't have before, I remember when he was a youngster, an insignificant little guy, and you see him now and he speaks slowly, with pauses, without stumbling over a single word, when in the old days he was a scream. Well, there he was, sweetheart, with his big Citroën, piling up millions, I can't quite remember now where he told me he works but of course it was as a sales representative, that has something to do with all this fuss about the industrial park, don't pay too much attention to what I say. And how well he drives, Mario! why, it's a pleasure to watch him, he doesn't make a single movement more than he needs to, it seems like he was born with the steering wheel in his hands. But he did, you're not going to believe it, look at me out of the corner of his eye the whole time, and as we went past the picnic place he said, "You're just the same, little one," and I, "What foolishness! think how many years have passed," and he, very polite, "Time doesn't pass the same way for everyone," see, an empty compliment, but a person's glad of it, grateful for it, Mario, a woman may be as straight and narrow as you please but she's not made of cardboard, it seems like it's an effort for you to say a pleasant word to me. Then he stopped and said to me, all of a sudden, what I least expected to hear, did I know how to drive, take note of that, and I said very little, hardly at all, and he said that he always saw me in line waiting for the bus, among ordinary people, imagine how humiliating, I assure you I was more embarrassed than I've ever been in my whole life, but after all what could I tell him, why the truth, that we didn't have a car, I wish you could have seen him, "No, no, no!" really shouting, hitting himself on the head, as if he didn't believe it, see, in these times it's absurd that a lady has to wait for a bus, Mario, everybody's surprised by it except you, you neither feel nor suffer. Don't kid yourself, darling, today a car is a prime necessity, just look at Don Nicolás himself, a Fifteen Hundred, and if you pay so much attention to him in other ways, why don't you imitate him in everything, it makes me furious, it really does, that for everything bad he's a saint and for good things he doesn't count at all. The spirit of contradiction, that's what you are, I start to think about it and you've never done a single thing I wanted in my life, stupid, remember the wedding dress, of course I could have guessed that, but I thought, at first, that it was because of your brothers, or because of your father's illness, or whatever. And God knows I didn't want it just to show off, after all, with a white dress or without one, a girl doesn't stop being what she is, but after the thing about Julia, you tell me, people, the way they talk, you had to have heard it, and you, still, "So what?" Did you think, see, that they were going to say it to you? But white, Mario, in case you didn't know, is the symbol of virginity, for your information, and nowadays, taking a woman to the altar dressed in street clothes is like announcing to the four winds, "I'm getting married for the second time, or with a floozy," I don't even like to think about it. But especially for Mama, Mario, after all I, look, I'm neither more nor less because of it, but after what happened, Mama would have liked to have people think, "Here comes a little virgin," just because, Mario, because we're human, because of everything, because for a woman purity is her most valuable possession and it can't be proclaimed too often, and, whether you like it or not, it's always an example for the common people, because they, and I'm not the only one who says so, are getting looser and looser about that sort of thing. And to be dressed for the street, as if it was any old day, I'd like to know what they thought, and furthermore there was no reason for it, that's what infuriates me the most, I don't know if you had anything to hide, my boy, but I could go into the church with my head held good and high, in case you're interested in knowing it. I'm telling you the truth, but I think those people on the Council, instead of going around all the livelong day discussing those pills, see, this is a fine time to be talking about them after a woman's all out of shape and loaded down with kids, that's not fair either, it seems to me, either all of us women ought to have them or none of us, and now it's going to turn out that people are only going to have one boy and one girl, like those foreign women, that's the decent thing, well, instead of that, Mario, it defines me, the wedding dress, just like it sounds, but fundamental, like a uniform, for all women, and the one who's not worthy to wear it isn't worthy of getting married, throw her in the mud, if she wallowed in it before I don't know why it should disgust her later. A little bit of firmness, yes, that's what we need, make sure of that, if not the day's going to come when an honest woman can't be told from a fallen one, you should hear Valen, now, in Madrid, all the women of the streets dressed just like us, no overdressing, you tell me, if I was the government a decree, just like that, like I'm telling you, I don't know why in the world, nowadays everything's directed at protecting brutes, Protestants, and hussies, and meanwhile us honorable women can go off and die somewhere. Of course if you'd told me in time, my boy, then we would have seen! But no, three months before, after the engagement party, just to make sure, when a girl can't go back on her word. "Marriage is a sacrament, not a spectacle," glory be to God! and there you were, fresh as a daisy, like always, why not, you got your way, I wish you could have seen Mama, poor thing, how she sulked, after the thing about Julia, this was the last straw for her. But what do you know about charity? I'd rather not remember your lecture, Mario, and still you kept saying, "It's natural for her to fuss, don't worry about it; she'll get over it," have you ever seen such selfishness? You're a cynic, worse than a cynic! and pardon me, Mario, sweetheart, I don't know what I'm saying, I nearly go crazy every time I think about the dress I had in mind, the waist a teeny bit high, princess style, it would have made an impression for sure, mind you, you men don't have the faintest idea what that means to a woman.

But it made no difference, you sticking to your guns, things would have been different if you'd told me when we started going steady, you can be thankful it was after the engagement party and I couldn't blow up about it, otherwise . . . All things considered, I was the stupid one, because Transi, see, had your number from the start, she may have been a little bit you-know, there's no doubt about that, she even let Evaristo paint her half naked, and what I told her was, "You shouldn't have done it," but I could have saved my breath, and then she even married him and what had to happen happened, well, the fact is that she, the very first time she laid eyes on you, had your number and I'm not saying it just to be talking. And Paquito, in a different style, more of the same, Transi may have not have had other qualities but she certainly had a good eye for the boys, you look at Paco now and he's a man of the world, and I'm not saying the car, it's everything about him, his person, I don't know how to explain it to you. Men have all the luck is what I say, if you don't look good at twenty you only have to wait another twenty years, fine thing, if only we could. But you certainly pulled a fast one on me, Mario, who could have said, you sitting there with the newspaper in the August heat, hour after hour, opposite the balcony of my house, looking, and I'm not talking about one day or two, and I used to think, "This boy needs me; he'll kill himself other-wise," I always was a romantic and a fool, never had a bit of malice, as you well know. And look at the good it's done me! And it's not that I'm complaining out of bad habit, Mario, you can see that, twenty-four years of marriage, it's so easy to say, and not even a miserable set of silverware, every time I invite people, I get so tired of it, a cold supper, all canapés, what can I do, always the same old thing, I have to figure how not to use anything but knives and dessert forks, and lots of times I ask myself, Mario, if I really deserve this punishment. If a person could be born twice! From where I stand now, I can tell you, I'd have more foresight, we women are the stupid ones to spend our lives always thinking of our husbands and children, Valen's right and then some, she says you get farther by not showing too much interest, that's logical, and then if that doesn't work, you take and wham! be demanding, bring me this and that and the other thing, you men think that the world owes you everything, you're all cut from the same pattern, Mario, because even though the way you are is beyond everything, with outsiders all kinds of flattery and attentions, and at home, not a word, that's what's hardest to bear, mind you, it's like that business in Madrid. You know how much I like Madrid, Mario, I'm just crazy about Madrid, I adore it, everything I could tell you isn't enough, well, I prefer not to go, that's the point we've reached, because I'd rather stay home than to have a miserable time, there may not be money for furs and a few trifles, but for buying that filthy stuff for making bubbles, or for having our picture taken arm in arm on the Gran Vía, you've certainly made me ashamed lots of times, sweetie, or for buying jumping jacks and stupidities like that there was always plenty. "Everybody has to live!" how lovely, that's right, everybody has to live except me, I'm different, I'd like to have a Six Hundred and I could have saved my breath, like I was asking for the moon, I know, Mario, shortly after we were married that was a luxury, I know it, but today it's a prime necessity, I tell you and I repeat it, today a Six Hundred, even janitors' wives, and I won't go back on what I say, why, man alive, they call them navels, for heaven's sake, because everybody has one, that says it all. But you say no, and that poor wretch of a photographer, fine, so all right, he would have had to throw away a plate, what does that matter, you tell me, what do you call that, after all you were never going to see him again, God knows how many pictures they've taken of us at weddings and things like that, and can you tell me where they are now? And you, insisting that everybody has to live, that you had more than they did, see, more than that faker who was selling the jumping jacks, you had to have a nerve, it wasn't because you had more talent but because you'd had more opportunities, that's nothing but double-talk and trying to mix a person up. Good-for-nothings, that's what they are, a bunch of good-for-nothings, and while they're showing you their little dollies, if they can lift your wallet they won't think twice about it, believe you me. The best of them, take note, ought to be behind bars, and then you talk about those in authority, well, for me, if they have any faults it's being too soft, mind you, it isn't so much the expense as the spectacle you made of me on the Gran Vía, watching that jumping jack bouncing up and down, or the fellow with the soap bubbles, we looked like two yokels passing the time till the bus came to take us back to the country, how awful! And even so, those were harmless, but how about the prisoners? Heavens, dear boy, we spent months with the amnesties or whatever they were, our house was like a branch of the jail, I certainly would like to know what got into you, mixing yourself up in that business, what smells, and it wasn't so much the smell, but for helping a prisoner, as if you didn't know, they could arrest you, just like I'm telling you, as an accomplice or whatever it's called, Armando was simply amazed every time he heard about it, and he was right. And you saying they weren't common criminals, fine thing to come out with that was, why, it was a lot worse, smarty. After all, sweetheart, a criminal commits a crime in a fury, he's carried away, see, but the others, they do it with malice aforethought, mind you, in cold blood, it's not a question of saying I was confused, I should say not, they're bad by nature and that's all there is to it. Well, you not paying the slightest attention, that they had nowhere to go but the street, that's logical, where did you think they'd go, and lucky for them, my boy, they ought to rot in jail, and if they do turn them loose, get used to the idea, it's out of pure charity, misunderstood charity, of course, with this business about amnesties, let them give thanks that they live in the country they do, because otherwise, well! And that's what you and your kind don't understand, you rascals, you confuse generosity with weakness, and you've made me spend quite a number of years thinking every other minute that they were going to take you off with that rabble, smarty, I had a bad enough time with the business about the train, the devil himself wouldn't have thought of that one, up all night, actually not sleeping a wink, all because you ran off at the mouth, miserable words. Antonio says that having been in preventive detention for twenty-four hours adds up to a record, just imagine if that's true, I don't even want to think about it, some legacy to leave to your children, poor little things, the day they find out about it.

XVIII

·····································

Son of man, behold I take from thee the desire of thy eyes with a stroke: and thou shall not lament, nor weep: neither shall thy tears run down. Sigh in silence, make no mourning for the dead: let the tire of thy head be upon thee, and thy shoes on thy feet, and cover not thy face, nor eat the meat of mourners, and it isn't that I make a big point of seeing through you, Mario, but when your mother died and I saw that you were perfectly happy, as if nothing had happened, I realized how eaten up with pride you are. And that fool of an Esther could still say, "Your husband has great dignity in his grief," look, points of view, if I had to choose between Esther and Encarna I wouldn't take either one of them, mind you, because each in her own way, they haven't done anything else in their lives but lead you astray. Dignity in grief, what do you think of that? She was just trying to confuse everything. And when you cried because you read the newspaper, how about that? You were sick then, how lovely, I'll bet anything you please that if you'd burst into song the day your mother died Esther would have thought it was just fine, right off she would have found a reason to defend you, I'll bet anything you please. It's just like Luis: "Excess of emotional control. Nervous depression," don't make me laugh, when doctors don't know what else to say they blame everything on nerves, that's very comfortable. It's the same as when you stopped wearing mourning after two days because your black calves made you feel sad, who ever heard of such a thing, and on top of it Esther saying that she understood you, that mourning is a stupid routine that ought to be done away with. Well, and wouldn't it be a fine thing if your calves didn't make you feel sad, that's what mourning is for, you rascal! Mourning is to remind you that you have to be sad, and if you're about to sing, to shut up, and if you're about to applaud, to sit still and not do what you feel like doing, why, I remember Uncle Eduardo, when he was in mourning for Mama, at the soccer games, like a stone, not even when there was a goal, mind you, it was really remarkable, and if somebody said, "But aren't you applauding, Eduardo?" he'd point to his black necktie and his friends understood perfectly, what do you think? "Eduardo can't applaud because he's in mourning," they'd say, and all of them in agreement, see, that's what mourning is for, smarty, it's for that and so others can see it, so that others only have to look at you to know that you've had a very great misfortune in the family, understand? and now I, even crepe, and it isn't that it suits me, understand, black on black looks dreadful, but you have to keep up appearances. Of course, laws like this don't apply to you, or naturally to that no-good son of yours, now it's time for you to reap what you've sowed, naturally everybody knows that what children hear at home, see, he certainly embarrassed me to tears yesterday. But my conscience is very clear in that respect, Mario, when your mother died, I remember like it was today, I kept after you day and night, I wouldn't leave you alone, "Go on, cry, it'll come out later and be worse; go on, cry," and you not a word, like it was nothing to do with you, until you burst out with, "Because it's the custom?" That's no way to behave, it seems to me, you left me speechless, honestly, I had the best intentions in the world, I swear it, and if I told you to cry it was for the same reason that I won't let the children take a bath after eating, it seems as if a person was peculiar and weird. The logical thing, when a person's mother has died, is to cry, you saw me, and I'm not talking for talk's sake, I was inconsolable, what a time that was, merciful heavens! and you didn't even notice, a few pats on the back, a few kisses at random, that's right, the things that would involve you the least, not even making love to me, Valen says that's a consolation at a time of sorrow, and I was absolutely unaware of it, nobody's more innocent and ingenuous than I am, I understand it, you'd think I was stupid. You really do have the gift of doing things at the wrong time, sweetheart, just think at this stage in the game, wanting me to undress, imagine, you must be in your second childhood, with the muscles in my stomach ruined, my back all flabby and looking terrible. Well, no sir, I just plain don't feel like it, if you liked that you could have asked me at the right time, because, even though I'm not the one to say it, I had a great figure, a little bit too much bosom, maybe, it's not that I'm complaining about it now, understand, if I believed Eliseo San Juan a regular Venus, see, but a woman's too old for exhibitions and, especially, she's simply not in the mood. Things should happen in their own good time, Mario, and instead of turning over and "Until tomorrow," I went through a humiliation you can't imagine, you should have asked me then and everybody'd be happy, it's like that business of the prisoners, you have the spirit of contradiction in your blood, my boy, because what I say is, if you want to do something for others, there are heaps of poor people and, if you're a little bit clever about it, you can bypass Caritas, the way I do, because Caritas, no matter how much you defend it, what it's done is to keep us from dealing directly with the poor and the prayer before the coin we used to give them, I remember with Mama, years and years ago, how they used to pray with such devotion and kiss the hand that helped them. Fine shape the poor are in nowadays, goodness, look at them, all stirred up! And do you want to hear some more? Weren't you all taken up recently with the crazy people in the Asylum, what you don't think of, my boy, nobody thinks of, about how it was a shame the way they lived and a disgrace for the city, to the point that I was even ashamed to pick up *El Correo* on Sundays? But are you really right in the head, Mario? I oughtn't to tell you, but Josechu Prados, in case you'd like to know it, was laughing his head off at the Circle the other day and saying that what you wanted was to "make your own bed," as if he was saying you weren't in your right mind, get it? But Josechu is wrong, for you and your kind the point is to stick the knife in, even if it touches the bone, because to spend a pile of money on a new insane asylum is stupid, Mario, get that through your head, don't you realize what an extravagance it is, that it's throwing money away? How do those poor things know, stupid, whether the building's old or new, or whether the weather's hot or cold? If they're in the Asylum it's because they're crazy and if they're crazy it's because they don't know what's going on, they don't feel or suffer, they think they're Napoleon or God himself in person and perfectly happy, so there. And even though you're not convinced by arguments, what I say is, Mario, why anything more? Why throw money away on some poor devils who aren't even going to thank you for it? Yes, I know Esther was on your side and that bunch of miserable friends of yours, more of the same, nothing lovelier than to give to those who don't ask for it, but why throw money away on people who have everything? because if they believe it, Mario, it's as if they

had it, don't kid yourself, and if you give them a new bathroom and a game room and a garden, why maybe you'll ruin
them, who knows, because there's no way to come to an
understanding with them . . . And don't think that I'm not
sorry about their misfortune, but fortunately I still have my
head screwed on right and I agree with Armando that to try to
take on all the world's woe is simply an act of vanity. You stop
to look at it, sweetheart, and vanity is what has ruined you,
you yourself have admitted lots of times, that writing those
things and buying jumping jacks and letting us have our
pictures taken on the Gran Vía and assisting the prisoners,
you weren't helping others as much as you were helping
yourself, and then you'd start thinking it over and wondering
if the things you did, at bottom, were nothing but egotism,
which, actually, is what I've always maintained. Because if you
liked to please others, then why not Solórzano when he wanted
to appoint you to the City Council? Why, tell me that? After
that run-in of yours with Josechu Prados, and your articles in
El Correo, which carried a charge of dynamite, my boy, and
then the file on you, and after the record of your father and
your brother, that's another story, Fito Solórzano's attitude
couldn't have been more elegant, I think, he was holding out a
lifeline to you, "Here, grab hold, make a new start." And as if
that wasn't enough, you heard what Valen said, "To get into
City Hall as a cultural representative is to go in through the
front door." Well, even though that's the truth, stupid, you
said, no sir, "The price of silence," same old song. Because
even admitting that Fito Solórzano didn't invite you to sit
down, or started to smoke without offering you one, what
importance does that have? He was ready to make peace with
you, that's obvious, and I don't know why in heaven's name
you acted like that when you saw your name written up on

walls, because, I didn't dare tell you so, I was kind of excited about it, I admit it, to see it all at once like that, in such big letters. Praise be to God! Mario, even Vicente said it, "I've never seen Mario so worked up, it's as if they'd stuck a couple of darts into him," it wasn't such a big deal, goodness, and so stubborn, "They should have asked for my consent in advance," but for heaven's sake, are they going to have to consult with people to do them a favor? Because if it was a question of asking something of you it would be understandable, but goodness, a thing like that, no matter how you look at it, is an honor, well, you couldn't wait to turn it down, could you? I'd like to know what you said, you were so high and mighty when you went there, I'm not surprised that he didn't ask you to sit down or offer you a cigarette, I should think not, the strange thing is that he didn't give you a kick in the pants, you certainly deserved one, my boy, if the truth be told. And you still insisted that you were firm but polite, I'll bet, the way you stormed out of the house I doubt it very much, don't get angry, and after all, what he told you, that he didn't have to consult with anyone and that if you felt you couldn't handle the job, there'd be time to decide that after you were elected, that there was no use talking about it beforehand, it seems to me he couldn't have been more tactful. And if you think it was polite to say to him what you said, I'd like to know the way you expressed it, that you didn't like to bet where you couldn't win, then honestly I don't know what politeness is. And you saying he didn't even offer you his hand, well, I should hope not! If I'd been in his skin I'd have put you in jail then and there, just like you're hearing it, yes indeed, after a disrespectful attitude like that, and on top of it, in the outer office you really let off steam, with the delegate and Oyarzun, he must have heard you, mind you, saying that your name was there for the sound of it and not for real and God knows what other wild statements. I don't see how either one of them has looked you in the face since, the worst thing was that you yelled at them that it was common knowledge that Oyarzun himself, Arronde, the druggist, and Agustín Vega would be elected unanimously and by sheer chance you were right about it, the thing that provoked me the most, frankly, I was angry and everything, was that you didn't get a single vote, I was really surprised, mind you, because Filgueira himself, who was a councilman at the time, told me the day before, just like you're hearing it, honestly, "Tomorrow I'm going to vote for your husband," and then I don't know if he changed his mind or what, it was a strange thing. But you had no reason to get upset about that because you didn't even know it, I was very careful to keep it quiet, so it was all wrong of you to act the way you did, why, I could hardly speak a word to you for a month, what a fuss! but that's the way you are, just look at you and Encarna. If it repels you to see her eat and you hardly speak to her or anything, which doesn't surprise me, because your sister-in-law may be as active as you please but as for conversation zero, why in heaven's name do you invite her to come and spend time with us? Because look here, she's your sister-in-law and she's suffered, I don't say she hasn't, but enough's enough, my boy, we've really had Encarna in our hair. And let's not say that Encarna's an inexpensive guest either, Mario, because your sister-in-law eats enough for three, she never gets full, you should see the way she stuffs with fruit, like a glutton, my boy, at the price it is, and let's not mention fish, which is ruinously expensive, imagine bream the way it costs, and then she sneaks the bones onto the children's plates, it's something I can't stand, it drives me wild, I promise you. And then, those weird habits she has of shutting herself up in the bathroom to read, and saying the children make her feel faint, and that they have to be quiet, well, children are children, everybody knows that, and if she doesn't like them the door's close by, nobody made her come, like I say. And it isn't that I'm jealous, Mario, you know and you know full well that I never had that tendency, but even though she's quieted down now, it's always disagreeable to have to be under the same roof with a woman who's tried to snitch your husband, sweetheart, because after the thing about Elviro, nobody can get it out of my head that Encarna was after you. And when you finished the examination she was in a great hurry to hear the voting, look, what does she know about those things, she just likes to stick her nose into everything, and then to go and celebrate it, we'd better draw a thick veil over that, I'd like to know what you and she did that night, and as far as I'm concerned, God well knows that it doesn't matter to me, but just imagine if the children came to find out about it, and because of Elviro's memory, Mario, who after all, ugly or handsome, was your brother. No matter how little you cared about me, Mario, you should never have brought that woman into our house, with that rough way of talking she has, I don't know if she comes from a good family or not, but she acts like a fishwife, my boy, just like it sounds, a real mannish type, you had to have seen her shifting your father around in her arms, from here to there, always doing something, and that smell, I was three months pregnant and I remember it was a nightmare. And don't think Encarna did it out of charity, sure, sure, out of charity, it was so you could see her, my boy! so you'd be impressed! and, in passing, rub my nose in the idea that I was useless. No, Mario, no, I have your sister-in-law here in the house, and I do it because I have my reasons, but as for my liking it, not one bit, if that's what you want to know, and don't come and tell me about the kitchen, because that means very little, it's worse if you really want to know, because you have to see the arguments she gets into with me, on the grand scale, and then, absent-minded as she is, you've got to be right on top of her, reminding her about the salt, and the parsley, in a word I'd finish sooner doing it myself. But putting that aside, if you'd set the pesetas Encarna's cost us one behind the other, a Six Hundred tomorrow, Mario, what am I saying! A Fifteen Hundred, and even then maybe I'm underestimating.

XIX

....

*And being in an agony, he prayed the longer. And his sweat
became as drops of blood, trickling down upon the ground:* "My
God, I feel so alone; I'm so tormented," an obsession, eh?
What manias! But man alive, who's tormenting you, you're
only trying to give yourself importance. Yes, exactly, you were
the one who took such pride in standing up to everyone,
telling people that they were bad, that Christ wasn't like what
our interests tried to make him out to be. You're a fine one,
sweetheart. Do you think you're the only person who knows
what Christ was like? That is a diabolical piece of vanity,
Mario, don't kid yourself, we'd all be in a fine fix if Christ was
to return to earth to buy jumping jacks and soap-bubble pipes
from all the good-for-nothings in Madrid and have his picture
taken on the Gran Vía so the photographer could eat, what
ideas. Do you really believe, Mario, you stubborn thing, that if
Christ came back to earth he'd worry about crazy people,
whether they're hot or cold, when everybody knows full well
that crazy people can't be either good or bad? Do you think,
by any chance, that Christ would have thrown a lamb at
Hernando de Miguel down the stairwell, or worried about
whether a policeman had beaten up a juvenile delinquent, or
been insolent to a governor, just look at Pontius Pilate, or tell
Josechu Prados he had to count votes when the aim was

something perfectly good, why, the Pope himself says it, that in this country the monarchy is the only guarantee of order? Can you imagine Christ writing the articles you write about country yokels, people who do nothing but blaspheme, or attacking the Inquisition, or refusing to wear mourning for the dead? You have a pretty poor idea of Our Lord, sweetheart, "We've disfigured him; we've disfigured him," and aren't you the first to do it? In case you're interested in knowing it, Mario, Christ wouldn't ever have had a brother who was a Red, or a father who was a moneylender, and if he had had them, you can be sure he wouldn't have been so cool about it, and he wouldn't have been a troublemaker, nor, that's for sure, would he have talked about charity the way you did, you should have seen poor Bene, she was so excited about it, she spent weeks on end pressuring me, "Mario's the best one for the job; if only he'd do it," and it surprised me, honestly, how quickly you accepted. Because it's not right, Mario, to betray the confidence of the women who run the thrift shop, I was so embarrassed, a slight like that, because if you accept it's to talk about charity the way you ought to, you had an audience of the very best people, honestly, and you blew it in the first minute, criticizing charity benefits, what Valen said was, "What harm do we do playing bridge for the poor?" Well none at all, naturally, you rascal, if by playing bridge you cover a need, then blessed be bridge. Sinning and so on are what you can't do, but games and parties, why not? What's bad about that? And then the bombshell, I was stunned, I said to myself, "He's done it, today he's done it, where's this man going?" and you carrying on about "Today charity resides in supporting the demands for justice of the disinherited, and to shut their mouths with a chocolate bar and a muffler may even mean tricking them," and then the whispering started and I thought,

"They'll lynch him, they'll lynch him, and they'll be absolutely right." You certainly put your foot in it, like I say, about how charity must reach places where justice falls short, and everyone, and me first of all, couldn't understand a thing, during your whole lecture I was on hot coals, my boy, I thought I was going to have a heart attack, my God, what palpitations, and when they began to boo you, I wished with all my heart that the earth would open and swallow me, like I'm telling you, you couldn't even be heard, and poor Bene with tears in her eyes, and you gesticulating, all red in the face, it was awful! and in the midst of the uproar Arronde's wife, shouting, "Let's see what the press says tomorrow, how shameful!" and, as they left, you can't imagine the things they said, the least thing they called you was a Red, and I was quiet as a corpse. And what's more, the next day, downtown, with that miserable *El Correo,* may God confound it, praising you to the skies, how very brave, the language that has to be used in this century, along the lines of the Council, I'm telling you, they burned a dozen or so papers and yelled "Down with it," fortunately Bene, who's practically a saint, calmed the women down, they were in a great state. And thanks be, the other newspaper, *El Noticiero,* criticized you, that your speech was demagoguery and all that, which was the finishing touch for me, Mario, I swear, *El Noticiero* is reliable, mind you, a Catholic paper to the last ditch, right wing ever since it's been in existence. And now that you're alone, smarty, how could you be anything else! poor Bene, she was so excited about it, "Mario is a sweetie; thank him for me," she kept telling me, heavens, what a pitcherful of cold water, and you regretted it yourself later, don't say you didn't, just like the business about the lamb, asking yourself if using that language to talk about charity to people who didn't understand charity wasn't to lack charity, what gibberish, my boy, riddles, you throw the stone and then the bruise hurts you, like I say, and that you had doubts and doubt made you suffer, and if you keep your mouth shut your conscience reproaches you and if you speak out it reproaches you too, some problem that is, well, use good manners when you speak, my boy, what you ought to have done with Bene was the opposite of what you did, you should have encouraged people to give and go to charity benefits, and then at the end it would have been a nice gesture on your part to raffle off your cigarette case or something, a personal object. But nobody can give you advice, Mario, the airs you put on, I don't even dare any more to tell you to take off your suit so I can press it, and then, that you're alone, how could you not be, blockhead, wasn't that what you were looking for, tell me that. Didn't I tell you back when the thing about the apartment happened, at this rate nobody's going to be able to stand the sight of you, so much criticizing and criticizing, that it seems as if you and your friends really enjoyed rolling in the mud? It's like your books, when they weren't about weird things that nobody understands, they were about people who were half dead of hunger or the kind of yokels that don't even know A from B. And if yokels don't know how to read, Mario, and the right kind of people don't give a hang about yokels, do you mind letting me know who you were writing them for? And don't come out and tell me that things can be written for nobody, because that's not so, Mario, because if you don't say words to anyone they're nothing, just noises or scribbles, anyway I think so, I don't know. But nobody can make you come down off your high horse, sweetheart, not even a suggestion, look at the way I ran home to tell you about Maximino Conde and his stepdaughter, a regular movie script, mind you, and the whole city wondering how it was going to turn out, and all for nothing, and yes, it was a little bit you-know, I realize that, on the racy side, but in the novel, at the end, making him react decently, it could even have set a good example. But no sir, you prefer yokels and starving people, you got exactly what you deserved, darling! but then don't complain if you're all alone, if you except Esther, Encarna, and those friends of yours, that's it. And if we get down to cases not even them, mind you, you should have heard that Moyano, the one with the beard, about a month ago, with that little article of his, "The Redeemers," or whatever it was called, I didn't understand it all, I admit, but by reading it over I think I got the sense of it, but what I am sure about was that part that said, "All redeemers love their fellow man, some to truly redeem him and others to use him as a pedestal," it was a real bombshell, but for everybody, eh? Oyarzun was yelling, I understand, and that Moyano was just as bad, my boy, you could hear him out in the street. Heavens, the way he behaved! and then you, "Leave me alone; a man can't open his mouth without offending someone," the stock phrase, why not, it's all pretense, you rascal, look at yourself in my mirror, do I offend? tell me the truth, do I offend? I don't, do I? well, look, I certainly talk a lot, I never stop, a chatterbox, you tell me, sometimes if I don't have anyone to talk to, to myself, imagine how funny, anybody who saw me, but I don't care one bit. But you, everybody knows, if you open your mouth it's to make trouble, today, yesterday, and every day. Remember the file they opened on you, what could Antonio do? His duty, that's all there was to it, and you can still be grateful it was him, if they didn't fire you it was a real miracle, my knees still hurt from praying, they swelled up and everything. And if a student goes and complains, Antonio, see, has to inform Madrid, he didn't have any other alternative, but especially if you hadn't run off at the mouth, there wouldn't have had to be an Antonio or an Antonia either. Because Antonio respects you, Mario, I know he does, he even came to see me, "It hurts me as much as if I was doing it to myself, Carmen, believe me," do you need any more than that? and I, "You don't have to give me explanations, Antonio, I should say not," see, and yesterday, you saw him, one of the first, and he's canceled classes today and everything, how well he's behaved. You make your bed and then you have to lie on it, Mario, let's not discuss it any further, the devil himself wouldn't have thought of saying a thing like that. Do you think that a Christian can say right out, in the middle of class, that it was a shame the Church didn't support the French Revolution? Do you realize what you're saying? And that fool, Esther, saying that it certainly was a shame, great God in heaven! are you in your right mind, Mario, a blasphemy like that? Wasn't the French Revolution the one about those wild-haired old women who cut off the king's head, and the nuns', and all the good people's, the one with the Scarlet Pimpernel or whatever? Goodness, you have a nerve to say a thing like that, principles, my foot! God help us! how can principles be Christian if they consist in cutting off the right people's heads, and as for the end of it, you're seeing it for yourself, nothing's worse than France for shamelessness and unbelief, you take Valen last summer, and it isn't as if she was a prig, she came back scandalized, for your information, but it's all the same to you, you have a conscience the size of a sack, my boy, the things you can swallow! and the next Sunday taking communion, so cool and collected, as if nothing had happened, and Bene, who saw you, could hardly wait, "He must have confessed, didn't he?" and I, "I suppose so," you tell me what I could have answered her, God's probably pardoned you, Mario, because you didn't do it out of perverseness, I believe that, of course, but sometimes I used to think that you were taking communion sacrilegiously and it would be a quarter of an hour before I fell asleep, I promise you, I was so uneasy, because that's something that terrifies me. And the thing that hurts me the worst is to think that you weren't like this at the beginning, it's been that Don Nicolás and his gang who've filled your head with crazy ideas, it'd pass if a person was looking at it from outside, but when the man who thinks and does these things is your husband, it's an awfully bitter pill, I give you my word of honor, Valen laughs about it, I'd like to see her in my shoes. Of course, since Vicente is the best-balanced man who ever lived, he thinks that other people's affairs, no matter how fond of them you are, Valen has proved it to me, are like something in the theater. She told me, Valen I mean, take note, she told me, "Your husband and those people have a screw loose, honey. But I have to admit they amuse me, it tickles me to see them trying to make the world turn backward. They're quite something, but be careful, those are the ones who commit suicide or die of a heart attack." Like that, Mario, just like you're hearing it, I swear to you, as if she'd had a premonition, and honestly I can understand businessmen dying of a heart attack, the kind who win or lose millions on a telephone call, but to have you die of one, a man who never concerned himself with money, with a wife who does miracles on practically nothing, a man who's never lacked for anything, I don't care what you say, it's not fair, honestly, it's not fair and it's not fair, I'm telling you, I understand it in important men, but that you, Mario, a nobody, who are we trying to kid, should go and die because crazy people live in an ugly asylum, or because a policeman hit you, or because Josechu doesn't count votes, or because Solórzano wants to make you a city councillor, or because yokels don't have elevators, it's something I just can't get into my head, if the truth be told. Of course the stupid one was me, it was no- body's fault, your mother told me herself that you were a very introverted boy and so on, that as soon as you came home from school, first thing your bedroom slippers and sit down to read beside the brazier. What a way for a boy to behave, see, and then Encarna comes out with whether I do or don't do things, what does she know, if you used to do that when you were a kid, as a grownup more of the same, everybody knows, people don't change. "I'm alone, Carmen," you told me three days ago, do you remember? right here in this room, and I acted like I hadn't heard you, because if I talk it only makes things worse, but what did you want, after all? For Solórzano or Josechu to come and give you explanations? Mama, may she rest in peace, she never missed a trick, used to say, "We reap what we sow," what do you think of that? said like that, at first sight, it seems sort of stupid, but it's a very true saying, Mario, it certainly is. And it wasn't as if Mama talked just to be talking, nobody was more sacrificing than she was, see, when the thing about Julia happened she made a vow not to touch sweet things, she was crazy about them, if only she wouldn't have twins, you'll say that's another silly thing, but it's not a bit silly, Mario, there's a reason for it, because Mama, may she rest in peace, knew where the shoe pinched, and she told Papa so, and I found out later, and if there's only one, it's an excusable slip, but if there are two, that shows it was done in lust, take note of that, and in Julia's circumstances that would have been unpardonable. Although, if you stop to think about it, my sister's paid the price for what she did, poor Constantino may be as unfortunate as you please, but he's a very peculiar boy, I think he does yoga or something like that and sleeps with his head on the floor, and at night he walks all over the house, he's a nightwalker or a sleepwalker, or whatever that's called, imagine how scary. All for a moment of pleasure, Mario, not even that, because it's nothing, most times I don't even feel it, I'm telling you the truth. That boy's very peculiar, Mario. Julia wanted to push him off on me in the summers with Mario, I didn't even tell you, but I wouldn't so much as consider it, I wasn't about to take that on, let her manage for herself, she did the harm, let her find the cure. In general those children of foreigners are apt to turn out badly, Armando says they're an unknown quantity and I agree with him, I don't know if it's the mixture of blood or what, but all of them revert to type a little bit.

XX

·····················

But fornication, and all uncleanness, or covetousness, let it not so much as be named among you, as becometh saints: or obscenity, or foolish talking, or scurrility, but he was awful, Mario, would you believe that one afternoon when we were alone in the house he opened *Il Mondo* at an ad for brassieres and told me, with a little very characteristic smile he had, pointing, "Breast, eh? bambina?" Just imagine what a thing! With Galli, I'm telling you the truth, it would have been easy, whatever-I'd wanted, I don't know what there is about my breasts, honestly, but Eliseo San Juan, every time he lays eyes on me, goes sort of crazy, especially if I have the blue sweater on, "You're terrific, you're terrific, every day you get more terrific," he bores me, honestly, because if I'd give him a chance, well, but I pay absolutely no attention, not the least, I go on my way, heavens, what a man! And when I was a girl, I don't have to tell you, even though it's wrong of me to say it, I was sensational, one fine day I went with Transi to the old guys' studio, a filthy attic, and that disgusting pair wanted to paint us in the nude, and Evaristo said, "A bust is what would be right for you, girlie," I was dying of shame, I swear it, how embarrassing, all the portraits of nude women on the walls, but Transi was just as cool, you wouldn't believe, "This one's wonderful as to light," "The quality of the flesh is very well realized here," I wonder where she got all those things from, so technical, she never told me, didn't quite dare, mind you, as close as we were. And then Evaristo, the fresh thing, put his hand all covered with hair on my leg and kept saying, "And what do you say, girlie?" he took my breath away, Mario, like I'm telling you, though I didn't make a peep or move a finger, who would have. I was the one Evaristo wanted to marry, and if he married Transi when she was a little bit past her prime, not to mention him, he was older than old, it was a last resort and only a last resort, a woman can tell a mile off when she's attractive to a man, don't ask me how, I don't know, intuition, it's like a hunch. You should have seen Evaristo every time he stopped us on the street, "Now, now you're real stunners; last summer you were just kids," and he never took his eyes off my bosom, the brazen fellow, I don't know what it is about my bosom, Mario, but at this rate till I'm sixty, how disgusting men are, all alike, sort of cut from the same pattern. And Galli Constantino pointed to the tip, you're not going to believe it, those Italians are the very devil, though he met his match in me, but if it had taken us that way, whatever I'd wanted, I always said so, Galli liked me a hundred thousand times more than Julia, but you men can find a pretext for anything and, as poor Mama would say, you take what you can get, and if my sister gave him a chance, he would've been stupid, any woman would have served for what he wanted her for, that's what makes me the maddest, a humiliation like that, and then afterward, who knows, I wouldn't swear on a Bible, imagine Julia, seven years alone in Madrid, and with such a little child, the freedom that implies. But look, Mario, it didn't matter a bit to me, Papa and Mama didn't speak to her and I wasn't going to do less, just "yes," "no," "good," "bad," no more than that, it wasn't anything you could overlook either. Poor Mama, how she suffered! Do you know that she even tried to dissolve Galli's first marriage? She moved heaven and earth, she certainly did, but apparently, when there are children in the case, that's fatal, terribly difficult. And suddenly, boom! the earth swallowed him up, nobody could give any news of Galli and to this day we don't know if he was killed here, or during the world war, or if he's alive and kicking and doing his thing in his own country, you men are insatiable, Valen says that even old age doesn't stop you, so there. And maybe not in other things, but of course Galli Constantino was terribly handsome, you can't imagine, all us girls were crazy about him, and when he used to take Julia and me in the Fiat convertible, everybody looking at us. What great times those were! I had a marvelous time during the war, you can say what you please, why, it was like a party, my boy, I remember in the bomb shelter, what a scream with Espe, an awful Red, you can't imagine, and Papa, with that sly way he had, you know him, he'd talk back to God Almighty, "Those are greetings from your friends, Espe, don't be scared," just imagine, because of the bombs, and she'd say, poor thing, "Oh, don't say any more, Don Ramón, this war is a horrible thing!" I had a terrific time, Mario, why should I say anything different, the whole city full of people, such a hubbub, I still don't know, I'm telling you sincerely, why I didn't throw you over then, after we'd started to go steady, because every time you came from the front, with the thing about your brothers and all, you were a regular wet blanket, sort of thoughtful, or bitter, how do I know! But one fine day, for no reason at all, boom! the earth swallowed up our fine Galli, of course that happened very often, take Nacho Cuevas, Transi's brother, same story, they mobilized him halfway through the war and because he was sort of retarded, or had had meningitis or something, they placed him in auxiliary services, and one fine day, I don't know if they needed people or what, but Transi's parents found a little note under the door, all full of spelling mistakes, that said, "They're takin me," just think, without a g, "to the warr," with an extra r, "I'm awful scared. Good By," and then down below, "Juanito." Well, from that day to this, and they certainly moved heaven and earth, you know what the Cuevases were like, and nothing. Of course, the shape that boy was in, it's better that God took him, he was a burden, you can't imagine, incapacitated, and what a future! you tell me, that was the worst of it, a mason's helper or something of the kind. "Better off dead," as I said to Transi, but she, my boy, went all sentimental, and as if I'd said something bad, "Oh, Menchu, no, honey, a brother's a brother." Transi's awfully affectionate in her way, she's all heart, you ought to have seen the way she used to kiss me, strange kisses for a girl, of course, but not meaning any harm, just look who she wound up with, that old Evaristo, been around so long that people were tired of looking at him, a man fifteen years older than she was, without a job or anything, and a perfect scoundrel to boot, if I went to the ceremony it was only because of Transi, like I'm telling you, so as not to hand her a snub, and even so he was kidding around with insinuations I didn't like at all, you remember. Well, she was so determined that he had talent, sure, talent to catch a plane and go off to America, or Guinea or I don't know where, and leave her in the lurch with three little ones, I don't even know how she manages, mind you, the Cuevases have always been a terrific family but they've come down in the world a lot, they don't have a cent. Evaristo had talent for that all right, I don't doubt it, for that and for putting his big hands where he shouldn't, I was cold as ice, "And what do you say, girlie?" if I'd led him on that afternoon and gone along with him a little bit, Transi could have given up, and it's not idle talk either. Why, his eyes practically popped out of his head every time he said to us, "Now you're real stunners; last year you were just kids," but what he was looking at was my bosom, he never took his eyes off it, and here between us, Mario, I don't know what it is about my breasts but there isn't a man who can resist them, why just the other day, to give you only one example, there was a lout who was digging a ditch on the Calle de la Victoria, but really yelling, "Honey, with a front line like that the goalie wouldn't have a chance!" Yes, I know, it's coarse, naturally, but what can you expect from people like that, and frankly, that's why your attitude hurts me even more, mind you, if other people didn't notice, fine, but if men like me as much as they do, I don't care one bit for your indifference, I'll have you know. And nowadays, it can pass, but look when we were going out together! a little hand holding and that was a lot, of course I'm not saying you could have kissed me, I wouldn't have let you or anybody else do that, but a little bit more enthusiasm, you disaster you, even if you had to hold yourself back, of course you would have had to, but in case you'd like to know, us girls like to feel that you're impatient when you're with us, not as if you were sitting next to a fireman or something. But you, lots of "my own," lots of "sweetheart," but so stiff, as if nothing was happening, like a bump on a log, and in the end a girl doesn't know what's control and what's indifference, because don't tell me, my boy, if you tell a man about Evaristo that time, with his big hairy hand, and he doesn't react, he's made of cardboard, it seems to me. And it isn't as if I was asking for the impossible, understand, sometimes I wonder if I'm not overeager along those lines, but I try to be objective, and there's Valen, and Vicente is the most balanced person imaginable, don't tell me, well, Valen's told me ever so many times that the last few months, especially after the engagement party, are pretty heavy stuff, and I agree with her, see, I don't want to tell her that you hardly paid attention to me, so embarrassing, I give you my word, Mario, but every time I saw you sitting in the hot sun on that bench across from our house with a newspaper, it was then that I started to like you, see, I think it was because of that, I used to think, "This boy needs me and he must be very passionate," I really had daydreams about it, mind you, with no basis, of course, but to myself, and I tell you absolutely sincerely, I would have liked to have had to stop you in your tracks some time, I don't mean like Evaristo or Galli, because then I wouldn't have got married, for sure, but a little bit of passion, look at Maximino Conde with his stepdaughter, and at his age, completely unbalanced, to the point that she, Gertrudis, had to go abroad without even packing, goodness knows what happened there, because after all Maximino was her stepfather and must have had some scruples, and I'm not excusing him or anything like it, understand. What I want to make you see, Mario, is that there's an instinct between a man and a woman, and girls with principles, the ones who're the way we ought to be, enjoy arousing that instinct in men but without things getting out of hand, while bad girls go to bed with the first man they can lay their hands on. That's the difference, smarty, but if we see that you men don't react, why then we get complexes, and we think silly things, even that we're no good, because even if you don't believe it, we women are very complicated. And then, after twenty years, all of a sudden, come on! a whim, get undressed, look what an idea, you must be in your second childhood, well, I just plain don't feel like it, if you'd like to know, look at me now with my stomach all scarred and my back so flabby, well, no sir, you

should have asked at the right time. And Father Fando can
still say those stupid things, what consideration indeed, don't
make me laugh, I don't know how you manage it but, whatever you do, you certainly don't lack excuses, heavens, what a
slap in the face. You always were a little peculiar, darling, you
have to realize, I don't care if Esther does say that for an
intellectual, the flesh is an appetite like any other, he satisfies
it and that's that, it doesn't throw him off his stride, I think
that's funny, the year we went to the beach you certainly got
an eyeful, my boy, you gave me quite a summer, mind you,
enough not to go again, I wouldn't go back to the beach with
you tied hand and foot, with all the shamelessness there is in
everything today. I don't care if it hurts you to hear it or not,
I'm telling you that you have the gift of doing things at the
wrong time, Mario, don't come and tell me now, on the good
days not even look me in the eye and the bad days, we both
know it, a regular siege, "Let's not be stingy with God," "Let's
not mix numbers into this," how easy that is to say, and if we
didn't let a child be born because of it, big news! imagine, if
every man with every woman and each time had separate
children, just think of the children that would be going to be
born every minute in the world, millions of millions! awful,
you could lose your head thinking about a thing like that,
foolishness. The spirit of contradiction, that's what you are,
ever since I've known you you haven't done anything but wait
till I say white to say black, it seems like that's all you needed
to make you happy, see if it isn't.

XXI

For thou shalt eat the labours of thy hands: blessed art thou, and it shall be well with thee. Thy wife as a fruitful vine, on the sides of thy house. Thy children as olive plants, round about thy table. That doesn't keep me from suddenly thinking crazy things, Mario, such horrible things that in the middle of the afternoon I get out of the house and go to confession, it occurs to me, for instance, that if Mama were to see me all the livelong day washing out underwear, with only one maid for five children, mind you, because Mama, may she rest in peace, it shouldn't be news to you, was much more than a mother to me, you know it, she was my adviser, my confidante, my friend and everything that it's possible to be. And the fact is that this servant problem, Mario, has become impossible even though you men, because it's to your advantage, close your eyes and on top of that insist on encouraging the poor, as if it had nothing to do with you, you fools and more than fools, you're all utter fools, going on about wages, and about Germany, goodness, at this rate I think we're going to end up in total confusion, because it's not merely the fact that today you have to pay a maid more than a thousand pesetas, that's the least of it, but then there's what she eats, but even so, the worst thing is that there aren't any, you can't pull them out of thin air, Mario, get that into your head, you really amuse me, one day you get an inspiration and "Let's all put our shoulders to the wheel," it isn't a question of that, a house takes a lot of work, it's not child's play, sweetheart, you think about it and it's never ending, because can you tell me how it helps me to have the children make their beds during vacation and have you pick up a broom and sweep one room? What does that solve for me, tell me that? Is it, by any chance, a man's business in life? A house is a house, Mario, and I have to follow behind you straightening bedspreads, cleaning the corners for you, all of you make my job twice as hard, mind you, rather than helping me. And then you can still say that there's no greater satisfaction than looking after oneself, your help and your satisfaction make me laugh, you don't live in the real world. Like that about making Menchu do the dishes, since when does a nice girl have to be a scullery maid, tell me that? It's bad enough that I do it, but after all I'm her mother, and if I didn't have the sense to choose better, it's only fair that I should pay for it, but can you tell me why the child's to blame? No, Mario, no, don't kid yourself, a person has to put up with as much as she can and in the last resort, remember Mama, if we have to die, do it with dignity, just think how embarrassed I was the day Valen caught you with the shopping bag buying food, I wanted the earth to swallow me, mind you. Fortunately nothing you do surprises my friends any more, but you can be sure that Vicente, who's a man like a man ought to be, never thinks about doing those silly things, they don't even pass through his mind, heavens above, I'll bet anything you please. The trouble with you, Mario, you don't fool me, is that deep, deep down you feel remorse, the fact is you'll do anything except earn money, which is your obligation. It's not just nowadays, sweetheart, you always had ants in your pants, even Doro says so, you don't know how to stay still, I remember at the beach, you kept taking notes and looking at papers underneath the beach umbrella, or, if not, making a boat for the children, anything but lying in the sun and getting tanned, Mario, you were so white, and then with your bathing trunks practically to your knees and your glasses, it got on my nerves to look at you, honestly, sometimes I acted like you weren't anything to do with me, like I didn't know you, I oughtn't to tell you so but I was even ashamed. After all, Valen was right and then some, they oughtn't to let intellectuals go to the beach, because they're so skinny and un-baked looking, they turn out to be a blot on the landscape, more immoral even than bikinis. But the thing that makes me the maddest, I admit it, is that at the beach, if you weren't looking at the girls, of course, you were so intellectual, and then, at home, you'd pick up the broom and start sweeping, because one thing or the other, either you are or you aren't, but if you are, with all its consequences, my boy, I just hate in-betweens. Yes, sure, I know you aren't an intellectual, I know it all too well, by heart, mind you, intellectuals think and promote thinking, but if you can't think because your head's a mess, you can hardly make others think. Excuses, just phrases, like I say, because if you aren't why do you spend the livelong day with books and papers? What in the world made you so white on the beach, tell me that, the sun didn't do one single thing for you? And then, to make me suffer more, acting like such a big sportsman, that's funny too, you can't even keep your shoes decent and doing fifty kilometers on your bicycle every Sunday, don't tell me, all to make yourself feel younger . . . You'd take anyone aback, Mario, make sure of that, lots of times I think that your proletarian tastes come from the stingy way you were brought up, because look, a little while after we started going steady, when you told me we'd have to get along on one duro a week, you left me stone cold, honestly. Because, can you tell me what two people could do with one duro, even if things did get much more expensive later, I realize that myself, it's twenty times higher now? If I tell you that the soles of my feet still hurt from tramping the streets I'm not exaggerating, and how cold it was, holy God! I used to go home shivering, I had to wrap myself in the table cover over the brazier, head and all, to get warm, and Mama, "Do you mind telling me where you've been?" I wasn't about to tell her, poor thing, she had trouble enough already. And one fine day you felt generous and off to the café, like yokels, that white-haired waiter, don't tell me, every time you ordered a glass of beer, he'd say so slyly, "One glass for the two of you?" which was absurd, see, you made me suffer the tortures of the damned. How awful, sweetheart! I don't even like to think about it because I get so angry, I can't help it, it's too much for me, I realize how little I ever meant to you, because if you only had one duro, why take on a girlfriend? Did you have any right to do that? In those circumstances a man who's in love will steal, kill, or do something, Mario, anything except keep a nice girl in a situation like that, it makes me furious, mind you, even at this stage in the game, to have been such a fool, the tears even come to my eyes when I think about the insult, I had lots of time to find out what your weak points were, and even then I didn't catch on. What do you think of that? "One glass for the two of you?" Because that white-haired fellow said it so meaningfully, Mario, don't tell me he didn't, making fun of me, all dolled up, with a hat on even, so pretentious, pretending something I couldn't have, see, that's what drives me wild. I'd like to know what it would have taken for me to give you your walking papers. A real man would steal or kill before he'd keep a woman in that situation for three years, and you, still playing along, "For the young lady, I don't want anything," the heck you didn't, you were panting for it! How can you think he didn't notice, he was no fool, and especially I don't know why in the world you had to give so many explanations to a waiter, see, a nobody, that's the thing that disgusts me the most about you, that you humble yourself to working-class people when it's so easy to yell at them, and then, on the other hand, with the right people, even with the authorities, you let your tongue run away with you and go too far. What can a person expect of a man like that, can you tell me? And that wasn't the end of it, you didn't have a cent and still you could say that you were privileged, that you had enough to eat and were warm, the things a person has to listen to! a man who doesn't have a penny to his name, that's another story, you tell me now, if it wasn't for Papa, Mario, God only knows how much it's cost me to keep up appearances, you men, you're so proud of knowing all there is to know and then you swallow those stories about how more than half of humanity goes hungry, imagine, today the man who goes hungry it's because he damn well feels like it, Mario, just like it sounds, because what I say is, if they're hungry, why don't they work? Why don't the girls go and be maids the way they ought to, tell me that? Why? the thing is there's lots of immorality, Mario, nowadays all of them want to be ladies, and the one that doesn't smoke paints her nails or wears pants, and that just can't be, those women are destroying family life, just like it sounds, why I remember at home, two maids and a house-keeper for just a few of us, and they earned practically nothing, I'm not arguing about that, but why did they need anything more? Maids back then were like part of the family, Papa was wonderful about that: "Julia, not so much; leave a little so they can taste it in the kitchen too." There was solidarity then, time for everything and everyone in their own class, everybody happy, it wasn't like now when everyone wants to start as a general, I've never seen such ambition and such haste in my life, my boy. But no, you and your kind had to come along and improve things, a plague, Mario, like locusts, come on, got to tear everything down, this is unfair, got to cut a piece off the top and add some at the bottom, everybody knows that to make a phrase you'd be capable of selling your mothers, that wretched Don Nicolás, I'm earning stars in my crown with that man, take note, before, *El Correo,* I remember, was a pleasure to read, with that editor they appointed from Madrid, so loyal, and it's not just me that's saying it, everybody agrees, it was after he left that the troubles started. Because what I say, Mario, is, if after so much hue and cry you'd get some results, I'd understand it, but the truth is that it's no use, I don't understand how you can work so hard, because don't tell me that twenty duros, with the price of things today, is money, it's laughable, Mario, it's a swindle, that's what it is, you'd be better off writing for nothing. But on the other hand, when you wrote for Madrid, off with you, out, because you were so stubborn, that they'd changed your text and put Crusade instead of civil war, or some stupid thing like that, my goodness, the way you yelled over the phone, I'd like to know what poor José Mari Recondo thought, that was the way you repaid him, and all for one word, just think of the head-aches that words give you people, gracious heavens, that what did they mean that one was the same as the other, look, Crusade or civil war, I don't understand it, honestly, I'm not just playing dumb, I swear, if you say Crusade, all of us know you're referring to the civil war and if you say civil war we're all well aware that you mean Crusade, isn't that right? because not even the meaning is different. Well, then, stupid, you're more trouble than an idiot child, what was the point of that fuss, and throwing away six hundred pesetas, two articles a month were twelve hundred, and if you come right down to it twelve hundred pesetas could pay the household expenses? But no sir, out, I can't be blamed, what Valen says, and she laughs, but I promise you it doesn't strike me as the least bit funny, is that you'd rather they took your wallet than to take a word away from you, and it's true, Mario, miserable words. And do you know what that is? Complexes! for your informa- tion, all your kind are full of complexes, sweetheart, when what I like is ordinary people, normal, I don't know how to tell you, who don't give so much importance to foolish things, look at Paco, when he was a youngster he didn't care a thing about words, one was just like another to him, he confused "perspective" with "preceptive," he mixed everything up, he was a scream, well look at him now, he can laugh at the world, with a Citroën as long as from here to there and piling up millions. And a person doesn't need a university degree for that, I should say not, that was my mistake, all a person needs is contacts and being a little bit of a smoothie. You've heard Menchu, "Us girls, boys with a degree, not a bit of it; they're such bores," the up-and-coming generation is getting wise, Mario, make sure of that, they're not as silly as we were, they go straight to the practical angle and know that with a univer- sity graduate, in addition to going hungry, they're going to be royally bored. Imagine me with Paco now, to give just one example! A life like you see in the movies, heavens, trips to Madrid, abroad, and the best hotels, of course, he was telling me the other day, and no matter how well the Citroën rides, there are times when it's not enough, and every little while, a plane, to Paris, London, or Barcelona, everybody knows what business is like, anywhere. And then, in the pine grove, when he stopped the car, he put his arm along the seat behind me, meaning nothing bad by it, of course, he didn't even think about it, I'm convinced of that, and he was looking at me the whole time, "You're just the same," he said, and I, "What foolishness, just think of the years it's been!" and he, "Time doesn't pass the same way for everyone, little one," an empty compliment, you'll say, but a person's grateful for it, and I was a little bit stupefied, I swear, and when he took hold of me by the shoulders, my heart went sort of crazy, bam, bam, and I firmly believe that he hypnotized me, Mario, I give you my word, I couldn't move or anything, only the murmur of his words closer all the time, not even the pines, imagine, there are so many of them, and when he kissed me I couldn't even hear that, everything was blotted out, like I was unconscious, I swear to you, I could only smell, he smelled of that mixture, so manly, of good tobacco and cologne which is a smell, Valen can tell you, that almost makes you swoon, it's not an invention on my part, I could swear to you, I didn't participate in the least, I was half hypnotized, honestly.

XXII

....

Say to wisdom: Thou art my sister: and call prudence thy friend.
That she may keep thee from the woman that is not thine, and
from the stranger who sweeteneth her words . . . Let not thy mind
be drawn away in her ways: neither be thou deceived with her
paths, even though knowing men the way I do, Mario, I'm
absolutely certain that you've stepped out on me more than
once and more than twice, I'd bet anything on it. You only
have to look at the way Encarna turned up yesterday, some
little scene that was, I didn't know where to look, and Valen
said, "Why, you'd think she was the widow, dear!" and it's
true, my lad, she made me look ridiculous, what howls! It's
just like the business in Madrid, the point is to mix in where
nobody's invited her, like I say, because can you tell me why
she needed to be at the voting? And then, to celebrate, go off
and have a spree, and you saying that a beer and a few shrimps
at Fuima's, and nothing else, sure, as if a person was an idiot.
As the years pass, Mario, mind you, I'm more and more
convinced that man isn't a monogamous animal, that for you
men monogamy is a has-been. You look on us as such fools
that you take advantage of our humbleness, the knot's tied
and then you can take it easy, a faithfulness policy, of course
for you that doesn't apply, it's all one-sided, you men go off
and have a good time whenever you feel like it and live

happily ever after. And it isn't as if I was saying that you were a Don Juan, sweetheart, I should say not, but I wouldn't swear to it on the Bible either, that's the truth, no matter how often you say that you went into marriage as virgin as I did, I don't swallow that one, mind you, I'd be stupid if I did and I'm pretty tough now, I've had to be. "Don't thank me for it, it was out of timidity more than anything else," don't make me laugh, timidity's not in it! you men are pretty smart, the first chance you get, whoosh, so long, never saw you in my life, wife and children don't count for a thing. And that's if you aren't the ones who're looking for a chance, Madrid's quite something, my boy, it's disgraceful, after eight in the evening there are more hookers on the streets than decent people, it's been a mistake, see, to close the houses, I would have done just the opposite, I would have painted them in good loud colors so that nobody could make a mistake about them, and I would have shut the hussies up in there, but really tight, eh? and not let them even see daylight, they don't deserve anything else, I don't care how often you tell me that nobody's that way because she wants to be, when you men start making excuses you're impossible. Just look at you, and I couldn't have been nicer about it, "Tell me about your little flings when you were a bachelor, I forgive you in advance," but no indeed, and I give you my word, Mario, that I was prepared to drink the cup to the dregs, I swear to you, and after you'd finished, to give you a kiss, like an absolution, understand? and tell you, "What's past is past." But you sticking to your guns, same story as always, you're stubborner than a mule, my boy, and in capital letters, in case I hadn't grasped the point, like in your books, it doesn't make sense to use capitals, you people who pride yourselves on knowing things, when they aren't proper names and there isn't a period or anything, any fool knows that. "I WAS AS MUCH A VIRGIN AS YOU; BUT DON'T THANK ME FOR IT, IT WAS OUT OF TIMIDITY MORE THAN ANYTHING ELSE." What do you think of that? It makes me furious, Mario, but absolutely furious, to have you be so mistrustful, because if you'd told me the truth, I would have forgiven you just the same, I swear to you, sure as my name's Carmen, even though it hurt me dreadfully, mind you. And that's not counting after we were married, your infidelities in thought, that's adultery, just the same, see, remember the summer we went to the beach, just look at what a bad time I had, you couldn't take me back there tied hand and foot. And if it makes me furious don't think it's on my account, blockhead, you know me, and I may have other faults but I'm not jealous, but the children, think about the children, what a disgrace, Mario and even Menchu understand what kisses are, sweetheart, time passes, they're two adults, Mario, even though you're trying so desperately, with your bicycle and your silliness, to hang on to your youth. It's the way life is, sweetheart, and nobody can struggle against that, poor Mama, may she rest in peace, used to say, "There's a cure for everything but death," take note of that, it may seem like a commonplace, but there certainly is some truth in that little saying. Lots of times I think, a little bit foolishly, Mario, that if you'd been my mother's son, instead of being your mother's, she was so stuck on everything that was hers, you'd be a different person. Then everything would have gone much better, I'm sure, and it isn't that I'm complaining, understand, I know it's foolish to think those things, because if you'd been Mama's son, we'd be half brother and sister at least, see, and we wouldn't have been able to get married, and all that about the same blood and the Rh factor terrifies me, mind you, always has, and it's not that I'm saying it now, with Alvaro

you can't imagine what I went through, I can tell you about it
now, but because I bled beforehand, I imagined that it could
be something peculiar, that our bloods weren't compatible or
something and I almost got hysterical, I made a vow not to eat
ice cream for a month, think of that, you know how I adore
ice cream. Of course you didn't even catch on, and then, you
make a mountain out of every molehill, see, with Alvarito
himself, whether it isn't very strange that he should want to
go out to the country alone and build a bonfire, or that he
should call soldiers playing-card jacks and if he oughtn't to go
to the doctor, and if we oughtn't to this and that, just kid
stuff, Mario! the thing about Alvaro is that he has a vocation
to be a boyscoot, or whatever that's called, if you start thinking
about it he's never been sick, what you'd call sick, in his life,
measles and that was all, and very mild for measles, remember
we weren't even sure about it. Other things worry me more,
Mario, serious problems and not those silly things, look at
Borja, yesterday, and he didn't say it just to be saying something, it came straight from the heart, "I wish Daddy would
die every day so I wouldn't have to go to school," what do you
think of that? I gave him an awful thrashing, well, you saw,
and I know he's only six, but when I was six, I remember like
it was today, I felt veneration for Papa, real veneration, if
they'd told me something had happened to him I'd have died,
mind you. It's just like that other good-for-nothing and
mourning, no, those are stupid conventionalisms, see, "conventionalisms," he couldn't have found a fancier word, that
boy's going to be like you, Mario, so complicated, he's the spit
and image of you, he seriously worries me, just look last
Sunday, he didn't even ask me for his allowance, at his age I
can't allow that, whether he likes it or not he ought to start
going out with friends and leave those books alone for a while,

they're going to turn his brain to water, I don't know why you men need so many old books, they're nothing but storage places for dust, like I say. That's right, there was always money for books, but a Six Hundred, see, what a silly thing, a luxury, you had enough with your teaching, your papers, and those friends of yours, and let the rest look out for themselves. Take that business about Aran, and look how long I've been after you about it, my boy, a lifetime it seems, well, so she'll grow, she's three years old, well, of course she's three years old, stupid, but at three there are tall little girls and short little girls, and Aran's very short, and if there weren't precedents it would pass, but look at your sister, Mario, aside from her being so insipid, Charo, physically, is just nothing at all, she's like a little jug, don't tell me, she doesn't even know what she wants, you can see that, first a Slave of Mary, eight months and out, you look at her now and she isn't happy anywhere, it's not for nothing you're brother and sister, sweetheart, you're two people who've got ants in your pants, misfits or something, there's a reason why they're so much in style nowadays. But I'm telling you that I don't want my daughter to be like that, and I don't care if you laugh or cry, I intend to take her to Luis and have him give her a good going over, and prescribe some vitamin shots that will make her grow and develop. Everything that's in my power to do, I won't rest, sweetheart, stop telling me I'm strangling her personality, you take the other one, chatting with the janitor at all hours, fine personality that is, if personality consists in refusing to wear mourning for a father, then it's better for them not to have a personality. After all, my ideas aren't so bad, and either I'm not good for anything or my ideas have to be my children's, sweetheart, and if Mario wants to think on his own, let him earn it and go and think where there's a landlady, but while he lives under my roof, those who depend on me have to think the way I tell them to. Enough is enough, a person is or he isn't, as poor Mama would say, because you tell me what good it can do my son to chat away with the janitor, in his cubbyhole furthermore, to make me suffer more, it's like seeing you, Mario, he's your spit and image, my boy, remember that old fool Bertrán, every time he showed up with your salary, you'd encourage him to talk, asking him if he earned a lot or a little, you tell me, with an usher, and then from one thing you went on to others, I heard him, don't think I didn't, he said it good and loud, that he was still good for it, especially by changing mares, just imagine that old mummy, deaf to boot, you men would say anything to brag about being manly. I'm tired of telling you, Mario, that if you get chummy with these people you don't know where it will end, if you give them an inch they'll take a mile, it served you right, even if it bothers you to hear me say so, because if you blew your nose carelessly and you treat him as one equal to another, then he's perfectly within his rights to tell you, "You have some snot on your face," that's logical, I laughed to myself, but I thought, "Serves him right for being a fool, serves him right. Let's see if he learns from experience," and you didn't even know where to clean it off and he, "Higher, lower, there," and you, "Thank you, Bertrán," with such a mortified face. Well, if the truth be told, he was very much affected yesterday, he was one of the first to show up and straight to the dining room, what did you think, I let him stay there a while, but then I said, "Bertrán, go along to the kitchen if you don't mind, we can hardly budge in here," I should say not, since when is an usher going to be with the teachers? And I'm not saying the cemetery, that's his duty, but to come to the house is out of place, and then he embarrassed everybody with his deafness, poor Antonio wound up shouting, and the other one, "I can't hear what you're saying," a real spectacle, like I'm telling you, and Don Nicolás laughing, see, he couldn't have found a more opportune moment, it was a real miracle I didn't throw him downstairs, he may be intelligent, I don't deny it, but he certainly doesn't have the gift of doing the right thing at the right time, remember the business about giving you the decoration, I don't know what right he had to an opinion, "Don't do it, I know Mario and he's quite capable of throwing it in the pond," and you, what could be expected of you, "They want to make me into a tomb with a Grand Cross on top," good or bad there's just no way to deal with you, my boy, what a character. And the truth is that if they hadn't told you, "That's enough," namely that you were like a runaway horse, what articles, once your mouth heats up you don't know what you're saying or where you're going, like the time they told you over the phone to stop writing them, how did you want them to tell you, the quickest way, that's logical, and you, "In writing, in writing," do they have to draw up a legal paper to talk to you? I'm always on pins and needles with you, sweetheart, as if you were a little child, remember what happened on the train, of course it had to be with that Moyano, the best thing he could do would be to shave off those whiskers, I don't even know what he looks like, and you kept insisting that the severe regime he was talking about was for his stomach, sure, sure, you can't put that one over on me, you two could have been in real trouble, the man who complained was influential, see, with a political record I'd like to have for myself, Mario, he did exactly the right thing in calling the police, you never know, and all because the two of you ran off at the mouth, and I didn't sleep a wink all night, how could I help it, especially after hearing Antonio, and just imagine, I made phone calls to everyone, and he kept saying, "I'm not entirely sure, but I think that twenty-four hours of preventive detention adds up to a criminal record," heavens, as if that could be taken as a joke, as something unimportant, my poor children! With you the thing is that you talk when you shouldn't, and then, at parties, unless you have a couple of drinks, you're a gloomy Gus, heavens, what faces! Why did you always shut up, tell me? Of course, you're there against your will because, if you come right down to it, you don't know how to sing, tell racy stories, play the guitar or dance modern dances, you're a hindrance, so there. But it isn't as if I hadn't told you, Mario, ever since we got married, don't tell me I haven't, I realize myself that I was even tiresome about it, "Learn at least one social grace; without one social grace you're a lost man," but you, as usual, didn't pay the slightest attention, I don't know a single woman, mind you, who's influenced her husband less than I have, honestly, and that's lack of love, sweetheart, no matter how you look at it. You used to make me feel sick, eh? off in a corner, bored stiff, rolling one of those cigarettes that smell awful, I'd be so angry, I swear to you, I don't know which I prefer, because you don't have anything but extremes, either you're like a madman or like a dead man, just look the other night at Valen's, and I saw it coming, eh? word of honor, I saw it coming, as soon as I laid eyes on Solórzano and Higinio, the minute we came in, and you kept firing champagne corks at the streetlights, Valen may have enjoyed it and all that because she's a very open-minded girl, she's a darling, Valen is, but I, the time came, I promise you, when I didn't know where to look, to say I was embarrassed is an understatement.

XXIII

....

For as wisdom is a defence, so money is a defence: but learning and wisdom excel in this, that they give life to him that possesseth them, though admit it, Mario, if instead of spending so much time on those ridiculous books, you'd taken up something more profitable, a bank, for instance, anything at all, it'd be a different story. Because it's easy to say, my boy, the long hours you've spent in this study, toiling and moiling, not even taking time to pee, and in the end, what for? Very simple, to show us that yokels live without elevators, that the crazies have to have a new insane asylum, that all men ought to start from zero, I suppose you know what you mean by that, and that we have to cut some off the top and add some on the bottom. Well, here we are, and for that you've spent so many years, like I say? You have to be an utter fool, my boy, don't tell me, what I find awfully hard to take is that you can see me worked to death, up to my ears all day long, and you calmly sitting in your study, or chatting and smoking with your friends, I never saw such clouds of smoke, holy God, as soon as you all left, two hours airing out the house. I'm telling you that when you got sick, your nerves or whatever it was, it was a rest for me, praise be to God, everyone to his own house and everybody quiet, what a relief it was for me! And the same thing's true of meals, sweetheart, no gratitude and no reward, because can you tell me, you rascal, what good it did me to spend the whole blessed morning in the kitchen? All you do is gulp, like a turkey, you never looked at what you were eating, you disaster you, I don't know whether out of gluttony or what, but it certainly didn't show on you, honestly, I remember at the beach, skinny as a rail, my boy, and then so white, and with your glasses, you got on my nerves, enough to make anybody ashamed, no kidding, I'd forbid intellectuals to get close to the ocean, it's such an ugly thing to see! Because if just once you would have told me, "My, this is good," it would have been enough, I'm reasonable, anything would have done, see, but no, the only times were if there was a hair or a fly, that's not so awful, you just take them out and that's the end of it, but no sir, a regular scene, I'm the one who's a fool to take so much trouble over meals, even Encarna who's so soft on you, you've heard her, "A stew's the same as duck à l'orange for Mario," it's the truth, the way you act is enough to discourage any woman, what a bore, my boy. Those wretched books, they'd sucked out your brains, you couldn't think about anything else, heavens, what an obsession! you'd be eating or at a party with your head somewhere else, and on the street not even greeting people, you ought to see the reputation you have all over town for being disagreeable, nobody can stand the sight of you, and it's not just me saying it. And then the titles of your books, Jesus and Mary, you'd get so hot and bothered! and then wind up with something completely beside the point, "The Sand Castle" or some silly thing like that, I don't know if it's pretty or ugly, but it just simply doesn't fit, sweetheart, you take a good look and there aren't any castles anywhere in the book, that's such an easy thing to do, the point is that the title has to go with what's inside, just look how ridiculous, anybody can do the other thing. And then those capital letters: "THOUGH DIFFICULT, IT IS STILL POSSIBLE TO LOVE IN THE TWENTIETH CENTURY," look who's talking, practice what you preach, three years waiting to get married and in the end "Good night, until tomorrow," and that priest can still say consideration, a little less soft soap, it's an insult, that's what it is, a great big whopping insult, because a woman, and I know very well what I'm saying, can put up with a rape a thousand times better than a humiliation like that, it's the last straw, Mario. And of course I was a teeny bit frightened, why should I say I wasn't, I knew something had to happen, Transi and all the girls said so, but anything but that. Consideration! Don't make me laugh, a hopeless egotist, that's what you are, going on about how men don't love one another, how machines dry up their hearts, must be the bicycle, you rascal, you take those characters of yours, on the island or wherever it is, a person doesn't even know where they are, that's another thing, and it seems like they can't talk about anything else, I hardly thought they were there for fun, they're so tiresome, I laughed my head off with Valen, "All of Mario's characters, absolutely all of them, are wet blankets," and Esther, I hardly need to tell you, praising you to the skies, like a fury, "They're symbols," I suppose she knows what symbols are, see, but she says things with such seriousness, my boy, that you can't argue with her. To love in the twentieth century, look who's talking, a man who on his wedding night turned over and "Until tomorrow," why, you ought to have died of shame, heavens, a snub like that, and then later on that the waters were rising around you, that everything was frivolity and violence, you must not have been talking about yourself, miserable nerves, you men don't know what to think up next to give yourselves importance. Go on, ask Galli Constantino if he knew how to love in the twentieth century! And before he should have, too, nobody can understand you men, some want too much and others not enough, I'd like to know about Julia in Madrid, God knows, alone, seven years, just imagine, with American students in the house, she wasn't going to live on air, but it's a danger, frankly, because what Valen says is, that once a woman gets a taste for it, it's natural, between a man and a woman there's an instinct and what you have to do is avoid the occasion of sin. Well, you going on about how we don't love, that we're losing the habit of loving, you got obsessed about it, like I say, and then, to get it off your chest, that little article in the American magazine, "Absence of Feeling in Modern Literature," a hundred dollars, Mario, that's easy to say, six thousand pesetas, but once and never again, see, what an opportunity, a gold mine, but who was going to swallow a bunch of tripe like that? And furthermore, what I say is, my boy, if modern literature doesn't have feelings, don't you raise a hue and cry about it, modern literature is what you and your kind write, and it's up to you, then put them in, it's really funny, see, and if the novel ought to be a reflection of life, the way you say, there's Maximino Conde, there's a good strong feeling, you tell me, with the stepdaughter, if that isn't taken from life, but you not a bit of interest, not even to listen to me, eh? and I hurried home so fast. You complain out of pure bad habit, Mario, admit it, unless what you call feelings are how the guards behave with prisoners, or buying jumping jacks from all the good-for-nothings in Madrid, or feeling sorry for crazy people, in which case I'll shut up, but that's putting the cart before the horse, dummy, because love, love, real love is what's between a man and a woman, no two ways about it, and that's been true since the world began. The trouble with you, you lazybones, is that you never forget an injury, you're a malcontent, and secretly you're one of the kind that bears grudges, you still haven't forgotten that business about the policeman, that's where the trouble lies, and I don't believe what you say about his hitting you, not if you swore on a stack of Bibles, mind you, and I'm not the only one, just look at what Ramón Filgueira told you, that's logical, and furthermore in places like that and the hour it was, nobody's going to be too particular, they'd be in fine shape at the barracks and in the police station if they handled every delinquent who came along with kid gloves. And you saying that you thought, "I'll keep still; the time to talk will come," but they didn't let you either at the barracks or at the jail, naturally, they're the law and you keep your mouth shut, at a time like that you're a criminal, even though you resent it, neither more nor less. I remember that rule about not riding a bicycle in the park ever since I was a little girl, you couldn't do it, it isn't as if they'd thought it up just to annoy you. It made you furious to fall off the bicycle, I'll just bet it did! and if I were the police officer I'd have done the same, "You can't issue a countercomplaint unless it's certified by a doctor," it would have been enough for anyone else, but not you, stiff as starch, off to First Aid! to bother them at four in the morning, which is no time to do it, and then to have you say that you happened to find just the right person, it was that quack of a doctor who cooked it up for you with "Hematoma produced by the knuckles of a hand," that takes a nerve, what Filgueira said was, "The pedal itself," who knows, that can't be proved, but you, insisting on the countercomplaint, abuse of authority, a monomania of yours, "Here's the certificate," if you'd gone straight to Filgueira and said, "You're right, Filgueira, I was mistaken," things would have gone better for us later on, and neither he nor Josechu Prados or Oyarzun or anyone would have denied us the apartment, It was absolutely typical of you too, saying that furthermore we'd met all the requirements, it was a settled thing. And especially what Filgueira said, "I have to believe my policemen, a police- man at that hour is the same as the Minister of the Interior," naturally, Mario, sweetheart, in those circumstances the highest authority, you tell me what we'd do without them, chaos. But even accepting it as a fact that he hit you and that those fairy stories of yours about the pistol were true, you should have kept your mouth shut, Mario, because if a policeman in a fit of anger hits you with his fist don't think he's doing it for fun, of course not, but for your own good, just like we do with the children. There's one thing that's perfectly obvious, Mario, and we have to accept it whether we like it or not, and it is that a country's like a family, exactly the same, take away authority and wham! catastrophe. I'll never be thankful enough to God that your cousin Luisito Bolado called you to persuade you to withdraw the complaint, it was really something the way he behaved, anybody else would have taken for granted you were guilty and not bothered, it was quite a favor, and you, instead of thanking him for it, kept insisting it was a conspiracy, you wouldn't accept a milder word, that all of them were against you, same old song, you don't see anything but enemies everywhere, hallucinations, my boy, the man who fears has reason to fear, as poor Mama used to say. You're so stubborn! Like a little child, Mario, at bottom that's what you are, everybody in agreement except the doctor, a conspiracy of silence, it was no use trying to convince you, you get hold of an idea and no one can make you back down, no matter what the consequences. And after all, these things happen to you because you're so sloppy, because if you came along dressed like you ought to be, with your trousers pressed and your shoes clean, and if you left the bicycle at home, which is where it belongs, do you think there's a policeman who'd lay a hand on you? No, Mario, and they're not manias of mine, everyone ought to dress according to his class, and a gentleman's always a gentleman, and he gets a different kind of respect and a different kind of consideration, no two ways about it, and it's natural besides, but if you go out on the street dressed anyhow, with your lapels turned up and wearing a beret, can you tell me what makes you look different from a laborer, and even more if it's at night? And I'm not going to say that it served you right because that's not true, you could have fallen just the same even if you were well dressed, but the fact is that if a policeman, or half a dozen policemen, see you with your hat on, and with decent clothes, well turned out, it wouldn't occur to them, mind you, and they wouldn't have stopped you, I'm absolutely sure of it, because they'd be able to see a mile off that you were an influential person and a man of substance. But the way you go around, a person would think you did it on purpose, Mario, what's surprising about the fact that they take you for a nobody and even slap you around? No, Mario, that's something I won't be able to forgive you for if I live a thousand years, that sloppiness of yours, you glory in it, and then smoking that tobacco that you don't see anywhere any more, it stinks, my boy, because even supposing that they stopped you, if you smelled of good tobacco, you probably think it's foolishness, but do you believe the policeman wouldn't have begged your pardon? "Excuse me, I've taken you for something you weren't," that's for sure, why, it's what you'd expect, clothes may not make the man but they do count, I should say they do, I've seen it so many times, why, even in good society, you poor fool, you show up wearing a designer outfit and you're somebody, and the best people will say, "Who's that woman?" see, they get interested, "That girl's not from around here," and if you step out of a Mercedes, still more, we may all be made of the same clay, I won't argue about that, but after all we're human.

XXIV

·························

But they seeing him walking upon the sea, thought it was an apparition, and they cried out. For they all saw him, and were troubled, but I'll never get tired of telling you, Mario, to be frightened without knowing what you're frightened of is to be an idiot, but a drooling idiot, my boy, just like it sounds, and you kept saying that it was like when you were a youngster and going to take an exam, something like that, in the stomach, but don't you realize that you've finished with exams, you utter fool! But no sir, you went on and on, "It's the solar plexus, I can't ... " I don't know why in the world Luis, knowing you as he does, how apprehensive you are and so on, gives you explanations, ever since you learned that about the solar plexus, just like with the structures, my boy, more of the same, you never stopped talking about it, heavens, what a man! and then that insignificant Moyano could still say the other day, I heard him all right, I pretended I hadn't, you tell me, a tormented sensitivity or I don't know what kind of a tale, you and your kind, instead of talking so that people can understand you, it seems like you talk in code, my boy, like those people in counterespionage, that's what Armando said, "I can't understand why they think so much. They think as if there was something that had to be fixed, but I don't know of anything that doesn't work," that's natural. And even so he

didn't see you at nights, Mario, that was when the perfor-
mance used to start, "Are they coming?" and you'd be stiff as
a board, listening, sitting on the bed, and I was all upset, I can
tell you that, "Who's coming?" and you, "I don't know, they
were coming up the stairs," you'd say, and I didn't dare to
move a finger, my heart going bam, bam, bam, I swear to you,
"I don't hear anything, Mario," and you, "Not now, it was
before," see, you're not going to believe it, but then it would
take me more than a quarter of an hour to get back to sleep,
that wasn't living, it was a nightmare. Like the time when you
came out with that fool statement that you were afraid you'd
get the idea of committing suicide, who ever heard of such a
thing, to be afraid of your own self, well, just don't get the
idea, smarty, it's up to you, it's drawing a pretty fine line to be
afraid of an idea. And then that you were losing your balance,
and that you got dizzy just from thinking that you were on a
ball suspended in the infinite, I told it to Valen, "The things
he says, Valen; he's crazy enough to be shut up," and because
of that to lie in bed, you certainly led a great life at the expense
of your nerves, my boy, what Antonio said, see, if he could
have done what he wanted to, but he's only a small cog in a
big machine, he answers to the Ministry, and the only thing
was to give you a sick leave, with half salary, just what we
needed, I don't think a couple of hours a day at the High
School, repeating the same things as always, would have killed
you. But no sir, "I wouldn't be able to stand it," and "It's too
much for me," don't you think that's lovely? that your ideas
were all mixed up, take note of what I've gone through with
my sick headaches, something horrible, sweetheart, exactly
like I was being pounded on the head with a hammer, but no,
naturally, that wasn't important, "Take a couple of aspirins,
tomorrow you'll be good as new," how pleasant. And it wasn't

that Luis didn't tell you, "The best cure, a little willpower," of course since you've never had any, you don't have a clue as to what willpower is, and so, to bed, to rest from doing nothing, like I say. And even so, if being in bed had brought you closer to me, it'd pass, but not even that consolation, the same as if you'd gone to bed with a sergeant in the army, that's what's hardest to bear, mind you, and it isn't for the thing in itself, you know full well that I don't care about all that nastiness one way or the other, it's what it stands for, of course, it was an old story, Mario, after what happened in Madrid, that's right, don't think that every woman would have put up with it, an insult like that, I haven't even told Valen about it, see, it makes me so ashamed, and Valen for me, you know she is, like a sister. That's for sure, it wasn't for lack of tears you shed, to this day I still haven't found out what you were crying about, you used to ruin my nightgown, my boy, to the point I'd have to change it, and you kept on and on with your refrain, that you'd rather they cut off your arms and your legs if the part that was left could live happily, anything but living the way you were, what a crazy thing to say, who's going to live and be happy without arms and legs, who ever thought of such a thing, the first nights I used to think, "Is he drunk?" but heavens no, why, you never touched a drop. But there weren't any good days for you any more, or bad ones either, take the night I started to tickle you with my foot, remember? a little hint, see, and what a start you gave, dear boy, and then, for no reason at all, sobbing and sobbing like somebody was killing you, go on, leave me alone, you left me cold as ice, because, after all, if I did that it was for your own good, because as far as I'm concerned . . . And I'm telling you, it showed on me, eh? I don't know what there was about me during those months, but Eliseo San Juan went wild, "You're terrific, you're terrific, every day you get more terrific," but beside himself, much more than other times, at first it scared me, I promise you, what a persecution, but what Valen says, after all, honey, it's a tribute. And what about poor Valen? Don't tell me, Mario, twice you left her high and dry with the meal on the table, twice, Mario, it's so easy to say, she'd done the best she could, you know what she's like, and you with your nauseas or your fibs, and thank goodness Valen's a good friend and Vicente understands, if not I could have killed you, because after all, she did it to give you something to do, but that doesn't apply with you. "Why? Why? Why?" so many whys, you blockhead! Well, what are those things for, stupid, but to kill time, see, to make time pass without noticing it; that's what it's about, heavens, at least I think so. You were impossible then, Mario, like a spoiled child, "I can't stand another day like this; the same as yesterday. My God, give me peace of mind," that was a fine thing to ask God for, you utter fool, when we need so many other things, you aren't right in the head. Nerves, some excuse that is, when doctors don't know what to invent they go and blame it on nerves, because what I say is, Mario, if nothing hurts you and you don't have a fever, what are you complaining about? Of course, when you come right down to it, it's the fault of us women and nobody but us women because we're at your beck and call all the livelong day, we're a bunch of dummies, but if you men were afraid we were going to step out on you, you wouldn't even remember your nerves. Either that or working, this thing with the nerves, nobody can get the idea out of my head, is a lazybones' disease, if you were in an office or a bank, where you'd work eight hours straight the way you ought to, it'd be another story, in every sense, mind you. It's like the fuss about sleeping, smarty, why, you spent the livelong day, as you might say, lying in bed. If you'd moved around a little, you'd have seen what was good for you, but a person can't eat without working up an appetite, as poor Mama would say. You men really amuse me, Mario, you get sick when you feel like it and get well when you take the notion, because don't tell me, if when you felt dizzy you took it seriously, just imagine where I'd be, I can't even climb on a chair without feeling dizzy. Why, even in the bus, take note of that, what can you tell me about dizziness? I'd like to see you in Paco's big Citroën, Mario, sure, just for a minute, see, out of pure whim, so you'd know what dizziness was. Holy God! it seemed like you didn't touch the ground. Actually I didn't want to, I can swear to that, for no particular reason, but people are so evil-minded, and Crescente was snooping all the time from his delivery cart, but Paco opened the door for me and I didn't have the courage to say no. And imagine the coincidence, a few days later the same thing, he put on the brakes just like in the movies, Mario, "Are you going downtown?" right at the bus stop, such a coincidence, and then when I told him I didn't know how to drive, that we didn't have a car, you can't imagine how he hit himself, really hard, eh? "No, no, no!" like he didn't believe it, see, he thought I was kidding, and I didn't know what kind of an expression to put on, Mario, I felt so awfully humiliated. If you'd had Paco's talent you wouldn't have been frightened of routine, Mario, I can tell you that, saying you just have breakfast, work, eat, make love, sleep, every day exactly the same, "Like mules yoked to a treadmill," what did you think, what else is there to do, you chump, just the same but in different places, look at Paco, but as for the rest, we're animals of habit, big news that is, do you mean a person can be scared of doing the same thing every day too? Don't be cross, Mario, but I think that the thing that frightened you was working, because don't come and tell me now that writing is work, some soft job that is, you're so anxious to justify yourself that you'd say the sun came up in the west, there's no difference between writing and playing the violin. And especially, if you were so scared of it, you shouldn't have done it, as far as my wishes are concerned, you know that already, anything else was better, salesmanship, or a business, or construction, just think nowadays with the thing about the industrial park, even, anything, you say yourself that it makes you sick to your stomach to read the newspaper, who doesn't feel the same, in that *El Correo* I dislike so much you don't tell anything but miseries, I should say so, and then going on about frivolity and violence, coward, you're a miserable coward, and that men don't understand one another, and what do you care? We'd be in fine shape if we lost our appetites every time the Chinamen or the negroes had a fight. Let everybody take care of himself as best he can, sweetheart! After all, it's no one's fault if they're peculiar. But from that to writing the way you write, there's a great distance, *El Correo* makes me feel sick too and I don't think my nerves are in bad shape, you stubborn thing, lots of times I think that you were well when you were sick and sick when you were well, even though that seems like a contradiction. Nerves, nerves . . . nerves start to tune up when a person's too well off, that's right, when a person has everything solved and lives quietly and without worries. Then the nerves and everything else come to the fore, I don't know what in the world that fear of yours was, "Are they coming?" you used to scare me to death, my boy, and waking me up without the slightest consideration, I'd like to know who you were waiting for, I couldn't worm it out of you with a corkscrew, and it isn't that I approve of staying up late as a general thing, understand, not at all, but everybody has the right to go to bed when he feels like it. It was like that crying of yours, the first few times you broke my heart, eh? My God, what sobs! And "Why are you crying, darling?" and you, "I don't even know, for everything and nothing," do you think that was any way to behave? And Luis even encouraged you, he's nothing but an old softy, "Uncontrolled emotional activity. Depression," the first part, well, I admit it, but what I told him was, and I'm not sorry for it, Mario, he had it coming to him, "I won't accept your depression," you tell me if you had any reason, you really are something, meals on time, shirts always ironed, a woman looking after you, what more can a man want? Now if he'd told me that everything that didn't come out at the time was coming out of you now, that's another story, but he should have talked plain, without going round and round it, let him call a spade a spade, doctors talk the way they write, don't tell me, nobody understands them but the pharmacists, and even in that case only some of them, they're just trying to give themselves airs. Because what I say is, high or low, everybody has a lot of tears to shed in this life, it's like a factory, that's logical, and if you don't shed them at the right time you shed them at the wrong time, no two ways about it. And it wasn't as if I didn't warn you, sweetheart, remember when your mother died, I was always after you, everywhere, "Go on, Mario, cry; if you don't it'll come out later and be worse," like your shadow, and then you, suddenly, "Because it's the custom?" you left me cold as ice, honestly, I don't think that's any way to behave, if I gave you advice it was for your own good, with the best intentions in the world, I swear. And with the business of Elviro and José María, more of the same, a poker face and that was it, didn't shed a tear, I don't know but what all that hasn't given you a complex, the most likely thing, but

you, you just clammed up and not a word, and you had me
mighty close by to talk it all out with, and maybe not in other
ways, but nobody's more understanding than I am, and what
you ought to have done was to talk to me about them, because
I admired Elviro, I'm not just saying it now, you know that,
and José María, apart from his ideas, I really liked, honestly,
he impressed me, mind you, and after he asked me if I was
the girl you liked, I used to run away from him, see, I hid in
doorways, and Transi, "Are you stupid? Do you think he's
going to eat you?" but I don't know, I couldn't help it, it was
like he could guess what I was thinking about, I used to turn
all red, little-girl stuff really, but I couldn't even say a word.
Now I come to think about it, what you had was a complex, it
wasn't nerves at all, sure, a great big complex, and because
you didn't talk it out in time, if you'd talked to me about your
brothers I'd have been delighted, just imagine, nothing I would
have liked more, what I couldn't allow, understand, that's
ridiculous, was to have you come out with the tale about how
your brothers thought the same and that José María, from his
side, went too far, and Elviro, from his, didn't go far enough,
what an idea, see, Elviro was a lovely person, and José María,
no matter how you look at it, was a dangerous man. It's like
that about what he said, when they were going to shoot him,
imagine, that it wasn't the first time a just man was dying for
others, lies, half dead with fright is what he was and praying
My Lord Jesus Christ, naturally, it isn't that I'm blaming him
for it, understand, it seems logical to me, but you and your
kind, as long as you can make a phrase, are even capable of
betraying the memory of the dead.

XXV

I have strengthened thee, and have helped thee, yes, with you there, it's a help, I understand that myself, but if the girl doesn't take to studying, I don't intend to reproach her for it, you have to respect a child's personality, Mario, and each one is a different person, and if you stop to think about it the lower-level exam is more than the higher certificate used to be, everything else is the same, and just look at money, a peseta of back then is like a hundred nowadays, and maybe I'm putting it low, it doesn't seem so but the cost of living has gone up twenty times. An awful lot is asked of youngsters nowadays, Mario, don't kid yourself, and only the extra-bright kids, you look at the García Caseros, pigs, and most of the people who count are like them, farms and salesmanship, see, all in the best of taste, don't tell me, why even the girls themselves, you should hear Menchu's crowd, "Boys with degrees, not a bit of it; they're such bores," and they're right in some ways, Mario, because can you tell me what university boy nowadays is the life of the party? Not one, it's a sure thing, it never fails, why, they don't know how, they don't even know how to hold a glass in their hand, that's logical, it's either one thing or the other, forget about noble concerns, stubborn, you're very stubborn, because what the girl has to do, and thank God she'll have no lack of choices, is to find herself a fiancé of the right kind, as for privations her mother has had enough of those. Just look at Julia, fat lot of good her noble concern for music has done her, there she is, taking in roomers, see, you tell me, all the Americans you please, students and so on, that's true, the very best class of people, maybe so, but only up to a point, remember about that negro, I don't know why in the world you got so angry with Papa, it's not fair, Mario, you heard him in the survey on TV, he said it loud and clear, and he was marvelous, mind you, even the Vice-President for Commerce congratulated him, "We're all children of God; the racial problem is a problem of souls and not bodies," take note, I don't think you could say more in fewer words, Valen was thrilled, and I was too, of course, but from there to having one in the house . . . And there's no reason for you to take that attitude, Mario, none at all, see, apart from the natural repugnance, just think of the extra work a negro must cause, imagine, if only in the amount of laundry, and frankly, I understand Papa, "A supplement of thirty dollars or I won't take it on," just like everyone else would have done, naturally, but that doesn't change Papa's feelings, Mario, he said it on TV loud and clear, "We're all children of God," clearer than running water, my boy, and then outside, everybody saying how wonderful, see, and if those foreigners thought like Christians, like Papa, there wouldn't be any racial problems and so on in the world. I'm with Papa, Mario, completely in agreement, everybody equal, for God there aren't any differences, blacks and whites exactly the same, now then, the blacks with the blacks and the whites with the whites, everyone in his own little house and everybody happy, and if that university, whatever it's called, I never will learn how to say it, wants to shove a negro off on me, let him pay double, see, dogs are God's creatures too and nobody thinks about having them live in houses. Got to be reasonable, darling, and look at things with a teeny bit of objectivity, Papa said it loud and clear, "We're all children of God," but that's as far as souls are concerned, it has to do with eternal salvation, understand? but there's no divine law that forces you to accept a roomer of a different color, fine thing if there were. And stop dropping little hints and saying that there's a long way between word and deed, you're just trying to confuse the issue, you always did enjoy looking for your neighbor's faults, because what I say is, if there aren't any negroes in Madrid he'd better not come, if you stop to think about it nobody asked him, let him study at home, you're not going to tell me now that there aren't any universities in America, you've heard Vicente, perfectly good ones. Don't get angry, Mario, but I think the negroes must send Don Nicolás coconuts or something; if not, I can't explain it, just look at how he defends them, I don't know if he has a black grandfather or something, but he can say whatever he wants to, negroes, you only have to think about it a little bit, are made of different clay, for a different kind of work, sugarcane and all that, boxers at most, anything, but the point is jobs that take brute strength, don't tell me it's not so, all of them. That's why you made me angry, Mario, why should I hide it from you, when you wrote that letter to Papa, saying that it's one thing to preach and the other to practice, there's a long way between word and deed, he didn't deserve that, you're ungrateful, I know it's been twenty-four years, but if it hadn't been for poor Papa, who drew up such a terrific report for you, how would you have won the competition, of course that's not important to you, trifles, but if he charged higher rent for a negro, see, what do thirty dollars mean to those people, then it was a sacrilege, I'd like to know who gave you the right to butt in, what you can't forgive Papa for is that he doesn't like your books, that he should be candid about them, just look how you hated it when he said that the social factor or whatever is the refuge of people who don't know how to write, which, furthermore, let's not beat around the bush, is a big fat truth. I've only seen you as upset as that when Recondo put Crusade instead of your civil war, what difference does that make, like I say, or when the business about the policeman, or when the thing about the apartment happened, I'd like to know what you were thinking of, you're always putting your foot in it, and then to keep insisting that, since the apartments were for public servants, preferably married and preferably with large families, legally they didn't have a leg to stand on, it makes me laugh, you men only pay attention to laws when they suit you, and then in the end, why, Canido didn't have any children, look, how many children can a widower sixty years old and I don't know how much more have, or Agustín Vega, he's a bachelor, and all of them were like that, at least they're people who're politically reliable, don't argue about that, but what a person can't do, you rascal, get it into your head, no matter how much of a public servant he is and how large a family he has, is to bluster about things, taking the attitude of "Here I stand," that's why there's a commission or whatever it's called, and it chooses this one yes and that one no, especially because of their past behavior, so there, even though the law doesn't say so, everybody understands it, and that whole story about appealing was ridiculous, you tell me, you get into a quarrel with the authorities and you'd have no apartment at all and, if you really want the truth, you'd even have to sell the bedroom furniture. Stupidities, Mario, you're such an innocent, you talk just to be talking, "It's a question of justice; I'll go as high as I have to," you scare me, mind you, you scare me half to death, yelling, "It's a question of justice," all over town, and thank goodness Luisito Bolado dissuaded you, because after the thing about the policeman, as soon as I saw him, I said to myself, "Mario's going to throw him out, he's perfectly capable of it," honestly, I still don't know how he had the nerve, I was terrified, and what he said in the end was, they've given you a three-room top floor, they haven't broken the law, you're the one who doesn't accept it, well, that was for sure, what were we going to do with three rooms, I agree, but before the council met, at the time they finished roofing the building, I could have done something, Mario, and you stood your ground, you're so obstinate, just look at Josechu, his parents on visiting terms with mine all my life, I could have thought of something to soften that whole business about the minutes, and exactly the same with Oyarzun and Solórzano, we could have collected plenty of recommendations, I don't know what that stubbornness of yours is good for, "If you do a single thing, I'll withdraw the application," I could have killed you, crying for a month, I skipped a period and everything, I swear, because the delegate came out in your favor and however little Josechu, Oyarzun, Solórzano or Filgueira himself would have supported you, the apartment was ours, you can be sure of that, imagine, six rooms, central heating and hot water, would've changed my life. But it served you right, Mario, after all you reaped what you sowed, neither more nor less, if you hadn't been so tiresome about insisting on a vote count, or set yourself up against Solórzano, when after all, it was all the same to you, and if you hadn't taken the attitude you did about the policeman and if, instead of that, as the saying goes, you'd gone to Filgueira and said, "You're right, Filgueira, I was mistaken," there wouldn't have been a force in the world strong enough to take the apartment away from us, I'm telling you from where I stand. And even with that and everything else, Mario, why kid ourselves, if you'd left my hands free, you'd have seen! a woman has a lot of ways, my boy, even without having to lower herself, to make people feel sorry for her, nothing's lost by trying, I don't know who you people think you are with a university degree, see, a university degree sounds so important, and when you come right down to it, what's a university graduate? a poor half-starved fellow, that's what, look at Paco, he hasn't needed degrees to be a personality, you people think that you can get somewhere with books and the only thing that books are good for is to fill your head as tight as a drum, I don't know how many people of that kind who've denied God, and you, to give just one example, see, saying it was a pity the Church didn't support the French Revolution, a blasphemy like that, when I saw you take communion the next day, I was cold as ice, I promise you, even Bene, for your information, said, "He must have confessed, didn't he?" and I, "Why, I suppose so," look, what was I going to answer her, you place me in the most difficult positions, just like the lecture, you tell me what's so bad about charity parties, they collect a lot of money and they're for very good purposes. You really amuse me, Mario, well, amuse me, you know what I mean, there are times a person laughs so as not to cry, you don't know how to do anything but make objections, and then, remember what happened with Hernando de Miguel's lamb, you don't know yourself if you've done right or wrong, and you start to have scruples, that's natural, saying you can't move a finger without offending someone, what nonsense, look in my mirror, do I offend? I don't, do I? Well, of course I don't, and look, even if I do talk a lot, I never stop, you tell me, a chatterbox, lots of times, if I don't have anyone to talk to, to myself, just think what a laugh, if anybody were to see me, but I don't care at all, if I have a clear conscience then gossip doesn't bother me. Complexes, that's what you and your kind have, you're full of complexes, Mario, it's just like the thing about the napkin rings, when we've got so little to do, you ought to teach other things to the children, thank God none of them has a contagious disease. But no sir, each child has to have his napkin ring, things always have to be the way you say, a mania, it could still pass when I was at home, with just a small family, but here, would you like to tell me what we gain by that? It's spreading lack of trust, neither more nor less, even Doro herself, and you know she adores you, you ought to hear her, "I don't know what our master is thinking of; it isn't as if somebody was sick in the chest," which is what I say, if, thank God, we're all well, why so much formality? You don't take any responsibility, which is the thing that makes me the most furious, and then, one fine day, you take a notion, "Have to put our shoulders to the wheel," you have to start by taking things as they are, stupid, and if certain things can't be they can't be, we've got a lot of kids and a lot of problems, a house doesn't run itself, and if you ever saw me sitting still you might complain, but you tell me, I don't stop working by day or by night, I don't have a minute even to breathe, you have to listen to reason, Mario, and as for not having things, there's not even space to store clothes, you can see that yourself, the shape we're in, look at yesterday, couldn't even budge, and you could still say, "If you do a single thing, I'll withdraw the application," look, how lovely, we had it right in our hands, and if I'd had an apartment like that it would have changed my life, just like it sounds, I should say so, and after all, there wouldn't have been any harm in reminding Josechu that his parents used to visit mine, anything rather than trusting to the fact that you're a public servant with a large family, everybody knows, Mario, it's nothing new, that requisites are passed over when it suits the powers that be, I remember poor Mama, may she rest in peace, "If you don't set up a howl you don't get fed," take note, but I get furious with you, Mario, honestly, it seemed like the heavens were going to fall if you asked for a recommendation, when in this life everything's recommendations, you scratch my back and I'll scratch yours, it's always been like that, that's what we're here for, I've heard Mama say so many times, "The man with sponsors gets baptized," but you can't do anything the ordinary way, we know that, the requisites, "I'm a public servant and have a large family; they don't have a leg to stand on," what's the use of counting on you, my boy, you and your kind seize on the law when it suits you, and you don't want to recognize that the law's administered by men, and it isn't the law, which neither feels nor suffers, but those men that you have to cultivate and play up to, that doesn't disgrace anyone, blockhead, you spend your whole life sticking darts in people and then, just because the law says so, you think everybody has to go on their knees to you, and if they don't give you the apartment, a lawsuit, an appeal, isn't that lovely, against the authorities, just what we needed, I don't know the kind of a world you live in, dear boy, it seems like you've dropped from the moon.

XXVI

....

And the vision of all shall be unto you as the words of a book that is sealed, which when they shall deliver to one that is learned, they shall say: Read this: and he shall answer: I cannot, for it is sealed. And the book shall be given to one that knoweth no letters, and it shall be said to him: Read: and he shall answer: I know no letters. It's the same as you, Mario, you made me laugh, honestly, how serious you were in that interview saying that people didn't read in Spain today, you think because they don't read you that the same thing's going to happen to everybody else, I'm sick and tired of telling you that as far as writing, you know how to write, you write easily and all that, but, my boy, about things that are so boring and about people who are so unattractive that your books fall right out of a person's hands, honestly. And it isn't just me saying it, remember Papa, and Papa's somebody in these matters, goodness, I think so, well, you heard him, he didn't exactly mince words, "If he writes to amuse himself, well and good, but if he's looking for fame or money he should try a different tack," it couldn't have been clearer, and Papa, you know that, an authority, at *ABC* they think the world of him, he isn't exactly a nobody, that was some report he made for you, a regular book, my boy, why, even though I never went in much for reading, I gulped it down without taking a breath, three times, you wouldn't believe it, I remember I was fascinated by all that stuff about the regressive method, all that about studying history backward, like crabs, because everything has its what-for, as the saying goes, things don't happen by chance. Even apart from his being my father, you should have had the report published in the House of Culture, mind you, it would have been a big success, I'd bet anything on that, because even though it was short and so on, you could fix that with a little bit larger type, there was a lot to it, today what people want, don't kid yourself, is books about love or books with substance, one or the other, but you can be sure nobody buys a book to be bored or to waste time, that's what I'm getting at, stupid, can you tell me who was going to read your things, and pardon my frankness, if your characters are either poor or dumb? Think about *The Sand Castle,* to give just one example, and I say that one though it could be any other, a yokel who has his land stolen from him, piece by piece, until he hasn't anything left but the clothes he stands up in, a dirty savage who, to put on the finishing touch, has a toothless wife who spends all her time insulting him. And that can still pass, but *The Inheritance* is even worse, just imagine at this time of day, who's going to be interested in the story of a common soldier who goes to war in a country that doesn't exist and doesn't want to kill anyone, or get killed, and as if that wasn't enough his feet hurt. I'm telling you, Mario, sweetheart, if you searched high and low you couldn't possibly find weirder characters, and especially now, see, saying that soldiers are nothing but savages, mind you, why, the boys from families that are a little bit you-know, lower class, with these new militias, are all officers, I promise you that when you started *The Right Arm,* the day you told me the main character wasn't poor, I was so tickled, I swear I was, that for a moment I thought, I must seem like a fool, that you were going to write the story about Maximino Conde to give me a surprise, because whether you like it or not, it was a plot for the movies, but no, of course not . . . That Ciro Pérez, you couldn't have found a more vulgar name, my boy, is a kind of mentally retarded person, and the little he does think might as well be Greek, a ridiculous person who doesn't know what he wants or where he's going, that was so mixed up, sweetheart, that I didn't understand a syllable, but I had the willpower to learn parts of it by heart, long ones, eh? and I could rattle them off like a parrot, so as to discuss them afterwards with my friends, one passage was like that thing about the farmer from Villaloma, the one who wrote to Valen, yes, you know, he met her during a hunting party, she was married and everything, the letter was so funny that we all learned it by heart, it began, "If your interest in me is negative to the point that you do not wish to answer me, I implore you Valentina to hear me, though it be only out of friendship," do you remember? terrifically funny, well, I did the same, Mario, I took and learned a paragraph, one that said, "In doing good, Ciro felt a complaisance, an unconfessed satisfaction, from which was automatically excluded any meritorious interpretation of his actions and one open to the possibility of a later correction. Hence his torture . . . " What do you think of that? doesn't it make you think awfully much of the letters of that fellow from Villaloma? Tell me the truth, Mario, that was quite a paragraph, don't tell me, not even if you'd done it on purpose, Valen nearly died laughing, but, my boy, Esther got mad for no reason at all, imagine how she reacted, what did it have to do with her anyway, and she kept on explaining, but impolitely, eh? calling us all kinds of things, telling us what Ciro Pérez meant by it, and I only had to hear Ciro Pérez and fall off my chair

laughing, and Valen I hardly need to tell you, and Esther more
and more furious, and that we were a couple of illiterates,
well, what Ciro Pérez meant, according to Esther, was that
every time he made room on the sidewalk, or gave up his seat
on the bus, and my goodness, here between you and I, what a
nuisance he is, he feels satisfaction and thinks, "I'm good,"
sort of with a little bit of pride, do you understand what
Esther meant? Well, the minute he starts to feel proud, making
room on the sidewalk stops being a meritorious action and
can even be sinful, you can see how he ties himself in knots,
even you would never have thought of such a thing, I'm sure
of that, and then Valen began to yell, "But that man's stupid,
honey!" and I started to laugh, an attack, Mario, just like
you're hearing it, and Esther I don't have to tell you, more and
more excited, until all of a sudden, she'd turned all red, and
she began to scream at me, "Don't laugh like that, Carmen,
don't laugh like that, that man may be your husband!" look
what a dumb thing to say, it was to embarrass me, so there,
and I, "Listen, sweetie, please," I was laughing my head off, I
couldn't hold it in, Mario, it was impossible, too funny, holy
God! and she said it was useless to try to make us understand
tensions like that, I think she said tensions, you know she
always uses such fancy words that nobody can stand her, and
that instead of giving up a seat I should substitute refusing to
sign some minutes or buying a jumping jack in Madrid, as I
was saying that you'd done, and then Valen came out and
said, "Mario might do it, but then he doesn't hand himself
idiotic problems," and Esther saying that what did we know
about the internal conflicts of any man, you tell me, some
conflict, so what I said was, "Esther, sweetie, don't exaggerate,
I know my husband better than you do," but Valen kept on
laughing and then Esther cleared out and went away scream-

ing that we didn't have the slightest touch of sensitivity, see, it annoyed me, what does she know, and maybe not in other ways, but sensitivity, my God, it's one of my things, you know it, sweetheart, why, when I'm unwell I can't even make mayonnaise, everything curdles on me, I have enough trouble without that, and Esther may be a very good friend and everything else you please, but just because she went to the university she puts on such airs that nobody can stand her, I'm absolutely perplexed when I start wondering how she gets along with Armando, they couldn't be more different, he has that vitality, why he thinks about nothing but eating, but the truth is he's crazy about her, he's not about to let anyone touch his little wifie, just look at the fuss he raised the other night at the Atrium, and really about nothing, about whether somebody looked at her or didn't look at her, I don't know, sometimes the thought comes to me that you might have done better with Esther, and other times I think not, too much alike doesn't work out either, I don't know, it's a complication, but the sure thing is, Mario, let's not kid ourselves, that you're not the type of man who's attractive to women, physically you surely aren't much, let's be frank, but you must have something, some hidden charm, because if a woman does like you, you bowl her over, eh? if the truth be told, there's Esther and there's your sister-in-law Encarna, it's a good thing I'm not the jealous type, because otherwise . . . I'd like you to hear Esther at the Thursday teas, if your books come into the conversation, everybody knows, they're gospel, symbols, theses, whatever, she's some advocate, my boy, I don't know why your ears don't buzz till you go deaf on Thursdays, gosh, what sermons, saying lots more than she has a right to, God help us, you tell me, that I shouldn't encourage you to look for another kind of job, see, that would mean destroying your

potential, imagine, honestly, I don't know where she found all
that talent in you, what I said one day, she was furious, of
course, with Armando's factory she doesn't have to worry
about money, what I told her was, "If talent's no good to earn
money with, then it's not talent, honeybunch," because that's
the honest truth, Mario, don't tell me, always praising and
praising you, I get sick and tired of it. That fool Esther prides
herself on knowing you better than anybody but she doesn't
know the half of it, I'd like to see her in my shoes, she
wouldn't last two weeks, I can assure you of that, because
books are one thing and the person's another very different
thing, there's nobody more obstinate than you are, and it isn't
just me saying it, "Gardenia" said it already, and loud and
clear too, remember? the handwriting expert there was at *El
Correo* before Don Nicolás came, when *El Correo* was still
readable, it was a pleasure, well, I sent her a sheet of your
writing without your knowing it, and she really drew a portrait
of you, my boy, I've never seen anything like it in my life, I
thought, "This woman knows him, for sure," she couldn't have
said more in fewer words, even Valen, see, "Why, she's made
a portrait of him," she was laughing so hard, and then she'd
read it, "Persevering, idealistic, and impractical; cherishes dis-
proportionate ambitions," what do you think of that? You put
"obstinate" where it says "persevering," and "deluded" where
it says "idealistic," and "lazy" where it says "impractical" and
you have your complete description, nobody would say,
sweetheart, that a person could get so many things out of
anyone's handwriting. And that fool Esther can still say that I
didn't have the sensitivity to appreciate you, look, what does
she know, sensitivity of all things, if she'd said something else,
why I remember Mama, may she rest in peace, "Child, you're
like a barometer," if I started to make mayonnaise when I was

unwell, everybody knew, it'd be ruined, and don't tell me, Mario, you were right beside me, when my tooth fell into the swimming pool, I shook and everything, eh? and then a week in bed throwing up, I was sick all over, what a miserable thing to have happen, I could have killed that wretched Chucho Prada, "Your own teeth'll fall out before the one I put in for you does," as if I could have trusted him. If that isn't sensitivity, let Esther say what sensitivity is, the stupid woman thinks that sensitivity is reading, stuffing herself with books, the more boring the better, it isn't that I'm going to say that I'm so cultivated, Mario, I don't even have time to be, you know that, but I'm no illiterate either, Mario, look, your report, well, Papa's, three times, and it wasn't exactly an amusing book, and Canido's, you can say whatever you want to, I love them, and yours, Mario, don't tell me, all of them, one after another, and learning paragraphs by heart, from A to Z, and before I was married *The Scarlet Pimpernel* and, ten times at least, *He Will Come by Sea,* I just adored it, I've never enjoyed a book so much, honestly, it had a special charm, that fool Esther gives herself such airs, as if she'd been the only one who ever read. And now that I remember, Mario, I also read from start to finish the book of poems by that friend of yours, Barcés, or Bornés, remember? the one we happened to meet in Madrid on our wedding trip, from Granada I think, he talked all the time about García Lorca, he was sort of red-haired and she was plump, very dark, you'd known him, I think, during the war, don't pay too much attention to that, I'm not sure, he was kind of shy, well, it doesn't matter, but I read the book all in one sitting, there were some awfully weird lines, some were really short and others really long, no connection between them at all, jumbled up, when I finished it I got a horrible headache, do you remember? different from other times, sort of in the middle of my head. What was the name of that friend of yours, goodness, I have it on the tip of my tongue, he spoke very low, like he was confessing, with a little bit of an accent and you and he spent the afternoon reciting poems to each other, sure you did, in a café on the Gran Vía, it was on a corner, what a memory I have! all full of mirrors, when you went in you'd bump into them, it was like a labyrinth? What an afternoon, holy God! the only thing, if you'd recited the one about my eyes, I remember that every time you started on a poem I'd think, "He's going to say the one about my eyes," but no, no, just a daydream, what I wouldn't have given, if Elviro hadn't told me I wouldn't have known a thing, mind you, "Does Mario read you his poems?" and I was so aston- ished, "Does Mario write poetry? It's the first I've heard of it," and he, "Since he was so high," and then he told me that you'd written one to my eyes and I was half dead of curiosity, mind you, every woman's dream, but when I asked you, "A weakness, they're mushy and sentimental," and nobody could budge you from that, and that's something that just makes me sick, Mario, because to write poems to nobody doesn't make sense, it's like going out on the street and yelling at random, it's for crazy people, Borrés! No, it wasn't Borrés, but some- thing like it, anyway it began with a B, don't you know who I mean, Mario? He was sort of sloppy, very plainly dressed, like you, and she was Andalusian, dark, her hair pulled back, and she used the formal mode of address to us all the time, "Because you," "Because coming from you," and she told that story that was so funny about the fair in Seville, the one about the horse, that one, one of the times I've heard you laugh the hardest, don't you remember? Yes, of course, how maddening! we were sitting near the entrance, sort of on the right, on a red sofa that ran along one wall, and you and he opposite, and he kept hitching up his trousers, and then, after he'd left, we remarked on how hairy he was, sort of dull . . . Barnés! That's it, Barnés, Joaquín Barnés, I think it was Joaquín, Mario, I'm sure, what a relief, goodness, what a weight that's taken off me!

XXVII

To put off, according to former conversation, the old man, who is
corrupted according to the desire of error. And he renewed in the
spirit of your mind: and put on the new man, really a different
man, I'd love to have you see him, Mario, just for the pleasure
of it, he's acquired a presence you wouldn't believe, with an
English sport jacket, sticking his elbow out the car window,
sort of very tanned and then, those eyes . . . absolutely dreamy!
he doesn't seem like the same person, you men have all the
luck, like I say, if you don't look like something at twenty you
only have to wait twenty more years, I don't know how you
do it. And I realized right away, just think, a big red Citroën
here, imagine, unmistakable, it couldn't be anyone else, and
though I tried to act like I hadn't seen him, wham! he stopped
dead, braking like in the movies, eh? and the car stopped for
a while, idling, and Paco kept smiling, "Going downtown?"
and I was all embarrassed, see, there was Crescente snooping
from his delivery cart, "Yes," "Well, climb in," and with the
door already open, what could I do, I slipped inside, and I
was more comfortable than on the sofa in our living room,
Mario, I promise you, and what I said was, "I'm crazy about
your car," which is the truth, it doesn't seem like you touch
the ground or anything. And then he turned the car around
and started off like a rocket for the road to the pine woods,

and I said, "Go back, are you out of your mind? What are people going to say?" but he didn't even pay attention, he stepped harder and harder on the gas and said, do you know what he said, he said, "Tell them to mind their own business," and both of us started to laugh, just imagine how crazy, the two of us alone in a Citroën at a hundred and ten kilometers, why, my head even started to spin, I swear it did, there are things that can't be explained, take note, that insignificant little kid who even used to mix up his words, you can't imagine now, a poise, a calmness, speaking quite low, no shouting, but just loud enough, like somebody who's been around, if you didn't see him you wouldn't have believed it, just look, in no time at all, what that man has accomplished, he's never stopped moving, my God, that ridiculous little shrimp! Actually, Transi had told me already, that afternoon I met her, take note, it was barely a month after Evaristo up and left, and she acted like nothing had happened, she's the kind who doesn't die of grief, of course she was always a teeny bit you-know, I don't know how to tell you, she never took things too seriously, imagine what a situation to be in, with three little ones, well, she was just the same, "Have you seen Paco? Kid, he's ever so attractive." And it's true, Mario, my, what a change, no matter how much I told you, you can't even imagine, such manners, such politeness, really a different man, I remember way back when, "diocese" for "dose" and things like that, he was an absolute disaster, I don't know about his parents, the father was a construction foreman if that, working-class people in any case, nobodies, though, if the truth be told, Paco was always intelligent and he behaved wonderfully during the war, his body's like a sieve, full of shrapnel wounds, you can't imagine. Well, you see him driving now and you're absolutely bowled over, what skill! he doesn't make a single unnecessary movement, you'd think he'd been born with the steering wheel in his hands. And then that smell he has, sort of good tobacco mixed with cologne, you can tell a mile off that he does sports, tennis and that, and when he smokes he doesn't even take the cigarette out of his mouth, see, at a hundred and ten, he must be crazy, and he blinks his eyes just like in the movies, and I said to him, I swear I did, "Turn around, Paco, I have heaps of things to do," but he kept on laughing, he has all his teeth, just imagine how lucky, "Let's make time; life's short," and off he went like a crazy man at a hundred and twenty, and just then we crossed with Higinio Oyarzun in his little ashcan, I'd like to know where he was coming from at that hour on that road, and I tried to scrunch down but I'm almost sure he saw me, imagine how fussed I was, and Paco, "Is anything the matter, little one?" and then, "Why, you're just the same," and I, "What a silly thing to say! Just think of the years it's been," and he, very polite, "Time doesn't pass the same way for everyone," an empty compliment, you'll say, but a person's grateful for it, why should I say anything different. And when he stopped the car he didn't take his eyes off me and he asked me, all of a sudden, I was so rattled, if I knew how to drive, and I said very little, hardly at all, and he went on saying that every day he saw me waiting in line for the bus, with all the ordinary people, and I didn't know where to look, I was more ashamed than I'd ever been in my life, I promise you, but what was I going to answer him, Mario, tell the truth and shame the devil, that we didn't have a car, that you were the kind of person who couldn't accept anything modern, and you can't imagine the way he behaved, I wish you could have seen him, "No, no, no!" like a crazy man, honestly, hitting himself on the head, naturally, that's what I say, sweetheart, years ago maybe not, but nowadays a car isn't a luxury, it's a working tool. And Paco kept lighting cigarettes one after the other, he must have smoked twenty if he smoked one, and "What's become of Transi?" and what I told him was that she hadn't been lucky, and if he remembered the old guys, well, Evaristo anyway, the tall one, he married her, when she was older herself, and five years later he'd abandoned her with three little children and gone off to America, to Guinea, I think, and then Paco said, "We all make mistakes, it isn't easy to choose right," I was so taken aback, his eyes misted up and everything, Mario, I can swear they did, it made me feel sorry for him, a big man like that, and I couldn't do less than ask, "Aren't you happy?" and he, "Let's not talk about that. I'm alive, and that's a good deal," but he kept looking at me more and more closely and I was all bewildered, see, thinking about the best way I could help him, and then I thought about recalling the times when we used to go walking on the promenade, back in our time, Mario, when that lout of an Armando used to put his fingers to his temples and bellow, remember? before we were engaged, well, I mentioned that, and he, "What times those were!" the way people do, and suddenly, "Maybe I lost my chance then. After that, you know, came the war," sort of sadly, but what I told him was, "But you behaved so awfully well during the war, Paco, don't say that," and then, for no reason, he unbuttoned his shirt, he doesn't wear a sweater or anything, in the middle of the winter, and showed me the scars on his chest, it was horrible, you can't even imagine, among the hair, who would have said, so masculine, as a boy he was sort of sissy looking, I felt cold as ice, I promise you, that was the last thing I expected, and I said to him, "Poor boy," just that, no more, I swear, but he put his arm across the back of the seat, I thought it was with good intentions, I swear, and before I realized it he was kissing me, all of a sudden, and yes, certainly, very hard, I didn't even know what he was doing, like a vice, yes, pressing so hard and very long, that's the truth, but I didn't respond at all, just like I'm telling you, I was sort of hypnotized, I swear to you, he'd been staring at me without stopping for I don't know how long, and then that smell that's partly cologne and partly good tobacco, it'd turn anyone's head, Valen can tell you that, she's mentioned it to me heaps of times, I only love you, I don't have to tell you that, but I was sort of stupefied, maybe it was the speed itself, not being used to it, who knows, could have been anything, I was like a bundle, just exactly, and my heart going bam, bam, bam, like it was out of control, you simply can't imagine, that was instinctively, my principles, of course, and I couldn't even wiggle a finger, I was like anesthetized, just exactly the same, I couldn't even hear the trees, just imagine, even if there were so many of them, only the murmur of his words, very close, of course, practically on top of me, it was like being up in the clouds, such confusion, and he opened the door and said, very softly, "Get out," and I was like a sleepwalker, I got out, but, like I'm telling you, no willpower or anything, it was a kind of weakness, of course it was, I obeyed him without knowing I was doing it, and we sat behind some bushes in the sun, a lot of them, yes, they hid us of course, and imagine at that time of day, a working day, there wasn't a soul, not anybody at all, if I'd been in my right mind I wouldn't have done it, and Paco kept saying, "Here just as I am, it seems as if I have everything, I'm alone, Menchu," and I, "Poor boy," again, but really sorry for him, Mario, that's the funny part, like I didn't know how to say anything else, of course it wasn't me or anything like me, I was hypnotized or whatever you want to call it, I'm sure I was, just imagine, I'm not like that, and he went sort of crazy, he began to hug me and press me down on the ground, and he said, he said, do you know what he said? after all, Mario, it's no novelty, after all it was sincere, others think it and don't say it, I told myself, look at Eliseo San Juan, always, and even Evaristo, I'd like to know what it is about my breasts, what I am going to do about it, and Paco more and more frantic, he said, do you know what he said? he said, "Twenty-five years dreaming about those breasts, little one," just imagine, and I, like an idiot, "Poor boy," that'll give you an idea, he was sort of beside himself, he tore my clothes and everything, Mario, but I wasn't myself, I don't have to tell you, forgive me, it wasn't my fault, I turned him down, I swear, I reminded him of our children, I don't even know where I found the strength because I had absolutely no willpower, hypnotized, honestly, but I sent him packing, he must have been awfully surprised, I promise you, may I drop dead if it's not so, I'd like to know if you and Encarna, in Madrid, forgive me, Mario, forgive me, I didn't mean to say that, but absolutely nothing happened, you can rest easy, I swear to you, I reminded him about our children, or maybe he was the one, who knows, I can't even remember now, but it's the same thing in the end, Mario, he took the words right out of my mouth, I couldn't even talk, I was out of my mind, sweetheart, you have to realize, I only want you to understand me, do you hear? because even if I had done something bad it wasn't me, you can be sure of that, the person who was there didn't have anything to do with me, I should say not, but nothing happened, absolutely nothing at all, I swear by what you hold most dear, Mario, believe me, and if Paco hadn't stopped in time I would have, you know me, even though I was a rag, but after all, he was to blame, and he was the one who had to stop, and when he pulled away his eyes were frightening, flashing, Mario, like a crazy man, but he said, "We're both crazy, little one, forgive me, I don't want to get you into trouble," and he stood up, and I was ashamed, yes, that's the way it was, when you come right down to it, he was the one, but whether it was him or me, sweetheart, the important thing is that nothing happened, I promise you, that would have been the last straw, the respect I owe you and our children, but please, don't just lie there, don't you believe me? I've told you everything, Mario, sweetheart, from A to Z, just like it was, I swear it, I'm not keeping anything back, like I was in confession, honestly, Paco kissed me and hugged me, I admit it, but it didn't go any further than that, fine thing that would have been, I swear it, and you have to believe me, it's my last chance, Mario, don't you understand? and if you don't believe me I'll go crazy, I promise you, and if you just lie there it's because you don't believe me, Mario! Aren't you listening to me? Listen, please, I've never been more honest, I could swear that to you, never with anybody, mind you, I'm telling you with my heart in my hand, listen, having you forgive me is a matter of life and death for me, do you realize that? it's not a question of a whim, Mario, look at me, come on, even if it's only for a moment, please, don't go and confuse me with my sister, it terrifies me just to think about it, I promise you, look at Julia, a bad girl, don't tell me, with an Italian, there's no excuse for her, right in the middle of the war, you tell me, she did it deliberately, after all Galli, a stranger, quite a difference from Paco, he might have lost his head and everything you please, but a gentleman when you come right down to it, Mario, "We're both crazy, little one; forgive me," it was fine of him, he took the words right out of my mouth, I swear to you, Mario, I swear by what you hold most dear, I was going to tell him, even though I was sort of stupefied, completely hypnotized, no willpower or anything, like a bundle, but I was going to tell him, honestly, and in a flash, he said it first, of course the important thing, whether it was one or the other of us, was that nothing happened, you know that, Mario, but look at me just a little bit, say something, don't just lie there, it seems as if you don't believe me, that I was deceiving you or something, and no, Mario, sweetheart, I've never been more honest in my life, I'm telling you the whole truth, all of it, absolutely, I swear to you, nothing else happened, but look at me, say something, come on, please, you're really something, I can't lower myself any further, it's the most I can do, Mario, sweetheart, after all, if you'd bought me a Six Hundred in time, there wouldn't have been any question of Citroëns, that's for certain sure, what you do with these restrictions is to push us women to the far edge, see if you don't, anybody could tell you that, but forgive me, Mario, come on, I'm asking you on my knees, there wasn't anything else, I give you my word, there's never been anyone but you, I swear, I swear, and I swear, by everything that's sacred, Mario, by everything you hold most dear, Mario, by Mama, mind you, I can't do better than that, but look at me, even if it's only for a second, come on, do me that favor, look at me! Don't you hear me? What more do you want me to say? Mario, may I drop dead if it's not true! nothing happened, Paco, after all, a gentleman, of course if was me he was dealing with, but if I'd had a Six Hundred, there wouldn't have been any Pacos or Pacas either, I swear it, Mario, I swear it by Elviro and José María, what more do you want? I can't speak any fairer than that, Mario, I can hold my head good and high, I want you to know, but listen to me, I'm talking to you! Don't act like you can't hear me, Mario! come on, please, look at me, one moment, only one second, even if it's one-tenth of a second, I beg you. Look at me! I haven't done anything bad, honestly, for the love of God, look at me one little moment, even if it's only a little moment, come on! do that for me, it's so easy, I'll beg you on my knees if you want, I don't have anything to be ashamed of, I swear to you, Mario, I swear to you! May I drop dead if it's not true! but don't shrug your shoulders, please, look at me, I'm begging you on my knees, come on, I can't stand it any longer, I can't, Mario, I swear to you, look at me or I'll go crazy! Come on, please . . . !

Carmen gives a start when she hears the creak of the door. She turns her head, sits back on her heels, and pretends to be looking for something on the floor. Her eyes and hands express extreme nervousness. Though the light of the new day is already coming through the window, the lamp is still lighted, projecting its pale luminous halo over the chair and the corpse's feet.

"What's the matter, Mother? Get up! What are you doing there on your knees?"

Carmen stands up, smiling stupidly. She feels defenseless, soft, and malleable. Her eyelids have taken on a bright pink, almost violet, color, and when she looks at him she looks sidewise, as if frightened. "I was praying," she murmurs, but she says it unconvincingly, not wanting to be believed, "I was only praying," she adds, and the boy leans toward her, puts his young arm around her shoulders, and notices that she is trembling.

"Are you all right?" he asks her.

"Fine, dear, why?"

Overnight Carmen's cheeks have sagged, and at the sides of her chin and under it, soft, gelatinous pouches have formed, like bags in which some sort of secretion has accumulated. Carmen also has soft, purplish, wrinkled swellings under her eyes. Mario persists:

"Are you cold? It seemed to me you were talking to yourself."

He pushes her gently toward the door, but Carmen resists leaving the room. She dissents without expressing it and without knowing it, but with a quiet, tenacious persistence that makes Mario relax the pressure he is exerting. Then she looks all around her as if, instead of having spent the night there, she were seeing the study, doubling as a funeral chamber, for the first time. Through the window the house opposite is clearly visible now, with its green-tiled balconies and its closed blinds painted white. And when one suddenly opens, with a dry rattling noise of slats striking together, it seems as if the house had yawned and stretched. Before the blind has been fully opened, the first motorcycle explodes in the narrow street below. And when the racket stops, the murmur of conversations and the crackle of early risers' footsteps, going to work, are clearly audible. A sparrow crosses the windowsill in little hops, as if he were bouncing, peeping joyfully, as birds do in spring. Maybe he is deceived by the bit of sky which closes off, like the back of a stage set, the workshop of Acisclo del Peral, and which has changed from black to white and from white to blue in a few minutes, almost without transition. Carmen looks at the black mourning swags, the books with their spines to the wall, the geometrical engravings of bicycles —circumferences, triangles, dotted lines—the blue globe of the world on the table, the lamp, Mario's armchair with the leather seat worn at the edges, and finally, and slowly, as if she had just realized what the situation was, her eyes rest on the corpse, on the face of Mario's corpse. She sighs, looks at her son, mechanically closes the collar of his shirt with trembling fingers, and says in a low voice, imperceptibly tinged with pride, smiling, "He isn't changed, do you realize that? He hasn't even lost color."

Mario squeezes her shoulders. "Come on," he says, and pulls at her, but Carmen seems fastened to the floor.

"Without glasses it doesn't seem like him," she adds. "When he was young he didn't wear glasses and he used to stare at me in the movies all the time, do you know? That was ever so many years ago, I don't know how long! I don't know if you'd been born yet, I'm talking about the year one, but it was nice,

I can tell you that, though I don't know how it happens that everything in life gets spoiled in the end."

Her voice has risen like an airplane about to take off, and when Mario simply says, "You oughtn't to have stayed alone. You're very upset. Have you slept at all?" Carmen, without any previous warning, bursts into sobs, hides her eyes in her son's tweedy blue sweater, snuggles close to his chest and murmurs a string of incoherent words, out of which Mario can barely distinguish a few phrases or fragments of phrases ("It's hopeless . . . " "His ego first and foremost . . . " "Not so much as a look . . . "), but Carmen's tension has dissolved and she docilely lets herself be led to the kitchen, sits on the white kitchen stool and watches Mario as he fills the Italian coffeepot with water, stuffs in the filter, and switches on the burner. As the burner heats, the wet base of the coffeepot hisses loudly. The kitchen is in shadow. Mario settles himself on the other stool, beside her. The first noises, the first voices of the morning echo in the airshaft of the building.

Carmen is bent over at the waist, as if defeated, as if the breasts which strain stubbornly against the interstices of the black wool, and which it has always supported proudly, weigh too much now. She furtively pulls the sweater away from her armpits. She says, "I just can't believe that for other people today's an ordinary day, a day like any other, mind you. I can't get used to the idea, Mario; it's impossible for me to."

Mario hesitates. He is afraid to upset her equilibrium again. At last he says, "It happens to everyone. Everybody goes through this ordeal sometime, Mother . . . I don't know how to express it."

The faint light coming through the window fills Carmen's face with shadows. When she speaks, an even darker hollow opens, almost in the center.

"Things aren't like they used to be."

Mario clutches his knees with his tanned, young, vital hands. "The world changes, Mother. It's natural."

"For the worse, son, always for the worse."

"Why for the worse? It's simply that we've realized that the things a person's been thinking for centuries, inherited ideas, aren't necessarily the best ones. More than that, sometimes they're not even good ones, Mother."

She looks at him, wrinkling her brow. "I don't know what you mean."

They are speaking in low voices. Mario's tone shows that he is very anxious to make her understand.

"You have to listen to others, Mother, that's what I mean. Don't you think it's significant, for example, that our concept of what is just always coincides suspiciously with our interests?"

Carmen's gaze is duller and more bewildered by the moment. By contrast, Mario's ingenuous self-importance increases as he speaks:

"We're simply trying to open windows. In this miserable country of ours the windows haven't been opened since the first day of its history, you can be sure of that."

Mario's color has risen. He is a little embarrassed. To hide it, he gets up and comes back with the coffeepot. He twists the button to turn off the burner, which in a few seconds turns gray. He takes two cups and the sugar bowl from the cupboard. He serves his mother, who has not moved, her eyes half closed, as if she were looking at something very far away.

"I don't understand you," she murmurs at last. "You all talk in code, like you were trying to drive me crazy. You read too many books."

Mario pushes the cup toward her. "Drink it," he says authoritatively. "Drink it before it gets cold."

Carmen slowly stirs the sugar with the spoon and drinks, at first without wanting to, closing her lips, as if she were afraid of being burned; but when she has tested the temperature she drinks eagerly. When she finishes, she keeps looking at her son, trying to explain him, not intellectually but as a simple biological phenomenon, as a consequence of herself.

"It isn't possible," she says finally. "It isn't possible that you're that little fellow, when he started to go to school and I used to say to him, when I saw his grades, 'This child's a scholar!' and he'd say, 'Mama, I'm not a scholar, I'm a philosopher.'"

Mario is drinking to try to fight down his embarrassment, but he tips the cup too suddenly and the coffee spills down the sides of his mouth. He sets the cup on the white marble of the table and hastily wipes his mouth with the back of his hand.

"Stop it, can't you," he murmurs. "It seems as if you enjoy embarrassing us with our ridiculous bright sayings, as if we'd been child prodigies."

Carmen opens her eyes, surprised; sincerely surprised. "Another thing I don't understand, honestly," she says, "is how you all despise the years when you were better. Even your father . . ."

Mario puts his hands to his head. "Oh!" he says emphatically. "Better! For God's sake, Mother! There's our savage Spanish Manicheanism, the good and the bad." The smell of coffee and the attention of his audience seem to carry him to the bar at whose tables the students of his year chat and edit their magazine, *Agora*. His voice rises. He gets excited. He lights a cigarette. "The good ones on the right and the bad ones on the left! That's what they taught you, didn't they? But you people prefer to accept it without question, rather than taking the trouble to look inside yourselves. We're all both good and bad, Mother. Both things at the same time. What we have to get rid of is hypocrisy, do you understand? It's better to recognize it than to go through life inventing arguments for ourselves. In this country, ever since the revolt of the Castilian Communities, we've been doing our best to stop up our ears, and the man who shouts too loud, to cure us of our deafness and wake us up, we eliminate and that's the end of it! 'The voice of evil,' we say, to reassure ourselves. And then, of course, we're perfectly satisfied."

Carmen stares at him, frightened. Her eyes are flat. Her whole face is flat now. She explores him. Mario realizes that it's useless, it's like expecting the wall of a jai-alai court to suck in the ball and make it stick to its smooth surface. Carmen's face is as flat as that wall, and like a wall she returns the ball in stronger and stronger bounces. There is a pause. In spite of everything, Carmen doesn't get angry. She feels inclined to benevolence. Doro begins to stir in her room beside the kitchen. The airshaft has filled with noise: sounds of sleepy conversations, the dragging of garbage cans, bumping on tiles. Carmen says, obstinately shaking her head as if she were trying to frighten off an idea, "And how about you, son? Have you slept?"

Mario finishes his coffee. Every time he draws on the cigarette he does so with such avidity that he seems to want to absorb it whole.

"No," he says. "I couldn't. A strange thing. Every time I tried to, it felt as if the mattress was collapsing, understand? An attack of dizziness. Here," and he points to the upper part of his stomach with his right hand. "It's something like when you're going to take an exam and you're waiting for them to call you."

Carmen's face stiffens. The slackness of those bags—the pouches and the puffiness under her eyes—disappears.

"No!" she screams.

But just then Doro comes out of her bedroom. "Good morning," she says listlessly. A door bangs at the end of the hall. Then another. Immediately after that the doorbell rings. It is Valentina. Carmen feels hurt by her relaxed features and especially by the flaunting of the white streak in her hair. Valentine approaches her and the two cross heads, first on the left side and then on the right, and kiss the air mechanically, kiss nothing, so that both feel the muffled explosions of the kisses but not their warmth.

"You must be half dead, Menchu, aren't you? Don't you find that you're feeling it now? Haven't you slept at all, at all?"

Carmen doesn't answer. Valentina tells her to hurry. It is a quarter to eight. While she is dressing, Bene and Esther arrive. It seems like a Thursday tea. Among them all they drag her off to the funeral mass. When they return, the house is in an uproar. Carmen's mind connects it with a previous period of time which now seems very far off. "You don't know what an impression it made on me." "So young, my dear." "I found out about it in the newspaper; by pure chance." The edges of her right hand begin to hurt at the first pressures. She leans forward, first to the left side, then to the right. She feels as if her lips have gone to sleep, lacking the strength to kiss. But even so, she kisses and kisses without respite. Esther reads the obituary in *El Correo*. "May he rest in peace, the good man who placed before . . . " "Good, for whom?" "In a materialistic period like ours, Mario Díez Collado gave, with his writings and his example . . . " "It's a real portrait of him, eh?" "Very deeply felt." "So sorry. I'll wait downstairs." "Health to pray for his soul." "It's not your fault, Carmen. I came for your sake." "Thanks, Josechu, you don't know how awfully much I appreciate it." Today the shapes' eyes are dull and sunken, as if they had been screwed in, but they respond to the same stimuli and are loquacious or laconic by turns. "Do you mind if I go in to see him for a minute?" "After this you ought to go to bed, Menchu. Mustn't abuse your body." "Not at all." "He isn't altered; he hasn't even lost color." "I'll wait downstairs." Silence. Mario with his tweedy sweater, Menchu and Alvaro, rove from group to group like lost souls. They come and go without finding a place to stay. "The heart's very treacherous, everybody knows that." Sighs. "Don't wait for Charo. She's stayed with Encarna." "You won't go to the cemetery, will you? I don't advise you to, sweetie, take my advice, I'm sure I wouldn't . . ." "Do you know if the children slept well?" More and more shapes come in and it seems as if the exit is blocked. "Bertrán, would you mind waiting downstairs? Here we can't even budge." "The ones who go fast, my dear, are the lucky ones." "Please, Doro, tell the janitor's wife and all those people to go to the kitchen." Carmen leans forward, first to the left side, then to the right, and kisses the air, kisses nothing, perhaps some stray strand of hair. "I can imagine what you must be feeling, poor thing! I still can't believe it." "Health to pray for his soul." "Why, I can't believe it myself . . . Last night . . . night before last he had supper just as usual and read till all hours. How could I imagine anything like this?" Now the shapes cannot fit, even by squeezing together, into the study and the dining room. They continue to pile up in the little entrance hall. "We men are nothing." "These sudden deaths really upset me." "Can you move over a trifle?"

When the undertaker's people arrive, the pace becomes

brisker. Carmen, Mario, Valentina, and Esther come and go, open and close, but a leftover shape or two still detains Carmen inappropriately. "I found out about it in the newspaper; by sheer chance." "Thanks, Higinio, you don't know how awfully much I appreciate it." Higinio Oyarzun stays in the entrance hall next to Arronde, the pharmacist. He is not wearing an overcoat, though it is early and the day is still chilly. From the study, whose door is open, sighs and sobs can be heard. "There was nobody better." "Who could have said it?" "We men are nothing." Higinio Oyarzun watches Moyano, inside his rabbinical beard. Arronde also looks at him sidewise, and then leans over and says to Oyarzun, very low, "A revolutionary." "Ha," Oyarzun laughs or pretends to laugh. Then he whispers, "I know those kinds of revolution. That one wants to get rid of me and take my place. Revolutions that turn out to be favorable for one person but of very limited general value. We're all a bunch of rascals." "The heart's very treacherous." "He didn't even have time to confess." "Poor thing!" Moyano shakes his head slightly. His eyes are wet and his Adam's apple, above the top of his black sweater with no shirt under it, rises and falls with increasing rapidity. "A man of integrity has died," he says to Aróstegui, but the words are scarcely out of his mouth when Oyarzun, although the remark wasn't addressed to him, answers him sharply from behind, shoving his short body against Arronde's shoulder. "Integrity? Ha! That man didn't have integrity for integrity's sake, but to enjoy rubbing the noses of the rest of us into the fact that we didn't have it. He was a hypocrite." Moyano turns on him furiously. "Disgusting Nazi," he says. And Oyarzun thrusts away Arronde, who is trying to hold him back, and yells, all restraint lost, "Let go of me! I'm going to smash that guy's face in! That . . . !"

Vicente's head appears around the study door.

"Ssh!" he hisses. "Please, they're bringing out the body."

There is a silence. The undertaker's men, with the coffin on their shoulders, open a path through the crowd, and behind it, framed in the doorway, Carmen is visible for a moment. She is not crying. She tugs at the armpits of her sweater and docilely lets Valentina put an arm around her shoulders and draw her close.